THE METROPOLITAN MUSEUM OF ART

THE DECORATION
OF
THE TOMB OF PER-NĒB

THE TECHNIQUE AND THE
COLOR CONVENTIONS

BY

CAROLINE RANSOM WILLIAMS, PH.D.

NEW YORK

MCMXXXII

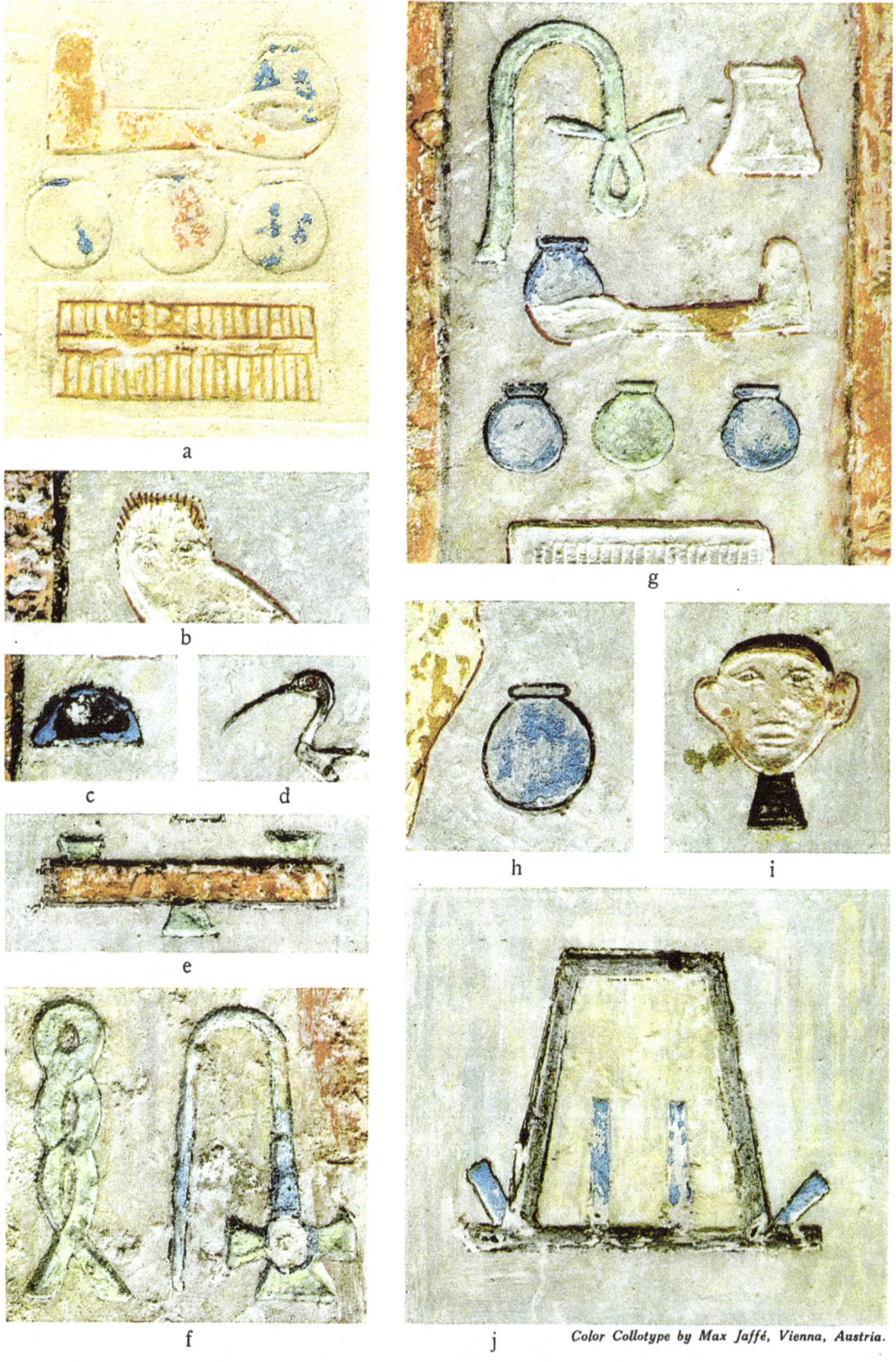

a

b

c d

e

f

g

h i

j

Color Collotype by Max Jaffé, Vienna, Austria.

PLATE I

Details of hieroglyphs with final surface partially preserved. Tomb of Ka-em-snēw. Metropolitan Museum. Scale 2:3. See pp. 40, 44, 47 n. 62, 88.

a. Bas-relief, top lintel, line 2. See pp. 24 n. 16, 42, 48, 65, 72.

b. Sunken relief, main false door, right inner jamb, top sign. See p. 42.

c. Sunken relief, main false door, right outer jamb, under front of ibis perch. See p. 33 n. 71.

d. Sunken relief, main false door, right outer jamb. See pp. 33 n. 71, 55 n. 112.

e. Sunken relief, main false door, left outer jamb, the lowest of three signs. See p. 45 n. 49.

f. Sunken relief, main false door, right outer jamb. See p. 45 n. 49.

g. Sunken relief, main false door, right outer jamb. See pp. 41 n. 21, 65, 72.

h. Bas-relief, main false door, inner small lintel. See p. 34 n. 74.

i. Sunken relief, main false door, left outer jamb, second example. See pp. 6 n. 15, 59 n. 130, 66.

j. Sunken relief, main false door, left inner jamb, third sign. See pp. 6 n. 13, 60.

The Decoration of the Tomb of Per-neb, by Caroline Ransom Williams
First published 1932 by the Metropolitan Museum of Art.
This is a semi-facsimile reprint, with no relationship to the Metropolitan Museum of Art.
© 2012 Coachwhip Publications

CoachwhipBooks.com

ISBN-13 978-1-61646-122-5

PREFACE

THE tomb of Per-nēb was discovered at Ṣaḳḳāreh in Egypt in 1907 by J. E. Quibell. It was presented to The Metropolitan Museum of Art in 1913 by Edward S. Harkness, who generously provided for its purchase from the Egyptian Government, its removal in large part from Ṣaḳḳāreh and transportation to New York, and its reconstruction in the Museum. It was first opened to the New York public in February, 1916. At that time an illustrated pamphlet, *The Tomb of Perneb*, was issued, of which chapter I was written by Albert M. Lythgoe, chapter II by me. A complete description of this tomb is now in preparation and will appear as part of a volume covering the Museum's four maṣṭabeh tombs of the Old Kingdom. Consequently, in the present book, I have made only such general references to the tomb as are essential to an understanding of the technique and color conventions of its decoration. Illustrations from other sources are also used to supplement the principal evidence.

My text, based on a study of Per-nēb's walls before their installation and before measures were taken for the preservation of their colors, was nearly completed in first draft in 1915-1916, while I was still on the staff of the Metropolitan Museum. I have, however, much reworked the manuscript, introducing here and there data gathered in later years. In March, 1927, through the courtesy of Professors G. A. Reisner and Hermann Junker, I was able to continue the study of the art of the Old Kingdom decorator in the Gīzeh necropolis. I am indebted to Cecil M. Firth for permitting, and to Battiscombe Gunn and J. E. Quibell for facilitating, as far as circumstances allowed, my study in the Ṣaḳḳāreh necropolis, and to R. Engelbach for aid in pursuing the subject of Old Kingdom decorations in the Cairo Museum. In the Metropolitan Museum, in 1929 and subsequently, I had the opportunity to examine a west wall from one of the chambers in the tomb of Ka-em-snēw, also before its colors had been treated by any preservative application.

My greatest debt is to Mr. Lythgoe for his kindness in arranging for me to revise, complete, and publish this book. I have further to acknowledge gratefully numerous helpful suggestions which H. E. Winlock made long ago on my first text and again recently on the revised manuscript. And I am under obligation for much kind coöperation and criticism on the part of other members of the Museum's Egyptian Department. In particular, Ambrose Lansing, Ludlow Bull, and Lindsley F. Hall, in my absence from New York, have several times collated proofs of the colored plates, and Dr. Bull has aided in the determination of the English forms to be used for the Egyptian personal names occurring in this book and has followed the progress of the manuscript with many a useful correction and comment. I shall express my thanks to various scholars for help on special questions in the course of the following pages.

Egyptian hieroglyphs are referred to by the letters and numbers of the Sign-lists in Alan H. Gardiner's *Egyptian Grammar* and the fourth edition of Adolf Erman's *Ägyptische Grammatik* and, in the case of forms not represented in one or both of those books, by the letters and numbers with the addition of an asterisk given in Gardiner's *Catalogue of . . . Printing Type*. All abbreviations used in this work for titles of publications may be interpreted by means of the List of References Cited.

C. R. W.

Toledo, Ohio
December, 1930.

TABLE OF CONTENTS

LIST OF PLATES

THE DECORATION OF
THE TOMB OF PER-NĒB

THE DECORATION
OF THE TOMB OF PER-NĒB

THE TECHNIQUE AND THE COLOR CONVENTIONS

I. THE TECHNIQUE

THE tomb of Per-nēb affords considerable evidence with regard to the technical methods of Egyptian wall decorators of the close of the Fifth Dynasty, in the twenty-seventh century before Christ. Although the decoration of the main chamber was once complete, the subsequent loss of much of its final surface has uncovered traces of preliminary processes which were never intended to be revealed; and the antechamber and the passage between the two rooms were still unfinished when work on the tomb ceased. The record, then, which Per-nēb's chambers contain invites careful study, and the more because hitherto attention has been focused on the content of the inscriptions and scenes found in tomb interiors, with very little attempt to understand and define the artists' procedure.[1]

The process of decorating a private tomb of the Old Kingdom when built of stone falls into three main divisions, namely, the placing of the first preliminary sketch to guide the sculptor, the carving of the stone, and the painting of the sculptured walls. The last-mentioned division is somewhat complex, for it includes the laying down of a second sketch and some washes before the application of the final colors.

A. THE FIRST PRELIMINARY SKETCH

The earliest stage of the work, that which preceded the sculpture, is preserved on the unfinished walls of the west side of the outer chamber (pl. vi) and the passage between

---

[1] See, however, Reisner, writing briefly in regard to the technique of Queen Mer-es-ᶜonekh III's decoration in *Bull. of the Mus. of Fine Arts*, 1927, p. 70. Valuable articles by Ernest Mackay on the methods used in the hewing out and decorating of Theban tombs have appeared in *J. E. A.*, 1917, 1918, 1921, and in *Anc. Eg.*, 1920, and illuminating comments on technique are scattered through the publications of Norman de Garis Davies. The latter also deal principally with decorations later than those of the Old Kingdom; references to some of them will be made in succeeding pages.

the two rooms (pls. VII, VIII). Several fragments of the first sketch are left also on the north wall of the main chamber (pl. IX).

In the building of tomb walls, both those of the exterior and those of interior chambers, according to the investigations of Clarke and Engelbach, only the rising and bedding joints were dressed before the blocks were laid, a method economical of labor and of stone.[1] The same mortar used as an aid in setting the blocks and leveling the courses was then, after the fronts of the blocks had been roughly dressed, spread as a plaster over breaks in their faces and along the joints to fill them out to a surface even with the rest of the wall.[2] There was not at this time any coating of fine plaster added. An examination of the west wall of the antechamber (pl. VI) makes evident that here, at least, the filling of coarse plaster did not extend to the minor unevennesses of the surface. The actual stone, noticeably pitted and showing the marks of the pointed chisel[3] with which the blocks were dressed, is visible, as the first sketch was laid on the bare wall. The blocks composing the walls of the passage to the inner room (pls. VII, VIII) were even more roughly dressed; and here there was need of much more plaster,[4] which varied from less than a millimeter to five millimeters in thickness over somewhat large areas, in addition to the deep masses once filling many of the present breaks in the stone. In the main chamber so little of the original surface is left that one cannot determine the initial condition of the walls.

The mortar and the coarse plaster to which we referred in the preceding paragraph are identical in appearance, being somewhat pinkish in the mass and strewn through with minute white, red, and dark particles.[5] Following the researches of A. Lucas,[6] we may be-

---

[1] *Masonry*, chaps. VII, IX (in particular, p. 100). Roeder has called attention to certain blocks within the cult chamber of Wehem-ka, the joints of which afford evidence that the blocks were set in place before their faces were dressed (*Uhemka*, p. 8).   [2] cf. Lythgoe, in *Perneb*, pp. 34-35.

[3] See the actual stonemason's tools of the IV Dynasty published by Reisner, *Bull. of the Mus. of Fine Arts*, 1928, p. 87, lower cut. Engelbach calls attention to the one ancient Egyptian representation of the dressing of stone building blocks known, namely, that in the XVIII Dynasty tomb of Rekh-mi-Rēᶜ (*Annales*, 1929, p. 22); cf. Newberry, *Rekhmara*, pl. XX; also Clarke and Engelbach, *Masonry*, p. 106, fig. 113.

[4] Small patches of coarse plaster are numerous on the wall from Ka-em-snēw's tomb; see pl. II, a, d, e. In "a" the plaster underlies preserved portions of the first sketch.

[5] A part of the corresponding plaster on the wall from Ka-em-snēw's tomb (pl. II, a, e) is of a more pronounced pinkish cast and is scattered through more prominently with black, red, and white grains. Another and whiter mixture is shown in the lower left corner of detail "d" in plate II.

[6] *J. E. A.*, 1924, pp. 128-131, and *Materials*, pp. 20-22, 23-26, 230; cf. Clarke and Engelbach, *Masonry*, p. 79. See also the results of analyses of plaster and mortar of the late IV Dynasty summarized in Jéquier, *Mastabat Faraoun*, pp. 11, A, B, and 12, note 3, and the clear statement and additional analyses given in Junker, *Giza I*, p. 90.

lieve that this binding material, as was generally the case in pre-Roman times in Egypt, was derived from crude gypsum, which occurs abundantly in the Egyptian deserts bordering the Nile and can be calcined to yield an impure plaster of Paris at a much lower temperature than that necessary in obtaining quicklime. The white and red particles are probably grains of sand and bits of burned clay, sand and clay being present naturally in crude gypsum, and the dark particles, for the most part, tiny remains of unburned fuel. The faint pink color of the mass may be ascribed to the presence of iron compounds in the gypsum.[7]

The Egyptian artist, being at this time, so far as we know, without crayon or other dry medium with which to execute his construction lines and drawing[8] and being obliged, therefore, from the outset to use wet colors, employed commonly the brown-red pigment which to this day in Egypt is used for humble purposes,[9] and which perhaps needed to be mixed only with water.[10] This pigment in Per-nēb's time was probably derived from natural deposits of red ocher.[11] Just as in the case of rapidly and casually executed quarry marks, here the brown-red water color attached itself readily to the stone or plaster; and as it was laid on in heavy line, the roughness of the ground was no special drawback. In some tombs, however, instead of red pigment, black was used for the first sketch;[12] in others, two sketch lines may be traced, the first in red being supplemented by finer lines

[7] Fisher, however, ascribed it to the addition to the plaster of Paris of "some red matter, possibly powdered pottery" (*Minor Cem.*, p. 15), and Lucas referred only to a superficial red, due, he thought, to chemical changes which took place in the iron compounds of the plaster "by exposure to atmospheric influences during thousands of years" (*Materials*, p. 24). But in mortar and plaster used in the Old Kingdom at Gīzeh and Ṣaḳḳāreh, pink color often, as here, permeates the entire mass; see Junker, *Giza I*, p. 90.

[8] Mackay raised the question in respect to Theban walls whether "a very powdery colour was sometimes employed for drawing these guiding lines," which could be "brushed off after the outlines of the figures had been painted," but did not himself much favor the idea (*J. E. A.*, 1917, p. 81; cf. *ibid.*, 1921, p. 165).

[9] Petrie called attention to the use of this pigment for marking baggage on Egyptian railways (*Abydos*, II, p. 34).

[10] This statement is made on the strength of the experiment described by W. J. Russell: "I took one of the specimens [an ancient bit of red coloring matter] with a curved smooth surface and rubbed it in a large porcelain mortar with a little water, and thus with the greatest ease obtained a wet powder which at once could be used, without addition of any other medium, as a pigment; for it adhered to paper, to wood, and to the fingers, with wonderful pertinacity ..." (in *Medum*, p. 44). Modern artists, with whom we have talked, however, have doubted whether this color would adhere permanently if no binding medium were used.

[11] Petrie stated, on the authority of Spurrell, that the ancient Egyptians sometimes ground the mineral haematite and sometimes utilized natural deposits of ocherous clays to obtain red coloring matter (*Medum*, p. 28); cf. Spurrell, *Archaeol. Journ.*, 1895, p. 226. Lucas, however, questioned the employment to any extent of haematite (*Materials*, p. 137).

[12] So in the tombs of Ne-kau-Ḥor, Raᶜ-em-ka, and Sen-nu-ka (pls. III-V; cf. pp. 14, 15 with note 1, 16).

in black.[13] Very rarely the first lines were yellow, the final lines red.[14] And several ways of working, including the use of solid black, occur even in a single restricted area.[15]

The sketches in the passageway and outer room consist of: (1) lines mapping out the composition by defining the height of the dado and marking out the borders, the different registers, and the spaces for the long vertically written inscription; (2) guiding lines to aid the artist in drawing the figure of Per-nēb and many of the smaller figures; (3) outlines of figures, objects, and hieroglyphs accompanied by a limited amount of inner drawing.

The lines of the first sketch have all the appearance of brushwork. They spread in some places and are narrower in others, thus varying from 0.5 to 5.0 mm. in width, and here and there they are broken; now the color is very thick as it dropped from the full

[13] This was noted long ago in the early days of interest in ancient Egypt, for instance, in 1822, in Belzoni, *Narrative* (3d edition), I, p. 272; Belzoni assumed that "the first lines were done in red by a scholar, or one not so expert as the master, who examined the outlines, and corrected them in black." Such double work is now exemplified in the Metropolitan Museum by some of the sketches remaining on Ka-em-snēw's wall; see excerpts, plate II, a, b, e, especially detail "b," where one may analyze the two drawings and see how, for example, in the middle sign (O 51) representing a granary, the red sketch renders the superstructure in broad single lines, with no inner details and with much fumbling at the right to place the granary's sloping side, and the black sketch is executed in fine double lines, with base closed at the ends and details added; compare, too, this final black sketch with the finished sign of plate I, j. It is a little puzzling to find on this wall where the two sets of sketch lines coincide, or cross one another, now the red, now the black, apparently done first, as if one man had operated alternately with two brushes. Probably this observation rests on a false appearance, due to the sinking of the pigments into the absorbent stone, for the black sketch is certainly the more competent and complete, and in places one can see that the sculptor followed the black line in preference to the red. In plate II, e, for instance, a red rectangle first indicated the area to be occupied by the three papyrus-roll-signs (Y 2), but the right end of the middle sign, as carved, followed a black sketch line to the right of a red line (once present, as its prolongation shows, but now cut away). Further, no example among Old Kingdom sketches has come to our knowledge of guiding lines, horizontals and perpendiculars (category 2 in the next paragraph), done in black; when present, guiding lines are always red, whether the figures themselves are red or doubly drawn in both colors. Lepsius, be it remarked, found in the tomb of Ma-nofre that the black sketch sacrificed the accuracy of the red as regards the proportions of the human figure (*Denkmäler, Text*, I, pp. 233, 235), but this may mean simply that there the craftsman responsible for the black lines was impatient of guides.

[14] So in the tomb of Ḥesy-Rēᶜ; see Quibell, *Hesy*, pp. 17, 33. Davies made the same observation with regard to certain later sketches (*El Amarna*, IV, p. 32), and Daressy, with reference to ostraca of the Cairo collection, in one of which all three pigments, yellow, red, and black, were employed successively in the order named (*Ostraca*, p. 29, no. 25144, pl. XXIX; see also no. 25043, executed first in yellow, then in red, and no. 25197, drawn in yellow and corrected in black).

[15] On the wall from Ka-em-snēw's tomb, in addition to the corrected sketches, there are sketches in black line alone (pl. II, f); here the sketched hieroglyph of a face in front view (D 2) may be compared with the same sign in its final and painted form as exemplified in plate I, i. The wall shows also a number of signs in black silhouette, other hieroglyphs of the same inscription being already carved; even the detail of plate II, f, exhibits a tendency towards the silhouette in the mud seal of the papyrus roll (this sketched example of sign Y 2 may be compared with the partially carved papyrus rolls of detail "e."). Further, the religious texts in the burial chamber of Pepy II's queen were done first in red line, then in solid black; see Jéquier, *Oudjebten*, p. 5, with note 2.

brush, and again it becomes thinner. That a ruler was generally used for the vertical and horizontal lines seems from their appearance unquestionable. With the possible exception of the horizontal line at the top of the west wall of the outer chamber, they have a regularity of direction which could hardly be achieved free-hand, and they could not have been produced by snapping a string wet in color against the wall, as was a common practice in the Eighteenth Dynasty,[16] for they exhibit no such occasional spluttering of the paint as this method would promote.[17]

We may begin our analysis of the guiding lines used in Per-nēb's tomb by examining the slight traces of the first sketch to be seen in the larger room. Here, on the north wall, is a spot where the ground between figures was not removed, and the gray paint which formerly rendered the careless workmanship unnoticeable has fallen away, revealing at the original level of the face of the wall two parallel horizontal lines in red, about 1.5 mm. in width and 5.8 cm. apart (pl. IX). The lower of these lines marks the level of the knees; the upper, the base of the hips. Lines in the same two positions may be observed in front of the first man in the register below. Besides the parts reproduced in plate IX,[18] a fragment of the guiding line through the knees may be seen in front of the last offering bearer in the fifth register from the top. Again in the lowest register of the wall, before the second offering bearer, traces of a line at the level of the top of the forehead are left. Elsewhere in the three lowest registers of the north wall, the background when not cut away to the normal level has nevertheless been worked over enough to obliterate the guiding lines. There remain here, as we have seen, slight vestiges of guiding lines in three positions in reference to the standing figures to be drawn, lines which once ran the length of the wall.

In endeavoring to picture the several registers as they looked before the design was sketched in, we must imagine not only the lines defining the registers above and below, but still other guiding lines within the registers to be inferred from the practice in other tombs of the period.[19] Quite probably three additional horizontals would

---

[16] Davies, *Five Theban Tombs*, pp. 5, 6; Gardiner, in *Amenembēt*, p. 12; Mackay, *J. E. A.*, 1917, p. 74.

[17] e.g., Davis, Maspero, and Daressy, *Harmbabi and Touatânkhamanou*, pls. XLIV, XLV, LII, LIII, etc.

[18] The entire north wall, of which plates IX and XI give details, is reproduced in Lythgoe and Ransom, *Perneb*, fig. 36, and in Capart, *Memphis*, fig. 346.

[19] The sketches longest familiar and most informing are in the V Dynasty maṣṭabeh of Ma-nofre; see Lepsius, *Denkmäler*, II, pls. 65, 68, supplemented by a diagram and discussion, *op. cit.*, *Text*, I, pp. 233-238; Berlin, *Ausf. Verz.* (2d edition), p. 53, no. 1108, d, e; also Schäfer, *Ägypt. und heutige Kunst*, fig. 81, and *Von ägypt. Kunst* (3d edition), fig. 260. For the few other published sketches of the Old Kingdom, see the following notes.

have been present, indicating respectively the level of the lowest ribs,[20] of the armpits,[20] and of the base of the neck.[21] Very probably there would have been perpendiculars, too, for each human figure,[22] if not for the jars and stands.[23] We do not postulate a line to mark the crowns of the heads such as is present in sketches in the tomb of Ptaḥ-ḥotpe, where it is additional to the six guiding lines enumerated above,[24] for a line in this position is exceptional in the Fifth Dynasty, and the crowns of the heads of Per-nēb's offering bearers are not strictly enough in alignment to suggest that such a guiding line was employed. Here, as generally in the Old Kingdom, calculations were made from the ground to the top of the forehead where the hair or wig begins, and the crown of the head was drawn in by eye.[25] Nor do we postulate a horizontal halfway between the knees and the ground, inasmuch as it has thus far been found only in sketches of the

[20] Present in every set of guiding lines known to us which dates from the V Dynasty with the sole exception of the partially published sketches in Ka-em-nofret's tomb; see Capart, *Memphis*, fig. 244.

[21] Present in all V Dynasty sketches, so far as we know, even those of Ka-em-nofret.

[22] We can mention but one instance of the omission of perpendiculars for human figures among published sketches of the V and VI Dynasties, that of the guiding lines for dancers in the tomb of Ne-kau-Ḥor; see Quibell, *Exc's at Saq. (1907-1908)*, pl. LXVI. In Davies, *Ptahhetep*, II, pls. IV (below on the right), XVII, they are omitted from the copy but present on the wall (so, *op. cit.*, p. 23). In the chamber of Ka-em-nofret, perpendiculars are to be seen in some registers but not in all.

[23] Found in Ma-nofre's tomb; Lepsius, *Denkmäler*, II, pl. 68. We noted them much used on the south wall of the tomb of Yasen.

[24] See references above, note 22; Ne-kau-Hor's dancers alluded to in the same note also have a line along the crowns of the heads, but the total number of horizontals exclusive of the ground line is only six, and the horizontal which normally defines the base of the neck and the shoulders here passes through the chins. One is perhaps warranted in regarding this as a case of maladjustment between the guiding lines and the subsequent drawing, the crowns of the heads and the chins of the figures being marked instead of the foreheads and shoulders. The diagram given by Lepsius is at first glance misleading, for in addition to the six horizontals actually present on the walls of Ma-nofre's tomb, he added in the diagram one level with the crown of the head (*op. cit., Text*, I, p. 234). As to its absence from the walls, he made the following express statement: "Der Scheitel blieb ganz aus der Rechnung . . . ; auch wird dieser Punkt nirgends, weder durch eine Linie noch durch einen roten oder schwarzen Punkt angegeben; man überliess diesen Teil dem Augenmass, daher er sehr wechselt . . . " (p. 235). A line is found also across the crown of the head in the similar diagram in Fisher (*Minor Cem.*, p. 16, fig. 2), but it is nowhere present in the plate 55 which is supposed to give in facsimile all that is on the wall. The line which strikes the crowns of the heads of the figures in the bottom register of the east wall (pl. 53) seems to have reference to the inscription, just as the inscription in the second register above this one is defined by horizontals to keep the hieroglyphs in even line.

[25] So Lepsius believed (see quotation in the preceding note), and this opinion usually holds good for the Old and Middle Kingdoms, although not, it would seem from Mackay's studies (*J. E. A.*, 1917, pp. 74 ff.), for the XVIII Dynasty and later. In the XVIII Dynasty the line marking the crowns of the heads is regular; the one along the tops of the foreheads appears indeed as a part of the system of squares, but is abandoned whenever only a few horizontals are employed.

Sixth Dynasty[26] and was presumably an innovation then, marking a tendency to increase the number of guiding lines, a tendency which ultimately resulted in a system of guiding squares. And finally, the degree of dependence which the designer of Per-nēb's decoration placed on the preliminary sketch[27] does not lead one to assume here the use of dots or checks for lateral measurements taken from the perpendiculars, such as are found rarely elsewhere in addition to horizontal guiding lines.[28]

In plate x is offered a tentative restoration of the guiding lines used in the portion of the north wall of the main chamber which has just been considered. The plate shows the outlines of the existent sculptured figures of men and offerings in black line and the guiding lines, which preceded the sketches for these figures, in red line, with the extant parts heavier than the rest. The details have been worked out by Lindsley F. Hall, and, conforming to the practice observable in surviving sketches, he has not begun the vertical guiding lines quite at the tops of the registers. Most often in extant examples, perpendiculars pass immediately in front of the ear, midway between the legs when striking the lower edge of men's kilts, and just behind the front third of the rear foot. They do not as a rule exactly bisect the body — now the front shoulder, now the other being nearer to the perpendicular. Actually the relationships between our restored perpendiculars and the sculptured figures cannot be carried through everywhere just alike. That the difference may well go beyond the sculptor's work to that of the draughtsman is evident when one examines the sketched figures with their perpendiculars in the passageway and outer room of Per-nēb's tomb (pls. vi-viii). As Lepsius observed, the lateral measurements were left more to the eye than the vertical proportions. Further, following the position of the sculptured figures on the wall itself, Mr. Hall has divided each register inde-

---

[26] Davies, *Deir el Gebrâwi*, II, frontispiece. This line occurs in the sketches of the tomb of Pepy-ʿonekh, whose "good name" was Heny the Black; the tomb, which dates from the reign of Pepy II, is still unpublished, but we have had access to a file of the photographs from Meir which the Egypt Exploration Society kindly permits institutions and scholars to buy, and the line is to be observed in numbers B 223, B 226, B 235, B 240, and B 243. Another unpublished sketch containing this line, now on exhibition in the Museum of Fine Arts, Boston (no. 13.4339, a), is dated by Reisner to the first half of the VI Dynasty, inasmuch as Nekhbu, the owner of the tomb, is a grandson of a known official of the reign of Isesy. We owe this information about the date of the tomb to the kindness of Dows Dunham; see further Reisner's statements about the career and date of this functionary in the *Bull. of the Mus. of Fine Arts*, 1913, pp. 53, 62-63, 65.

[27] See further on this point, p. 13.

[28] Recorded only for the tomb of Ma-nofre; see Lepsius, *Denkmäler, Text*, I, pp. 234-236. Checks are found on the passage walls of Per-nēb's tomb (see pp. 11-12), but placed on perpendiculars as substitutes for horizontals.

pendently of the one above and below it.[29] Possibly the pleasing absence of vertical alignment on the wall is to be accounted for by the ancient draughtsman's order of procedure. After blocking out the main divisions of the decoration, he may have begun at the top and have sketched in the design, completing the drawing preliminary to the sculpture in each register of offerings and bearers before executing the guiding lines in the next register below; thus his scaffolding would have required the least readjustment.[30]

In drawing the stands and jars, vertical lines were useful principally as an aid to keeping the two sides of each piece symmetrical. Perhaps they helped somewhat in laying out the composition. In the registers containing offering bearers, the vertical lines were an aid in maintaining a proper distance between figures, in planning the number which could be placed in a single register, and in sketching the outlines, while the horizontal lines helped especially in securing a likeness of proportions throughout the procession. But Lepsius's analysis of these guiding lines has shown further that they were placed in accordance with a definite system, to which the later systems of squares, at first eighteen and a fraction in number to the height of the standing figure, were intimately related.[31]

[29] This seems to have been the general rule when the artist was concerned with processions of bearers. See Lepsius, *Denkmäler*, II, pl. 65; Davies, *Ptahhetep*, II, pl. xvii (repeated in Lythgoe and Ransom, *Perneb*, p. 73, fig. 38), where, even without the reproduction of the perpendiculars present on the wall (p. 8, note 22), one may observe that the figures of the upper register are not directly over those of the lower register; also Steindorff, *Ti*, pls. 3, 31-44, 53, 54, 91-93, 101, 127; but in plates 102-104, the vertical alignment is such as to suggest that perpendiculars may have been carried through three registers at a time, and Fisher apparently gives actual examples (*Minor Cem.*, pls. 54, 55).

[30] Compare Gunn's conjecture of the fortuitous control of the final number of items in offering lists exercised by the draughtsman's method of laying out the decoration (in *Teti Pyr. Cem.*, I, p. 96, note 2); such lists are shown in small part to the left in plates ix, xi-xiii, and xvii of the present book.

[31] When these squares were first used is a question of considerable interest. Lepsius's opinion was that they came into use in the XVIII Dynasty, but examples of the XII Dynasty from at least two sites are now known; see Newberry, *Beni Hasan*, I, pl. x; A. M. Blackman, *Meir*, II, p. 21, pls. ii, x, xi, xv, and III, pl. xvii. Possibly with the foregoing examples in mind, Schäfer in 1923 gave as his opinion that guiding squares superseded the older system of lines and dots at the beginning of the Middle Kingdom (*Grundlagen*, p. 9), correcting the statement in *Zeitschr. für ägypt. Sprache*, 1923, p. 141; cf. now *idem, Von ägypt. Kunst* (3d edition), p. 318. Edgar (*Rec. de trav.*, 1905, pp. 143, 145) and Mackay (*J. E. A.*, 1917, p. 74) earlier, however, supposed the squares to have been first used in the Old Kingdom, although they did not name supporting examples, and the same opinion has also been expressed of late by Capart (*Memphis*, p. 259). We are unable to find on Old Kingdom walls networks of squares related to human figures which are not copyists' squares, later than the decoration itself. Thus the tomb of Nesut-nofre contains evidence of the ancient copyist's interest in unusual figures. To the right of the northern false door, in the third register from the bottom, a network of black lines lies on top of the sculptured figure of a dwarf. The lines are 0.5 to 1.0 mm. wide, the rectangles, 2.2 cm. square, and the network is 9 squares high by 5 wide. Junker calls attention to the fact that the copy was not made until after the painted surface had fallen away (*Gîza I*, p. 185). Other examples of copyists' squares are well known through publications. The correspondences between the system of guiding lines and the earlier of the two principal systems of guiding squares for first sketches are sufficiently explained by Lepsius's assumption that the system of squares was the outgrowth of the other.

THE DECORATION OF THE TOMB OF PER-NĒB

At least by the Fifth Dynasty, the Egyptian draughtsman was taught to draw the human figure with a prescribed length of limb and foot, and guiding lines in these preliminary drawings were so placed, following the accepted system of measurement, as to enable him easily to conform to the established standards.[82]

In the passage between the two chambers, the wall spaces were such as could be handled in the sketch each as a unit. Let us look at the east jamb (pl. VII). At the bottom of the field to be decorated, revision in the position of the ground line was required, and this construction line as first drawn is still to be traced. Four vertical guiding lines were dropped from near the top border to the ground line of the upper register, and four others, nearly continuous with the verticals of the first set, were dropped to the bottom line of the lower register. Their interspaces were made equal to one another, but their marginal spaces were made unlike each other and those of the central area. This is accounted for by the necessities of the design; besides the forward arm's projecting farther than the other, each figure has an inscription in front of it, but none behind it. More space is thus needed before the leading figures than behind the last ones. The proportions of the figures were indicated, not by horizontals, as in the main chamber with its long trains of men where it was more difficult to keep knees, foreheads, and other features in line, but more briefly by dots or checks on the vertical guiding lines.[83] The last three figures in the upper register and the second and third in the lower have the bases of the hips checked. Presumably all eight perpendiculars were marked at this point, but the figure of the leading man in the lower row is now broken through the kilt, and the dresses of the two remaining figures, those of women, are well covered with paint. Marks may be observed at the level of the knees on two figures, the first in the upper register and the second in the lower, and at the level of the armpits on the second and third figures below; a check is also to be seen at the level of the tops of the foreheads of the second figure above and

---

[82] On the subject of the earlier and later Egyptian canons of proportions, see Edgar, *Rec. de trav.,* 1905, pp. 143 ff., and the older literature cited there; *idem, Sculptors' Studies,* pp. ii, iii; Davies, *Ptahhetep,* II, pp. 22-23; Mackay, *J. E. A.,* 1917, pp. 74-85; Murray, *Sculpture,* pp. 20-28. Schäfer suggests that the proportions may have been derived from works of art which were considered standard at a given time or have been the creation of a single especially influential artist. He rejects, as improbable in early antiquity, the method of measuring numerous people and taking the averages of their measurements (*Von ägypt. Kunst* [3d edition], p. 326) Such a method of work, rare in our own day, as that of the sculptor R. Tait McKenzie, who made the measurements of college athletes the basis of fine ideal figures of nude youths, is not to be thought of in the case of the ancient Egyptians; see Hussey, *Tait McKenzie,* chaps. 3, 4, figs. 7, 9-12.

[83] So likewise in a part of Ma-nofre's sketches; see Lepsius, *Denkmäler,* II, pl. 65.

of all but the first below.[34] No doubt originally there were other marks which, because of the covering washes and the breaks, are not to be seen today; the checks extant indicate four of the six positions usually marked in guiding lines of the Fifth Dynasty (cf. pl. x). Special interest attaches to the facts that the women have the same height as the men and make the same stride;[35] the perpendiculars and guiding checks here, so far as we can detect, were all alike for the two sexes. This likeness in height and step between the figures of men and women is of course a concession to decorative effect. Generally in the Fifth Dynasty a normal difference is maintained, as in Ne-kau-Ḥor's decoration, where, to the right and left of the northern false door, the husband and wife stand together, and the wife's head and shoulders are well below Ne-kau-Ḥor's, and her feet are closer together than his.

The guiding lines of the west jamb are similar to those just described, even to the revision of the position of the lower ground line (pl. viii). Of the checks on the perpendiculars, the following may still be distinguished: those at the level of the base of the hips on the second and fourth figures of the upper register and of the third figure of the lower; one marking the base of the ribs on the second figure below, a position not represented among the surviving checks on the opposite wall, but probably once marked there also; those marking the top of the forehead on the second and fourth figures above. In the bottom register, the extant mark on the third vertical guiding line was placed a trifle too high, an error which was noticed and corrected in the outline of the figure.

We have seen that in the inner chamber all but a mere fragment of the preliminary sketch for the sculptor is lost, and that in the passageway one cannot know just how many positions were checked on the vertical guiding lines, but we probably have before us all the guiding lines used on the west wall of the outer room (pl. vi), and these are surprisingly few in number. The figures in the two upper registers were drawn in boldly without guiding lines whatever, merely the positions of the toes of each of the men's feet being checked on the ground line.[36] The figures in the other registers and the large figure

---

[34] Not all the checks mentioned above and in the next paragraph are easily discernible in plates vii and viii. They were studied under the most favorable conditions of lighting.

[35] Such a regular alternation of male and female figures personifying villages of the mortuary estate as occurs in this passage is rare. When an entire row of female figures is depicted, even if walking, the feet are generally somewhat closer together than those of men. See Murray, *Saq. Mast.*, I, pls. ix, x, xii; Steindorff, *Ti*, pls. 114, 115; also the interesting earlier figures given in Junker, *Gîza I*, pp. 221-222, fig. 51.

[36] Checks marking human feet are recorded elsewhere only for Ma-nofre's tomb; see Lepsius, *Denkmäler, Text*, I, p. 235.

of Per-nēb all have perpendiculars but no dots or checks. That the upper starting point[37] of the perpendiculars on this wall, too, was determined by eye rather than measurement is evident in the fact that these lines are of varying heights in the same register. Inasmuch as the proportions of the figures were estimated from the ground up, it mattered not if the vertical lines fell short of, or exceeded, the full height of the final figures. Always the verticals were carried above the highest of the six levels which were commonly checked, or marked by horizontals (pl. x), in the full sets of guiding lines of the Fifth Dynasty. In subordinate human figures and in hieroglyphs representing a human head, the omission of eyes, nose (when seen from the front), and mouth is consonant with the character of the drawing as a preliminary sketch.[38] The upward tilting toward the right of the ground lines of the two highest registers is odd; the abandoned ground lines, which were only partially erased, are more nearly horizontal.

Lepsius indicated at the right of his diagram giving the six horizontal guiding lines or checks of Ma-nofre's sketches slight variations observable in their position and laboriously explained the variations as due to a difference in the length of the unit — which he thought to be a foot-length — assumed in each instance.[39] He claimed to find the unit taken for a given figure carried through without error, and to see in this a demonstration of extreme care on the part of the draughtsman. But, if so accurate, why should the draughtsman have permitted his unit to vary from figure to figure? Moreover, the marks on the diagram do not bear out the statement that in each figure the unit was used without error. The variations seem rather to prove that the draughtsman did not place his guiding lines, or follow them, with great accuracy. And surely the sketches on Per-nēb's walls give the impression that artists of the Old Kingdom worked with much freedom. When he had passed beyond the apprentice stage, a man of talent would place little dependence on construction lines. One has the conviction in the presence of these sketches that the guiding lines were often used as a matter of routine and were not taken very seriously.

[37] The fullness of line at the top indicates that the start was made there, but in some cases the brush did not carry enough color to finish the line in one stroke, and a new start was made lower down.

[38] Inner details were more often given when the first sketch was in black line. Compare the signs of the full face (D 2) in plates II, f, and VI.

[39] *Denkmäler, Text,* I, pp. 233 ff. The question of the unit rests on a very uncertain basis. The fact that in modern times we can analyze these drawings in terms of a foot-length or the height of the head (Murray, *Sculpture,* pp. 20 ff.) does not prove that an ancient Egyptian operated with the one or the other of these measurements; he did not necessarily use any part of the human frame as a unit, but may have carried in memory an abstract series of fractions for the different levels of the height of human figures, which he often carried out, especially in the case of smaller figures, by eye alone.

The success of the sketch proper — the outlines of the hieroglyphs and the figures with their inner drawing — makes evident that Per-nēb's draughtsman did not venture too much in dispensing to a large degree with guiding lines. The sketch on the west wall of the outer chamber is especially admirable work (pl. vi). How expressive are the blocked-in profiles done with two strokes, how taut and well set up the men who advance on one another in the lowest register, how competent the curves of the wife's back and up-turned foot. Even the angle at which the lower hieroglyphs in the first column are set gives a look of piquancy and independence of trammeling rules to the drawing. Character is imparted to the sketch, too, by the short strokes at one or both extremities of a number of hieroglyphs, namely, M 17, S 29, U 1, and V 4, "nervous little jabs to stop off the line smartly and vigorously,"[40] which remind one of the short terminal strokes found to some extent in the signs technically termed "cursive hieroglyphs." Similar jabs are to be observed at the right end of two of the ground lines of registers (pl. vi, above at the right).

One may better realize the success of the preliminary drawing in Per-nēb's tomb if one takes a glance at a first sketch from the tomb of Ne-kau-Ḥor (pl. iii).[41] Here, in four registers, of which the two upper ones are now incomplete, offering bearers make their way toward the wife's false door. In the topmost register the sculptor has begun to cut the outlines of the figures, in the other three, the figures have been drawn and washes have been added, but there has been no carving. Much of the color has peeled off, exposing the bare stone. The sketch is in black line, varying from a mere hair's breadth to 2.5 mm. in width. The most precise examination with a magnifying glass fails to reveal any guiding lines. As the black outlines are well preserved, it is wholly improbable that guiding lines were used, and have since disappeared, leaving not a trace. Moreover, the man in the middle and the one on the right in the lowest register are out of balance, their bodies are tipped backward, as would hardly have happened had the draughtsman made use of perpendiculars, and there are other irregularities such as a knee placed too high. The conclusion seems inevitable that the figures on this short wall were drawn as they now appear without guiding lines. The draughtsman who made this sketch was not so well qualified to draw without construction lines as the artist who decorated Per-nēb's outer room, but he was overconfident.

[40] So described by Mr. Winlock, who, however, regards the two slanting strokes at the ends of the sketched *n*'s as imitations of the characteristic ripples of hieroglyph N 35.

[41] This particular section of wall is reproduced in line in Quibell, *Exc's at Saq. (1907-1908)*, pl. LXVI, 4.

THE DECORATION OF THE TOMB OF PER-NĒB

In the sketches of the outer room and passage of Per-nēb's tomb, the lines are not fine enough, or complete enough, to have furnished a detailed and absolutely definite guide to the sculptor. Rather, the sculptor would have been obliged to exercise discretion in the carving and to supply free-hand the eyes of the smaller figures and many other details. Possibly this way of working was due to the uneven surface; very fine sketch lines would have been difficult to execute on the roughly dressed blocks, and even the plastered areas of the passage were scarcely less difficult to paint on, because of their coarse granular surfaces. But even if finer sketch lines could have been made, the sculptor would have found difficulty in following them closely in such poor stone. We shall see, however, as we pass on to the later processes, that at no stage of the decoration, even when it might have been practicable to do so, was the decorator willing to keep meticulously to the work which preceded his own. There is a certain independence between processes which is astonishing, and whatever the excellencies of one stage of the work, they were likely to be lost in the next. There is no reason to believe that had the wall of plate vi been sculptured, we should necessarily have had preserved more than the general composition and the pose of the figures which it now bears. The spirited character of the drawing, that which constitutes its charm, might easily have been sacrificed. On the other hand, in the tomb which furnished the sketch of plate iii, the sculpture which has come down to us is of better quality than the sketch.

B. THE SCULPTURING OF THE WALLS

Per-nēb's tomb does not afford any evidence with regard to the early stages of sculpturing a wall, as the inner chamber was brought to completion, and the carving of the decoration of the passage and outer chamber was never begun. As an example of the sculptor's very first strokes, an excerpt is given in plate iv from the passage leading into Raꜥ-em-ka's cult chamber. Only a few traces remain of the first sketch in black line,[1] but one can see that the sculptor began by following the sketched outline with his instrument—possibly a mallet-driven copper chisel[2]—making an incision some 3 mm. wide,

[1] The black sketch line of the dragging rope for statues may be seen in plate iv in front of the first partially carved pair of legs.

[2] Much Egyptian limestone is soft enough to be carved by hand pressure, but work would proceed more easily and quickly with the use of a mallet. No ancient pictures of a sculptor of reliefs at work are known, but the mallet and chisel are depicted in the case of men sculpturing wooden statues (Davies, *Deir el Gebrâwi*, I, pl. xiv; this and further references are enumerated in Klebs, *Reliefs des a. Reiches*, p. 82). We have tried cutting a carved outline in Egyptian limestone with a knife, with a chisel driven by a mallet, and by hand, and have obtained a result most nearly approaching this ancient work of plate iv by the use of chisel and mallet, the former being tilted to utilize

which was deepest along the contours of the figures. Other examples of this first process are preserved in the tombs of Ma-nofre[3] and Ḥetep-her-Akhty.[4]

We should note here that the plaster filling along the joints and the patches of plaster to make good defects in the faces of the blocks, mentioned on pages 4 and 5, could be cut just as the limestone was cut. The carving of Egyptian plaster apparently presented no special technical difficulty.[5]

The second stage of the sculptor's work is illustrated by an unfinished figure in a Fifth Dynasty relief from Gīzeh now in the Museum of Fine Arts, Boston (pl. v).[6] The figure is that of a maiden facing the left and holding a blue water lily to her face with her right hand, while her left arm hangs at her side. The girl's name is inscribed in front of her in a vertical column of hieroglyphs, and her titles are carved above her head. In this example, the sculptor has completed the broad cutting about his figure and hieroglyphs and has carved away the background, so that the design appears raised, having its contours, however, still angular in section and its surface flat, without as yet a vestige of modeling. The raised arm is not separated from the border of the field, and the eye, ear, and bracelet and the stem, sepals, and petals of the flower are not carved, but still remain in the preliminary sketch executed in black line. On the background the marks of the tooling are prominent, especially horizontal, or slightly oblique, square-ended strokes which are probably the work of a chisel[7] and broader smoother surfaces which

only one corner of the cutting edge. In so soft a stone, if the sculptor proceeds carefully, as is necessary in following a sketch, jump marks are not noticeable. We secured a smoother channel with the mallet than by hand pressure. For a possible example of a sculptor's chisel dating from the III Dynasty, see Petrie, *Tools and Weapons*, p. 20, pl. xxii, 51; the working edge is 8 mm. wide. A V Dynasty example in common wood of the mallet such as sculptors wield, one shaped like the hieroglyph U 36, is pictured in Petrie, *op. cit.*, pl. xlvi, 60; a mallet to be used by a sculptor would, however, be smaller than this extant specimen. The mallet was grasped at its narrowest part, and blows were delivered now on the bulbous main part, now on the flat butt of the handle below the hand; see Steindorff, *Ti*, pl. 134.

[3] Capart, *Memphis*, fig. 315.

[4] Holwerda, Boeser, and Holwerda, *Denkm. des a. Reiches*, pl. xii, two figures at bottom of left door jamb.

[5] In reference to the door jambs of the tomb of Kai, we made the following note: " . . . filling of joints a pinkish coarse plaster. On north jamb, now devoid of paint, one can see carving passing from stone into plaster; on south jamb, not only joints, but defects in stone, filled and carved." And we noted similar carving of coarse pink plaster in the tombs of Nesut-nofre, Ka-em-ᶜonekh, and elsewhere. This kind of carved plaster has not been commented on in publications, but is familiar to those who have studied reliefs of the Old Kingdom in position at Gīzeh and Ṣaḳḳāreh. Compare the technique of a later period described in Davies, *El Amarna*, IV, p. 32.

[6] From the tomb of Sen-nu-ka. This detail was first kindly called to our attention by Mr. Lythgoe. For permission to publish it here, we are much indebted to the authorities of the Boston Museum.

[7] cf. Capart, *Memphis*, fig. 185, at top.

we think were obtained by shaving off the chiseled surface thinly with an adze. Other examples of relief sculpture in which the background has been lowered, although as yet the figures are without modeling, have been published from the decorations of Me<u>t</u>en,[7] Ptaḥ-ḥotpe,[8] <u>T</u>i,[9] Ḥetep-ḥer-Akhty,[10] and Ma-nofre;[11] an especially early stage in the process of lowering the background about hieroglyphs has been made known in a relief from the tomb of Sekhem-ka,[12] and unpublished examples are probably numerous.[13] We have observed in Per-nēb's cult chamber places where the craftsmen did not cut the background to the lower level (see p. 7 and pl. IX); when covered by gray paint, these neglected areas were hardly noticeable.

The figures of men and objects were next worked over. In this process the last traces of the first sketch with its guiding lines were cut away, and at the same time the surface pitting, such as is visible on the west wall of Per-nēb's outer chamber (pl. VI), for the most part disappeared from the figures, as it had previously done from the background. But the actual amount of stone removed was not very great, although it probably varied in different parts of the decoration. Comparing the fragments of the original surface left on the north wall of the inner chamber with the adjacent sculptured figures, we find the lowering of the surface by the sculpture to be scarcely perceptible (pl. IX). The amount of projection of the relief is rarely over a millimeter, and clearness was secured rather by the depth of the original cutting around the contours. In Per-nēb's tomb, as in many another of the period, the modeling of the human figures is somewhat summary, being largely confined to the legs and face. The breast is quite flat, and the clavicles are not indicated;[14] the muscles of the arms are shown only in outline, the sculptor contenting himself with rounding the contours of body and limbs which had been left angular in the first cutting. In the majority of the figures, however, the curls of the wigs were worked out in full; and some able effort was expended on the modeling of certain hieroglyphs

[8] Davies, *Ptahhetep*, II, pl. III

[9] In Steindorff, *Ti*, pl. 43, the leading figure in the upper left corner is entirely flat, and of the second, the legs and the ribs of beef carried in the right hand have been modeled, but the remainder is unworked, except for an incised outline about the wig where it borders the face; in Steindorff, *op. cit.*, pl. 47, below, water lilies hanging over a man's arm are only blocked out.

[10] Holwerda, Boeser, and Holwerda, *Denkm. des a. Reiches*, pl. XII.

[11] Capart, *Memphis*, fig. 315.

[12] Steindorff, *Kunst der Ägypter*, p. 196.

[13] e.g., a relief in the entrance of Wehem-ka's tomb referred to by Roeder (*Uhemka*, p. 9).

[14] Contrast the exquisite modeling of these parts of the body in the panels of Ḥesy-Rēꜥ; see Quibell, *Hesy*, pls. XXIX-XXXII.

and details, as, for example, in the case of the calves' heads, which are extraordinarily subtle and vivid (pl. ix, above). The work is, indeed, very uneven, being poorest at the ends of the registers away from the large figures of Per-nēb, where in places the design is only scratched in, sometimes, as in various trays of offerings, incompletely.

The processes of lowering the background and modeling the figures were followed by the finishing of the walls. The loss of the coating of paint in many parts of Per-nēb's main chamber has exposed the completed sculptured surface, and one is able to observe the state in which the artist responsible for reliefs saw fit to leave his work. This is indeed the stage in the decoration of a maṣṭabeh chamber most familiar to the modern student because of the great number of fully sculptured reliefs, both in museums and still *in situ* in Egypt, which are entirely denuded of color. The sculptor did not carry the finishing process to the point of removing all traces of the tooling. On the contrary, one may see where the chisel stopped when pushed between the petals of a flower or follow its course along the band of the men's kilts; and the surfaces are full of fine scratches. This last is especially well seen in our plate xiv. Probably the difference in the appearance of the surfaces reproduced in this plate and those about the girl's figure of plate v was effected by rubbing with a piece of sandstone.[15] The fact that the walls were to be covered with paint may well have influenced the sculptor's technique, and the finishing process may have been carried no farther in order to avoid unnecessary labor. But aside from this consideration, we should note that the softer material, limestone, did not invite, or reward, an expenditure of labor in polishing, as did the harder stones employed by the Egyptians. Far from detracting from the charm of the work to the modern eye, we may remark in passing, the less finished surface makes a special appeal in its emphasis of essentials and its unmistakable traces of human handicraft. One admires the lively modeling of the tiny hieroglyphs (rough as the planes are), the correct placing of the knee muscles, the very elimination of details, and the indifference to mere smoothness.

The sequence of processes followed in sculpturing a wall is the one given in this account, but we do not intend to imply that each in turn was carried out over an entire wall before the next one was begun. Rather, as unfinished decorations prove, two or more processes went on simultaneously; plate iv gives examples of the first process and completed work in juxtaposition; plate v, of the second process and the finished relief. And

[15] Again we may cite the practice in sculpturing statues, for the finishing of which the polishing stone was the customary tool; cf. Steindorff, *Ti*, pl. 134.

the examples cited above (p. 17) from the tombs of Ḥetep-ḥer-Akhty and Ma-nofre offer illustrations of the first and second stages occurring together, in Ma-nofre's work with a part of the preliminary sketch also remaining. Perhaps the explanation is to be sought in a division of labor, one man doing only one kind of work, and as many men as the chamber would accommodate being employed together. A, who was making the first cutting about the lines of the sketch, as shown in plate IV, may have stopped abruptly in order to give B, who was to lower the background, a chance to set to work. A transferred his activity elsewhere, C and D were able to model and finish the part done by B, but work on the tomb ceased before A had a chance to return to this wall.[16] Otherwise we must suppose A, or the foreman who controlled him, to have been very capricious, or very much pressed elsewhere, to break off the first process of the carving in so erratic a manner. If each sculptor was qualified to execute all the processes, the unfinished work of plate IV becomes even less explicable.

The final process of the sculptors before turning over the walls to the painter was to remedy in a comparatively fine plaster defects due to slips made in chiseling and to the occasional splintering of the stone and its supplementary coarse plaster during the carving. This finer plaster has been examined on the fragments of filling from the joints, which fell when the tomb of Per-nēb was taken down, and which were carefully collected and sent to New York. It can also be seen here and there on the walls where there are breaks and, consequently, edges visible. It differs from mortar plaster in its texture, which is closer and more homogeneous, being free from particles of sand, and in its color, which closely approaches that of limestone. That it is largely composed of powdered limestone seems extremely probable.[17] This finer plaster was not carved, but spread on in a soft state and worked while still soft, for it looks smeared, and under it the sharpness of the previous cutting is often obscured. Although in Per-nēb's tomb intended to

[16] Engelbach has recently suggested in the case of a sarcophagus of hard stone that the different stages of completion of its interior decoration indicate the employment of several men to do different kinds of work at the same time (*Annales*, 1929, pp. 23-24).

[17] Specimens of this fine plaster kindly tested for us by Dr. H. H. Willard, Professor of Analytical Chemistry in the University of Michigan, showed the presence of both the carbonate and sulphate of calcium. On the occasional artificial mixture of powdered limestone with gypsum to improve the color of a plaster, see Lucas, *J. E. A.*, 1924, p. 129; generally, however, according to this authority, calcium carbonate when present in ancient Egyptian plaster is there as an impurity. The corresponding plaster on the west wall from the tomb of Ka-em-snēw (pl. II, c, d) is less fine than the plaster from Per-nēb's tomb and contains some grains of a contrasting color, its main mass being very pink. It may well be composed of a larger proportion of crude plaster of Paris than that in Per-nēb's decoration. In detail "c" the plaster may be seen in the depths of a hieroglyph done in sunken relief, that is, on a surface not yet exposed before the wall was carved.

cover only defective places, it overlapped more or less the adjacent carving. But that it was not spread over the whole wall is clear from the fact that the washes and sketch lines discussed in the next section are again and again found resting on limestone with only the thinnest intervening layer of whitewash.[18]

C. THE PAINTING OF THE WALLS

The sculptors having finished their work, the cult chamber was now given over to another company of men, the painters. Their first procedure was to whitewash all the walls with a preparation of brilliant white color and of such fluid consistency as no doubt to be laid on with a brush. The loss of the final surface has exposed this wash in many places where it now appears as a film which could be peeled off or as a thin powdery layer. Like the sculptor's repair plaster discussed at the close of the preceding section B, it tended to gather in the depressions of the carving and thus partially to obscure the relief. On chemical examination this whitewash in Per-nēb's tomb proves to be "a high grade of calcined gypsum."[1]

[18] The Egyptians were past masters in the manipulation of plaster, and only a beginning has been made in understanding the skill and the extent of their use of it. In the VI Dynasty and later, entire walls were often decorated with reliefs executed in plaster. See Junker, *Anzeiger*, 1913, p. 25, pl. VI, and *ibid.*, 1927, p. 143, and A. M. Blackman, *Meir*, I, p. 7, and IV, p. 27, pls. XXII, 2, XXIII, 1, XXIV, for the VI Dynasty; A. M. Blackman, *op. cit.*, I, p. 9, and III, pp. 11, 14, etc. (principally in the footnotes), and pls. XXXVII, 3, XXXVIII, 2, XXXIX, for the XII Dynasty; Davies, *El Amarna*, IV, p. 32, for work at El ʿAmarneh; Mackay, *J. E. A.*, 1921, pp. 166-168, for Ramesside times. Whether modeled plaster merely supplemented the carving of the walls, as in Per-nēb's decoration, or almost entirely repeated the labor of executing the design, as in the later ʿAmarneh technique, depended on the quality of the stone. Mackay regards the reliefs of Ramesside times as modeled while still soft, so far as time permitted, and finished by carving after the plaster had set. This technique, he states, "appeared first in the Eighteenth Dynasty, but does not seem to have become popular during that period." He thinks it was derived "from the compulsory use" of plaster "in filling up flaws in the rock walls of tombs that were to be sculptured in the usual manner." But all the conditions were present for its development in the Old Kingdom, at Meir in rock-hewn tombs and at Gīzeh and Ṣaḳḳāreh in maṣṭabeh chambers, whenever poorer grades of stone, incapable of being well carved, were employed. The poorer grades were increasingly used in the VI Dynasty, and the tombs of this dynasty are the ones dating from the Old Kingdom which are most copiously supplied with reliefs in plaster. These questions among others need to be studied. Was modeling in plaster ever undertaken in preference to painting on a flat surface in the case of stone walls unsuitable for carving, or was it always supplementary to inadequate stone reliefs? How was the plaster applied, at one time or in successive layers? We observed that the plaster reliefs in the tomb of Ka-ḥi-ef were peeling in layers; the modeled top surface of now a leg, now an arm, of human figures had come away, leaving incised outlines in the level below it. The composition of the decorator's plaster of the Old Kingdom needs further examination; some of it is only slightly less coarse and pink than the typical mortar plaster (cf. p. 4), and at the other extreme is a glistening white, powdery plaster which seems like a thicker application of the whitewash discussed in the first paragraph of our next section. No doubt we shall be well informed on these matters when once Junker and Reisner complete their publications of the Gīzeh cemeteries.

[1] So described by Dr. B. A. Soule of the Department of Chemistry of the University of Michigan, who was so kind as to examine samples of it. Contrary to Raehlmann's view (quoted in Eibner, *Wandmalerei*, pp. 49, 51, 586)

THE DECORATION OF THE TOMB OF PER-NĒB

Considerable change is observable within the Old Kingdom as to the surface to which pigments were applied. Data are not yet published for the technique of the reliefs of King Djoser, which were found at the Step Pyramid and belong in the earlier part of the Third Dynasty about 2975 B.C.,[2] but it is certain that at Meidūm in the early Fourth Dynasty the stone sculptures of Raᶜ-ḥotpe and Nūfer-maᶜet in part received the paint directly, for the "coat of colours" is said to have been "in some instances apparently rubbed into the stone so thoroughly as to become adherent."[3] At Gīzeh, in the cemetery west of the Great Pyramid, the burial chambers of the Fourth Dynasty had their limestone lining blocks painted in imitation of granite. In one tomb believed to date from the reign of Khufu, Junker found the paint laid on bare stone, in others ranging from the time of Khufu to that of Men-kau-Rēᶜ, he found a whitewash underlying the red and black pigments.[4] Junker also observed at Gīzeh that in the cult chamber of Ka-ne-nesut I, attributed by him to the close of the Fourth or beginning of the Fifth Dynasty (around 2750 B.C.), the colors were laid on bare stone, but in the later decoration of Nesut-nofre they were placed on "eine dünne weisse Putzschicht, die als Untergrund auf die ganzen Wände gegeben war."[5] And in a relief of the Old Kingdom at Munich examined by Eibner, red pigment was laid on the bare stone, green on a layer of gypsum of considerable thickness.[6] The technique of Per-nēb's wash of white is typical of the later Fifth Dynasty work. In the Sixth Dynasty, with the increasing use of poorer stone, pigments were

that a gypsum ground was always used in the Old Kingdom and a lime ground in the New Kingdom, Eibner has shown that both gypsum and carbonate of lime occur in the Old Kingdom and that gypsum occurs as late as 150 B.C. (*Wandmalerei*, p. 580, sample from the tomb of Raᶜ-ḥotpe of the early IV Dynasty, with pigment "auf einer dünnen Kalktünche," and p. 581, samples from the Sun temple at Abu Gurōb dating from the V Dynasty, for both; also statement, bottom of p. 586). What is actually found by chemical analysis is gypsum or calcium carbonate, and it is a matter of inference whether the latter was put on the wall as such, perhaps in the form of whiting, or as a lime wash which has since altered. Compare our page 19, note 17, for the same question as regards plaster, and Lucas, *Materials*, p. 24, as to whitewash. Lucas, in his earlier book, *Antiques*, p. 52, refers to ancient Egyptian plaster as "ranging from crude gypsum to fine plaster of Paris," hence the identification of a fine grade of plaster of Paris in Per-nēb's tomb need awaken no distrust.

[2] Firth, *Annales*, 1927, pl. III, and 1928, pl. II; Capart, *Memphis*, figs. 90, 138, 140; *Illustr. London News*, November 12, 1927, p. 861.   [3] Petrie, *Medum*, p. 28.

[4] *Gîza I*, pp. 48, 167.

[5] *Anzeiger*, 1913, p. 20; for Junker's latest opinion on the date of Ka-ne-nesut I's cult chamber, see *Gîza I*, pp. 9, 36, 79, and *Kultkammer* (3d edition), pp. 15-18.

[6] See *Wandmalerei*, pp. 54, 55, 586; Eibner gave the date of this relief in round numbers as 3000 B.C. (*op. cit.*, p. 53). Professor Dyroff, kindly responding to our inquiry, expressed the opinion, after consulting with Eibner, that the piece in question is in all probability number 1034 of the Egyptian section of the Münchener Museum für antike Kleinkunst, namely, a limestone fragment from the funerary temple of King Ne-woser-Rēᶜ, published in line by Borchardt in *Ne-user-reᶜ*, p. 82, fig. 58 c. Against this view seems to stand Eibner's record, *op. cit.*, p. 53, that the piece is in sunken relief.

often laid over, or more rarely in,[7] thick beds of plaster, the primary purpose of which had been to supplement or take the place of carved stone.[8]

This whitewash or plaster, which commonly intervened between the stone and the pigments and is such an outstanding feature of Egyptian painted wall reliefs, seems to have had a number of purposes. When, unlike the compact, firm blocks of the early tombs, which received their paint directly, the stone was very porous and much patched with plaster, the whitewash probably served as a pore filler to prevent the absorption of the paint and its fixative.[9] An important use in the case of such walls was also to produce a uniform and easy surface for the painter's brush. And whitewash may well have been found to brighten and improve the quality of the painted surface wherever pigments were laid thinly enough to be affected by it. Further, Eibner regards plaster as technically necessary in binding in certain pigments.[10]

The walls having received their coating of whitewash, the next process was to outline the design, in whole or in large part, with red. This line is exposed again and again on Per-nēb's walls and in places may be seen to underlie the outlines of the top surface. It is for the most part broader than the final outlines, its width averaging nearly that of the lines of the first sketch (p. 6); its color is the same brown-red, more or less thinned, which was used for the first sketch, but that it is not itself a part of the first sketch is made certain by the fact that it may be seen here and there to overlie the whitewash and to appear on the lower levels, which were not by any possibility exposed before the carving was done. It may well be called a second preliminary sketch, as it doubtless served to facilitate the final coloring of the walls. Indeed its presence seems to us most probably attributable to a craving for an easy guide under a light which was in part necessarily artificial. In sculptured work the design could hardly have been so clear as in red line contrasting with the white ground.

Inasmuch as the existence of a second sketch has received notice only once briefly in earlier discussions of Egyptian painted reliefs,[11] we now offer a few specific illustrations

[7] So in the tomb of Yedu at Gīzeh, especially in the case of the jewels of the large figures of the east wall.

[8] cf. p. 20, note 18.

[9] Suggested by Mackay in regard to Theban rock-hewn tombs (*J. E. A.*, 1921, p. 164; cf. *ibid.*, p. 166).

[10] cf. p. 33.

[11] For certain XII Dynasty sculptures, Spurrell denied its existence: "The lines were usually regulated by the sculptor and did not require sketching by the colourists" (*Archaeol. Journ.*, 1895, p. 228). Reisner, however, recognized it in the tomb of Queen Mer-es-ᶜonekh III: ". . . and finally on the white plaster the design was redrawn in red lines and colored as in the main room" (*Bull. of the Mus. of Fine Arts*, 1927, p. 70).

of its survival on Per-nēb's walls. Plates xv and xvi show photographically and in line three offering bearers from the south wall; in the drawing in plate xvi, the broken lines indicate the second sketch, and the solid lines, the figures as previously sculptured. In plate xv one may discern on the front of the kilt of the last man the two levels, the upper with its final outline, and, where this has dropped away, the lower with its second sketch line. One may observe on this figure, also, the outlines of the arm carried in the second sketch across the carved stems of onions, which in reality would hide the arm. Likewise, in the case of the foremost offering bearer in plates xv and xvi the outlines of a shoulder and the front of the body are drawn over the carved stalks of papyrus plants which he carries, and, in the case of the offering bearer in the middle, the figure of the ibex which he carries is fully drawn in the second sketch, although the entire figure had been previously sculptured. Evidently at this stage of the decoration the draughtsman felt especially the need to keep without confusion before his eye the full drawing of the human figure, inasmuch as even the contours later to be covered were indicated in the second sketch. Among the offerings an interesting example of his feeling for form is found in the necks and mouths of tall jars rendered in the second sketch, even though in the finished decoration the tops of the jars were to be covered solidly by black pigment representing clay seals (pl. xiv).[12] Among the hieroglyphs the second sketch line is found repeatedly about signs outlined on the final surface in black. It is less easily detected in the case of the hieroglyphs outlined on the top surface with red, because of the danger of mistaking one kind of red line for the other when only one is present, but on hieroglyphs F 24 and U 21 (in *štp.t*) of the south offering list both may be seen, the second sketch appearing at a lower level (pl. xvii, lower left rectangle of hieroglyphs).

An underlying red wash is found among the hieroglyphs when black paint was to be used on the final surface.[18] Outside the hieroglyphs the available evidence is less obvious, but the wash certainly underlay many of the black division lines of the offering lists and registers and many details which were to be black in the final surface. Besides being used under black, the wash possibly was laid on the nude parts of some of the male figures,

---

[12] cf. Ransom, in *Perneb*, pp. 74-75, fig. 39.

[18] It is to be seen on most examples of hieroglyphs E 15, N 33*, N 35, N (35), U 31, Z 1 (in offering lists) where black has dropped off, also on parts of hieroglyphs, as on the beard of D 2, the wigs of A 1, A 40, D 1, and ⟨⟩; the sides, bottom, and inner mark of X 8, the greater part of X 2, the eyelids of D 4, the tops of W 21 and W 22, the handle of V 31, the cord of T 21, the mud seal of Y 2, and the horns of ⟨⟩.

later to be colored brown-red.[14] Below the scenes in Per-nēb's cult chamber ran a broad band of brown-red bordered by black. A light red wash apparently underlay both these pigments, although it shows principally where black has fallen away. It is possible that the practice was not uniform throughout the decoration, and we hesitate to believe that a red wash was laid everywhere under brown-red, inasmuch as there is frequently not a trace to suggest it when the top color has fallen away.[15] Even the partial use of a red wash requires explanation. We believe that it was essentially a part of the second sketch. The first sketch on the west wall of the outer room (pl. vi) shows a tendency on the part of the draughtsman to fill in here and there with solid color, as in the two upper registers where, for example, the tuft of an animal's tail and its horns and hoofs are tinted red. The wash now in question does not occur with sufficient frequency to warrant the view that it was essential as a foundation to brown-red, whereas if we regard it as a part of the second sketch, its somewhat irregular use is entirely comprehensible.[16]

The second sketch departed considerably from the sculptured outlines. In some instances the changes were by way of correction, as when the wrong hieroglyph had been sculptured.[17] Again on the north wall, under a table of trussed fowl, the draughtsman added to the pile of offerings two cucumbers and a bunch of grapes, which had not been included in the design as sculptured (pls. xi-xiii, at right of second register from bottom of plate), and there are other examples of additions made in the second sketch. There is further almost constant lack of correspondence between the sculptured and the sketched figures; and it would seem that the draughtsman of the second sketch must have used the carving only as a general guide, without endeavoring to repeat its outlines closely. There is evidence that in the final coat of paint, in turn, the decorator did not everywhere keep precisely within his second sketch lines, but the greater part of the difference between the final painted surface and the sculpture is due to changes made by the man who laid down the second sketch. The impression made by the decoration in

[14] In the third register from the bottom on the south wall, faint red color may also be seen on the eyes of the offering bearers and, here and there, on their kilts, which were not reserved so clean as in the other registers.

[15] On the legs of one of the large figures of Per-nēb (south wall), the under tinge of red looks quite as much like a stain from the brown-red as like a preliminary wash.

[16] Compare in plate i an example of the red wash as used in the tomb of Ka-em-snēw; in detail "a," it is to be seen on the central pot (W 24), which in the final surface was blue in color.

[17] Thus in the north offering list in the item *twȝw.t* the sculptor bungled the second example of hieroglyph X 1, and his work was set right in the second sketch. In the titles on the same wall, the sculptor omitted sign N 37 in *ẖry šštȝ*; the draughtsman of the second sketch then reduced the size of sign U 30, making room to draw in above it the missing letter, a modification which was perpetuated on the final surface.

THE DECORATION OF THE TOMB OF PER-NĒB

Per-nēb's tomb is of able, and at the same time very casual, work. Presumably in the comparatively dim light of the chamber, the draughtsman would have felt hampered had he tried to follow the sculptured outlines exactly. He had a sufficiently practised hand to sketch the figures with greater rapidity when working somewhat freely.

We have now brought our study of the stages of decorating Per-nēb's tomb to a point where the main chamber, already sculptured, presented a brilliant white surface with scenes and inscriptions picked out in red line and with certain details in solid red color.[18] Before taking up the last processes which yielded the final surface, we need to consider the pigments used. The colors found on the final surface of this decoration are red, yellow, green, blue, brown, black, gray, and white. All are earth and mineral pigments, organic materials being unknown for pigments in the wall paintings of Egypt which antedate the Ptolemaic period. The reds, yellows, and browns at this time were ochers; the black, a form of carbon, now soot, perhaps now charcoal; the white, gypsum or whiting. These have been so often determined as to require no special consideration here,[19] but we must take up more particularly the green and the blue of Per-nēb's decoration.

Green color occurs in the predynastic period long before the acquisition of a blue pigment by the Egyptians. Although green is not shown in the colored plates reproducing the predynastic wall paintings of Hierakonpolis, the text of the publication makes clear that all the boats in these paintings save one were once green, the pigment being a granular layer of crushed malachite laid over white.[20] Powdered malachite was used at Mei-

---

[18] We must qualify this statement by mentioning the possibility that the various successive processes went forward more rapidly in some parts of the decoration than in others. Compare what was said on pages 18-19 on the sequence of processes.

[19] The microscopical appearance of samples from Per-nēb's tomb submitted to Dr. Soule was such as to suggest, though it did not prove, that the black pigment of the finer details is soot, the gray of the background, a mixture of gypsum and charcoal. On the composition of Egyptian pigments, see Petrie, *Medum*, pp. 28-29, for the early IV Dynasty, a section founded on the chemical and microscopical examinations made by Spurrell, whose own presentation of the matter may be read in *Archaeol. Journ.*, 1895, pp. 226-227; for the XII Dynasty, Russell, in *Medum*, chap. VIII, and Spurrell, *ibid.*, pp. 227-229, who identified for black, in samples from Beni Ḥasan, in addition to the more common lampblack, or soot, the mineral pyrolusite; for the XVIII Dynasty, Spurrell, *ibid.*, pp. 230-235; Russell, *loc. cit.*; Petrie, *Tell el Amarna*, pp. 25-26; Lucas, in *Tut-ankh-Amen*, II, pp. 178-181; in general, Laurie, *Materials*, chap. II, and *Greek and Roman Methods*, Appendix I; more recent data in Lucas, *Materials*, pp. 136-146, and *Analyst*, September, 1926, pp. 442-443; and Lucas, quoted in Clarke and Engelbach, *Masonry*, p. 200; specific analyses in Eibner, *Wandmalerei*, pp. 578-589.

[20] Quibell and Green, *Hierakonpolis*, II, p. 21; nothing is said of a chemical analysis, but we must suppose that the green color was not attributed to malachite without an adequate examination. The use of malachite for eye paint in the predynastic period is well attested; see Petrie, *Prehistoric Egypt*, p. 43, § 113, and Lucas, *Materials*, pp. 146-147.

dūm as a green pigment,[21] and Eibner reports examples of it from the Old Kingdom, one on the relief in Munich already mentioned [22] and two others from the Sun temple at Abu Gurōb, a round seventy-five years earlier than Per-nēb's tomb.[23] The mineral malachite having been determined as the source of green color in these earlier examples, we are not surprised that an examination, kindly made by Dr. Soule, gives results favorable to the view that powdered malachite was used here also.[24] At a later time sporadic occurrences of the crushed mineral chrysocolla used as a pigment are known,[25] and by the Eighteenth Dynasty an artificial pigment, a by-product of the blue discussed in our next paragraphs had been developed.[26]

The greatest contribution of Egypt to the pigments of antiquity was the beautiful blue of which the tomb of Per-nēb affords the oldest examples in this country in a quantity to render the color's merits appreciable, examples that are also among the oldest and most abundant to be identified anywhere. Far from having been invented in Alexandria, as Vitruvius thought,[27] the "Egyptian," or "Vestorian," [28] blue goes back

[21] Petrie, *Medum*, p. 29; Spurrell, *Archaeol. Journ.*, 1895, p. 227.

[22] See references p. 21, note 6.

[23] *Wandmalerei*, p. 581, nos. 3, 5.

[24] We quote from Dr. Soule's report on the samples submitted: "I gave each a careful examination using both low and high magnification. The smallest fragment (8 mm. x 3 mm.) carried a layer of five darker green areas, possibly 0.2 mm. in diameter, and six or eight particles of the blue frit previously identified (see p. 27). The balance of the layer was pale green and looked as though it were faded or washed out. The large, more circular piece (35 mm. x 25 mm.) had only a few of the darker green areas and particles of frit. The body was distinctly lighter in color, not due to any apparent decrease in thickness of the layer or admixture of colorless or white particles. The third, oblong piece (26 mm. x 7 mm.) also carried a few darker green areas and blue particles, but the main portion of the layer was decidedly greener than on either other piece. Later I examined portions of the pale green coating from each of the three fragments, found that they were alike and that they were essentially copper carbonate, i.e. malachite. Since this is normally the end product of the decomposition of copper minerals I searched each sample with the microscope for any evidence of chrysocolla. I found none. Consequently, I am led to the conclusion that Per-nēb used malachite. After some experimentation I was able to isolate one of the darker green particles and break it open. It appeared to have a brownish center covered with malachite, i.e. it was possibly copper oxide, cuprite, partially altered to malachite. This is a common situation." For those whom it may interest we add the information that macroscopically the lighter green of the foregoing samples was like Maerz and Paul, *Dict.*, pl. 19, D 5, and *Munsell*, GY 7/4; the darker green we matched only in *Munsell* as G 4-5/4, but a different sample of dark green is equivalent to Maerz and Paul, *op. cit.*, pl. 29, H 10.

[25] Spurrell, *Archaeol. Journ.*, 1895, pp. 227-228. The occurrence of "veins of blue silicate of copper, chrysocolla," in the Eastern Desert (27° to 29° N. latitude) is mentioned in Barron and Hume, *Topography and Geology*, p. 259. We owe this reference to Dr. Soule.

[26] Lucas examined five specimens of the XVIII to the XXVI Dynasty (*Materials*, pp. 143-144), and Eibner, one of the XVIII Dynasty (*Wandmalerei*, pp. 582-583, no. 16 from Berlin no. 10338; cf. *op. cit.*, p. 589).

[27] Book VII. 11.

[28] The name is derived from the Vestorius who fostered its production in Puteoli; see Vitruvius, *loc. cit.*

to the Old Kingdom, and once the way of making it had been discovered, it became the principal, if not quite the sole,[29] blue pigment used down through the centuries until after Christ.[30] It has been found, not only in Egypt in later periods,[31] but also in Crete and other Aegean regions, in paintings of the Bronze Age, in Pompeii, Rome, and outlying parts of the Roman empire.[32] As a color, it is characterized by the absence of green; rather, it verges very slightly towards red.[33] In chemical composition, it is a double silicate of calcium and copper;[34] it has a definitely known crystalline form; and its usefulness was enhanced by its remarkable stability. This pigment has been a

[29] Raehlmann maintains that in wall paintings extant from antiquity only a single blue pigment occurs, the one known as Egyptian blue (*Museumskunde*, 1913, p. 227, § 23); indigo, so this authority states, has not been identified in any ancient painting (*ibid.*, p. 231, § 49), and ultramarine was not in use (Lucas, *Materials*, pp. 142-143; Laurie, *Materials*, pp. 47-48); see, however, on other blues, Swindler, *Painting*, pp. 426-427, and below, pp. 29-30. No reliable evidence exists, moreover, for the use of a cobalt pigment in ancient times. The supposed instance of the XX Dynasty mentioned by Lucas (*op. cit.*, p. 139), citing Wiedemann (*P. S. B. A.*, 1892-1893, p. 113), seems to us on examining Wiedemann's source (Hofmann, *Zeitschr. für ägypt. Sprache*, 1885, p. 65) to be not a pigment but a smalt. According to Raehlmann (*ibid.*, p. 229), cobalt pigment is modern, being characteristic of the XIX century; ancient forerunners of smalt are another matter which does not concern us here. Error all too easily creeps in, as in the attribution of Per-nēb's blue color to a cobalt source (Toch, *Journ. of Ind. and Eng. Chemistry*, 1918, p. 120), much quoted in Lucas's writings — in *Materials*, p. 63, however, with skepticism, on the grounds that cobalt minerals are not native to Egypt and are not blue in color and, therefore, were unlikely at so early a time to be recognized as capable of imparting a blue color.

[30] The latest examples known to Raehlmann are in the wall paintings of S. Maria Antiqua at Rome (*Museumskunde*, 1913, p. 228, §§ 31, 33).

[31] See the analyses reported by Lucas, in *Materials*, pp. 142, 238, citing also Crow, *Annales*, 1903, p. 242.

[32] See Swindler, *Painting*, p. 74; Raehlmann, *Museumskunde*, 1913, pp. 225-228, §§ 10, 17, 25, 27, 28, and *Über die Maltechnik*, pp. 67-68, 79-80; Micault, *Bull. de la Soc. min. de France*, 1881, pp. 83-84 (wall painting in Brittany near St.-Brieuc); Pisani, *Bull. de la Soc. min. de France*, 1880, pp. 197-198 (free pigment from a painter's stores found near Autun); Laurie, McLintock, and Miles, *Proc. of the Roy. Soc. of London*, 1914, p. 420 (examples from Rome, Syria, and Crete, and from Viriconium in Shropshire, England). These references might be greatly multiplied.

[33] We find it in Per-nēb's tomb, where the paint is broken and the real color is seen below the surface, to agree with *Munsell*, PB 5/6. Compare the following note and our plate XIII.

[34] We owe the following statement about specimens from Per-nēb's decoration to the kindness of Dr. Soule. "The samples of plaster from the tomb of Per-nēb have been examined with respect to the blue surface coating. This latter was scraped from the base and carefully washed about a dozen times, first with warm hydrochloric acid, then with water, until the residue appeared to be free from white particles, i.e., plaster. After drying, the color, macroscopically, was a pale blue — the same as fine crystals of blue vitriol ($CuSO_4.5H_2O$). Microscopically, there were opaque, pale blue masses in large amount, transparent crystals of a beautiful azure in moderate quantity, colorless crystals (sand) and brown particles in small amount. Direct chemical tests proved conclusively the presence of copper in the form of a silicate and the absence of cobalt (the test would surely have revealed the presence of 0.1%). Microchemical examination, including petrographic, confirmed the above and revealed optical properties corresponding to those given by Winchell [*Optic and Microscopic Characters*, pp. 126-127] for calcium copper silicate ($CaCuSi_4O_{10}$), made from fusion and called 'Vestorian blue.' I therefore conclude that the material is a calcium copper silicate."

subject of interest and investigation since the early part of the last century.[35] It has been produced synthetically by modern chemists again and again,[36] and certain students of it have suggested that its use might with profit be revived at the present time.[37] To the French chemist Fouqué is to be attributed the final recognition of its nature,[38] to Professor Laurie, the demonstration by definitely controlled experiments of the ingredients and conditions of its production.[39]

How then did the ancient discovery come about? Probably, as Laurie and his colleagues have set forth,[40] in the course of the development of copper glazes. As late as 1910, Laurie designated the Egyptian blue as a powdered glaze,[41] but after making his own experiments he pointed out that glaze when crushed makes a poor pigment, as it forms a gray powder.[42] First we need to bear in mind that the Egyptians did not develop the art of glazing pottery, the terms "faience" and "glazed pottery" so frequent in Egyptological literature giving a wrong impression. The materials at hand led rather to the development of glazes "consisting of silicates of the alkalies and of calcium, coloured with oxide of copper," according to one view of their composition,[43] and these ingredients do not run freely on pottery, but require a silicious base—actual sandstone and steatite or an artificial base consisting chiefly of quartz sand and only negligibly of clay.[44] Thus while people who glazed pottery never hit on "Egyptian blue," the very ingredients which presumably entered into the early Egyptian glazes even before the close of the predynastic period—quartz sand, malachite, limestone, with native soda as a flux—when heated together in proper proportions, develop at a narrow range of temperature, 840°-890° C., the scale-like blue crystals which compose the Egyptian

[35] A summary of the course of its investigation, including comments on Laurie's results, is given in Eibner, *Wandmalerei*, pp. 203-206.

[36] See especially Russell, in *Medum*, pp. 45-46, § 66; Laurie, McLintock, and Miles, *Proc. of the Roy. Soc. of London*, 1914, pp. 418-429. We are indebted to Dr. Soule for specimens which he made.

[37] So regarded by Fouqué, *Comptes rendus*, 1889, p. 327:"La beauté et la solidité de cette matière colorante, qui ne redoute ni l'air, ni l'humidité, ni la lumière, ni la plupart des agents chimiques, la facilité de sa fabrication, le prix très bas auquel on peut la produire font désirer qu'elle reprenne sa place dans l'industrie." cf. Laurie, *Materials*, p. 229.

[38] See *Comptes rendus*, 1889, pp. 325-327, and *Bull. de la Soc. franç. de min.*, 1889, pp. 36-38.

[39] For the full account see Laurie, McLintock, and Miles, *Proc. of the Roy. Soc. of London*, 1914, pp. 418-429. Reviews and summaries occur in *Anc. Eg.*, 1914, pp. 186-188; *J. E. A.*, 1914, p. 73; *Chemical News*, 1913, p. 300.

[40] Laurie, McLintock, and Miles, *Proc. of the Roy. Soc. of London*, 1914, p. 428.

[41] *Materials*, pp. 5, 23.

[42] *Archaeologia*, 1913, pp. 316-317.

[43] Burton, *Journ. of the Roy. Soc. of Arts*, 1911-1912, pp. 594-602, in particular, p. 597.

[44] cf. Lucas, *Materials*, chap. II.

blue pigment. Heated less, they form a bluish green glass, heated more, they give an olive green glass; but at the right temperature, the quartz is acted upon below the point of fusion of the whole mass, and the blue frit, as it is often called, crystalizes out. It is a friable substance which crushes easily as no glaze or glass, the product of complete fusion, does. At a later time the Egyptians learned to combine and manage their materials in a way to produce frits of other colors, such as the green pigment to which reference was made above (p. 26).

For the history of the art of painting, the possibility of tracing in Egypt as in no other land the emergence of blue, the last of the painter's primary colors to be acquired by man, is of high interest. Blue pigment was not included in the resources of the palaeolithic artist, so far as is known, and the Egyptians got on without it for many centuries. Blue color in nature was familiar to them from the earliest times, for instance in the ornamental rock lapis lazuli and the mineral turquoise, both of which they had in the predynastic period, before 3400 B.C. The earliest recorded instance of a blue which may be artificial (or mineral, as seems more likely and reduced to powder by crushing or grinding) is the inlay of "dark blue paste" found by Professor Reisner at Nagᶜ ed-Deir in a gold object of the First Dynasty.[45] No blue coloring matter is again on record until we reach the tomb of Ḥesy-Rēᶜ, generally attributed to the reign of Djoser, the builder of the Step Pyramid, in the early part of the Third Dynasty. Here blue color makes its first known appearance in wall painting—very sparingly, for only a single surviving occurrence of it is reported[46]—and here, too, nothing is known of the chemical composition or particular hue of the blue pigment. At Meidūm, further, in the early part of the Fourth Dynasty, about 2900 B.C., Egyptian blue was not yet in use. The walls here revealed a so-called blue described by Spurrell as "in some cases bright, but in most cases hardly blue but grey or slate coloured."[47] No samples for chemical examination were obtained, and the nature of this early pigment, too, remains uncertain.[48] Some use at this time, however, was made of a very beautiful blue mineral, azurite (or chessylite, as Spurrell designated it), powdered, two occurrences

[45] Reisner, *Early Dyn. Cem.*, I, p. 31; cf. Möller, in *Goldschmiedearb.*, p. 61, note 2, and *Metallkunst*, p. 25 with note 65.

[46] Quibell, *Hesy*, p. 22, § 13.

[47] *Archaeol. Journ.*, 1895, p. 227.

[48] Petrie's statement about it reads: "On the walls it appears much of a blue verditer tint, apparently derived from an impure earthy blue carbonate of copper" (*Medum*, p. 29); compare another passage: "No traces of green or blue frits have been found in all this early work" (*loc. cit.*).

being recorded, the free pigment in a shell used as a painter's palette [49] and the pigment employed for painting the pupils, eyelids, and eyebrows of the resin-soaked wrappings of an individual who was interred at Meidūm.[50] No other instances of the use of azurite as a pigment by the ancient Egyptians have been made known; we suggest, however, that there may be unrecognized examples of an original azurite blue altered to green in early works of Egyptian art.[51] In the days when the Great Pyramid was being built, the Egyptians were still apparently without a stable blue pigment which could be freely used, for a number of polychrome stelae and inscriptions dating from the reign of Khufu are totally devoid of blue color.[52] The earliest well-documented examples of Egyptian blue are those identified from the ruined Fifth Dynasty Sun temple at Abu Gurōb, which, as we have already said (p.26), was only about seventy-five years earlier than Per-nēb's tomb.[53] Laurie, to be sure, states that the pigment goes back to the Fourth Dynasty,[54] and Spurrell mentioned vaguely an example assigned by Petrie to the same dynasty,[55] but nothing precise is known of Egyptian blue in the Fourth Dynasty, and Lucas, writing in 1926, could not carry it farther back than the Eleventh Dynasty.[56] As the evidence now stands, the acquisition of this lovely pigment was an occurrence of the period of one hundred and fifty years covering the latter part of the Fourth and the earlier part of the Fifth Dynasty, that is, about 2875-2725 B.C., if we follow the extremely conservative minimum dates of Professor Breasted. We hope that the study of its early history will be continued, and to this end we mention here the

[49] Petrie, *Medum*, p. 29; Spurrell, *Archaeol. Journ.*, 1895, p. 227.

[50] Spurrell, *loc. cit.*, who said that the pigment had turned green with age. Compare Smith, *J. E. A.*, 1914, pp. 192-193, pl. xxxi, 2, who states that the pigment is malachite and the mummy perhaps of the V Dynasty; an original blue is much more likely for eyelids and eyebrows. Of course both authors are right, malachite being the end product of the alteration of copper minerals; cf. p. 26, note 24.

[51] Eibner remarked that on walls azurite tends to become green (*Wandmalerei*, pp. 200, 386). Its most successful use as a pigment was in illuminated manuscripts and tempera pictures of the Renaissance (Laurie, *Archaeologia*, 1913, pp. 317-318; Raehlmann, *Museumskunde*, 1913, pp. 230-231, §§ 41-48).

[52] Junker, *Gîza I*, pp. 155, 173-174, pls. xxiii, xxvii. See also Lutz, *Steles*, pls. 1, 2 (no. 2), 48, 49; on page 15, number 2 is stated to be devoid of color. In September, 1915, when the present writer had the privilege of examining this stela of Nūfer, it still retained considerable color, although not so much as the stela of Wep-em-nofret (no. 1). On the other hand, the blue occurring very sparingly in the somewhat later tomb of Seshem-nofre on the blade of the chisel-hieroglyph (U 23) and a small boy's collar may be the Egyptian blue.

[53] Eibner, *Wandmalerei*, p. 581, nos. 6, 7; compare the analyses of Old Kingdom blue by Raehlmann discussed on pages 48-49 of Eibner, *op. cit.*

[54] See Laurie, McLintock, and Miles, *Proc. of the Roy. Soc. of London*, 1914, p. 418.

[55] *Archaeol. Journ.*, 1895, p. 227.

[56] *Materials*, p. 141; his 1930 statement in Clarke and Engelbach, *Masonry*, p. 200, remains the same.

presence in the collection of the Metropolitan Museum of an unpublished cylinder seal formed out of this same artificial blue mineral, a cylinder dating from the reign of the Sixth Dynasty king, Pepy I (about 2600 B.C.),[57] and being fifty years or so later than the blue pigment of Per-nēb's wall decorations and very like it in color.[58]

As is well known, the one method of painting on walls which was customarily used in Pharaonic Egypt is painting *a tempera*.[59] So here in the Fifth Dynasty in Per-nēb's tomb the pigments were mixed with a binding material. The question of the exact vehicle or vehicles generally employed in ancient Egypt is one of the most baffling with which we are concerned. No microscopical tests have been developed to distinguish egg, casein, and various kinds of gums and glues from one another when immensely old, more or less altered, and at the best present in exceedingly small quantities; the chemical tests for telling such ancient substances apart are hardly more satisfactory, although the presence or absence of organic matter of an adhesive nature may be established. We are thrown back on considering what good binding materials were available to the Egyptians, and on supposing that different ones may well have been tried out. An instance of the use of gum in the Nineteenth Dynasty has been said to be proved by analysis,[60] and gum arabic was easily obtainable in the land. The ancient Egyptians are known to have possessed glue,[61] and therefore Lucas has suggested that size may have been used with whitewash.[62] Eggs were certainly available, for the early Egyptians domesticated geese and ducks, even though the common domestic fowl,

[57] Acc. no. 07.228.95. L., 7 cm.; diam., 2.5 cm. Another of the same dynasty in the British Museum is mentioned by Glanville, *J. E. A.*, 1928, p. 190; see also Hall, *Roy. Scarabs*, nos. 2603, 2604, and Ross, *Art*, p. 120.

[58] On the inside, where it is in best condition, its color is equivalent to *Munsell*, PB 5/8, and to Maerz and Paul, *Dict.*, pl. 34, F 9.

[59] Thus far attempts to identify in Egypt examples of true fresco, or painting on wet lime plaster, are untrustworthy; see Swindler, *Painting*, pp. 40, 421, 422. To be sure, even recently Glanville made the statement apropos of painted pavements of the ꜥAmarneh age "that the Egyptians had to some extent acquired the technique of true fresco at this time — clearly from Crete" (*J. E. A.*, 1928, pp. 189-190), and Eibner in 1926 regarded the question as still an open one, his own analyses, as he pointed out (*Wandmalerei*, p. 587), having been of painted stone reliefs, where the layer of plaster, even when of lime, as he thought, was too thin to admit of the fresco technique. He sustained, however, by a fresh analysis the old verdict of von Bissing and Reach (*Annales*, 1906, pp. 64-70) that pavements in the late XVIII Dynasty were decorated *a tempera*, not *al fresco* (*op. cit.*, pp. 589-590). If Lucas is right that the calcining of limestone to obtain lime was not practised in Egypt before Roman times (cf. our p. 5), obviously all possibility of finding the true fresco technique there in earlier centuries disappears. We should recall, too, that the dryness of the Egyptian climate is unfavorable to painting in wet plaster.

[60] Laurie, *Materials*, p. 22.

[61] Lucas, *Antiques*, pp. 13-14; Spurrell, *Archaeol. Journ.*, 1895, p. 239.

[62] *Materials*, p. 24.

now so plentiful in the land, had not yet been introduced.[63] The identification of wax and resins is easier, although the specific resins employed and their solvents have not been determined.[64] Spurrell found resin used at Meidūm as a binder — perhaps, as he thought, in an unsuccessful experiment.[65] For the Old Kingdom, the most interesting but, in the present state of knowledge, unprecedented, case is that of a wax binder employed with malachite.[66] Both resins and beeswax had an established use in Egyptian wall paintings of the Eighteenth and Nineteenth Dynasties, chiefly as varnishes.[67]

More attention has been given in Germany than elsewhere to the subject of vehicles used with Egyptian pigments, Raehlmann having studied the pigments by the microchemical method,[68] not merely in flat view or broken up, but principally in section, whenever the pigment layer would hold together. In the case of "Vestorian blue," whether of early Egyptian or of Roman date, he observed a crust of brownish color, which he likened to sprinkled sugar in its granular texture, and which is now referred to as the "Raehlmannfirniss" and supposed to be some kind of organic fixative or varnish. Whatever its nature, this crust is quite apparent in Per-nēb's tomb and perceptibly

[63] Eggs are frequently depicted among the food offerings placed before the deceased; and nests with eggs in them, in wall paintings in sporting scenes. Spurrell once thought that he saw indications of the presence of egg as a binder (*Archaeol. Journ.*, 1895, pp. 229-230); Lucas, however, discredits his evidence (*Materials*, p. 149), although in 1930 willing to include egg among the possible vehicles used (quoted by Clarke and Engelbach, *Masonry*, p. 200); Eibner, more recently than Spurrell, felt reasonably sure of having identified an egg medium (*Wandmalerei*, p. 585, no. 21).

[64] The evidence for apiculture in the Nile Valley during the Old Kingdom and later is perfectly satisfactory. For instance, among the details from Theban wall paintings exhibited in facsimile in the Metropolitan Museum first in January, 1930, and the property of the Museum, is one showing the smoking of the bees to stupefy them and the withdrawing of the honeycombs from hives apparently much like those used today in Egypt and Syria (Lansing, *Egypt. Wall Paintings*, p. 14, no. 31); cf. Klebs, *Reliefs des a. Reiches*, p. 58. For modern apiculture in the Near East, see *Illustr. London News*, April 19, 1930, p. 688. Beeswax, then, was available in the land; resins had to be imported, but that they were imported and used for a variety of purposes is clearly established, although, as Lucas has emphasized, the nature of the resins used requires further investigation (*Analyst*, September, 1926, pp. 444-445).

[65] *Archaeol. Journ.*, 1895, pp. 224-226; Petrie, *Medum*, p. 29.

[66] In the case of a relief in Munich; Eibner, *Wandmalerei*, pp. 54-55.

[67] Mackay, *Anc. Eg.*, 1920, pp. 35-38; Eibner, *Wandmalerei*, pp. 583-585, nos. 19-22; Lucas, *Materials*, pp. 147-155; Davies, *Nakht*, pp. 57, 58, *Puyemrê*, I, p. 11 with note 2, and *Ken-Amūn*, I, p. 60.

[68] See *Über die Maltechnik* for the exposition of his method and the discussion of Egyptian blue in Roman times. A book issued by Raehlmann in 1914, *Über die Farbstoffe der Malerei*, has not been accessible to us, but the author's analyses of blue pigments brought back from Egypt by Lepsius and the views he set forth in that book are reported and appraised in Eibner, *Wandmalerei*, pp. 45-53, 577-578, 586. Eibner himself examined about forty unimpeachable samples of pigments, ranging from the IV or V Dynasty to around 150 B.C. in date, furnished him by the Egyptian section of the Prussian State Museums in Berlin. In the case of every sample from a wall decoration he endeavored to determine the medium used. The usefulness of his work, however, is curtailed by the insufficiency of the data given for the individual samples, and we are greatly indebted to Professors Alexander Scharff of Berlin and Karl Dyroff of Munich for supplementary information about Eibner's Egyptian material.

affects the hue; only below the surface is the true quality of the blue color fully apparent today. Another striking result of German investigations is the view that in one and the same early Egyptian wall decoration more than one technique may have been employed, the pigments being individually treated and binder and ground suited to the nature of each. The ochers, which could be finely ground without suffering in quality, were laid directly on stone, or, as here, on only a film of whitewash, the coarser-grained malachite green and Egyptian blue, which did not bear being very finely powdered, were imbedded in an intervening thicker layer of plaster to unite them adequately with the stone.[69] Here we must leave the subject, samples and opportunity for studying it further in the case of Per-nēb's decoration failing.

When we began work on Per-nēb's decoration, under the best lighting and with the aid of hand magnifiers, we endeavored by noting the different levels of the final pigments to establish the order in which they were applied to the wall, and the results of this study are summarized in a passage in Lythgoe and Ransom, *The Tomb of Perneb*.[70] We still think the overlapping of the pigments a valuable criterion, but one to be used with caution, inasmuch as the observer can obtain only a surface, not a sectional, view and only a low magnification. The carelessnesses of ancient work, the possibility that the order of applying the pigments varied somewhat according to the nature of the design or the convenience of the painters, the possibility that some repainting was done in the course of the original decoration or subsequently,[71] the tendency of the pigments to penetrate one another,[72] all complicate the attempt to analyze the final procedures. The examples of Old Kingdom work which we studied at Gīzeh and Ṣaḳḳāreh presented many apparent contradictions; for instance, the background pigment now seemed to overlap slightly the painted objects, and now to underlie their outlines. But one of our early observations in Per-nēb's tomb we stand by with as much conviction as when first we made it, namely, that the last body pigments to be put on the

[69] Eibner, *Wandmalerei,* pp. 53-55, 577, 586, apropos of a relief in Munich.

[70] Pages 75-76.

[71] A clear case of repainting is illustrated in plate I, c, where blue is laid on top of black. Ka-em-snēw's false door has in all fourteen letters *t* (X 1). Blue color is undoubtedly present on top of black in ten, probably in an eleventh; in three cases blue is laid on the wall without having black beneath. In the same decoration the bill of the ibis-hieroglyph (G 26) was repainted blue, although the greater part of the blue pigment has peeled off (pl. I, d).

[72] This is an important factor, only to be studied microscopically in the case of detached samples. We suggest that it has a bearing on the problem of vehicles. Although we most emphatically do not suppose the fresco technique to have been used on Per-nēb's walls, we do not find, as has sometimes been assumed for painting *a tempera*, that the colors where they are superposed invariably lie in clearly defined layers one on top of the other.

walls were the green and the blue. Except for inner details which were rendered in black line or dots, no color is anywhere seen to lie on top of the green and blue pigments. We believe that they were by far the most precious of the pigments which entered into this decoration, and that both their costliness and the need of a special technique in utilizing them led to their being reserved as the last important addition to the walls, to be put on perhaps by the master painter. Everywhere they stand out in some relief from the wall as compared with the finer-grained pigments, and nowhere do they exhibit brush strokes; rather, their surface is granular and smoothed as if by a spatula.[73]

Taking up the processes of the decoration where we left them on page 25, we may say that the operations which yielded the finished surface included working the gray of the background in and out of the interstices of the design,[74] painting the final outlines and the top body colors, and last of all superposing lines and dabs of pigment to render inner details.[75] In Per-nēb's tomb the decorator was sparing with inner drawing; for instance, hieroglyphs which in the very finest Fifth Dynasty work are crossed with delicate black lines were here painted solid green or blue, without such inner drawing.[76] In intention, although sometimes streaked when unevenly laid,[77] the final colors were flat tones, either silhouetted against the gray ground or outlined in a contrasting hue.[78] The silhouette and filled outline, modified by more or less inner drawing in line, dots, and dabs, constituted the type of painted decoration characteristic of Per-nēb's day and indeed of all Pharaonic times; purely line drawing occurred in this tomb and

[73] Compare the passage in Spurrell, *Archaeol. Journ.*, 1895, p. 228: "The green before drying was pressed down by a bone or metal instrument so that a smooth and polished surface was given to it, the irregular edges clearly evince this pressure . . . . The pressed-out edges of the blue were trimmed off . . . ."

[74] In plate 1, h, a detail from Ka-em-snēw's decoration, one sees that the larger hieroglyph (G 43) was reserved when the background pigment was put on, and that the smaller sign (W 24), eventually to be blue, was painted over with gray. But the general practice was to reserve all hieroglyphs and objects. In rapid work, however, the background pigment rarely came just far enough and not too far. At the front of the wig of the large figure of Per-nēb on the south wall (pl. xvii), there is a bare space, two to three millimeters in width, where the gray was not brought far enough, an omission which was not made good later. The same figure's left arm exhibits gray intruding on brown-red. This last might be due to retouching to cover such a gap as the one previously mentioned. Or others might see in it an indication that the painting of the design preceded the painting of the background.

[75] Such as black dots on solid blue to suggest the individual grapes of a bunch of grapes, black on white and dark yellow to indicate the spots of a leopard's skin (see pls. xii, xiii, xix).

[76] e.g., M 17, N 41, Q 3, V 30, V 31. cf. pl. xiii.

[77] cf. p. 37.

[78] A discussion of the psychology and aesthetics of the use of outlines about designs sculptured in relief, the painter actually rendering less effective the work of the sculptor, who to some degree had introduced light and shade, lies outside the scope of this book; compare, however, the previous reference (p. 15) to a certain independence between processes.

generally only in preliminary sketches. In the Old Kingdom, pigments low in value[79] predominated; in the New Kingdom, many delicate pastel-like tints were employed, the value of the common pigments being raised by the addition of white. Shading was only a rare and sporadic phenomenon in Egyptian painting, and it is wholly unknown for the Old Kingdom.[80]

Brush strokes are in many places readily followed in the orange-red and yellow, only a trifle less easily in the brown-red, gray, and black, pigments. We think that brushes of the usual Egyptian type — reeds with ends frayed out — were used with all except the blue and green pigments. A typical example, one of the deep yellow rectangles of the border to the right on the south wall, may be described. Here a brush about 5 mm. wide was used. A stroke started at the upper left corner, passed horizontally across the top of the rectangle, and rounded the right corner without break, being carried down the right side of the rectangle; all the other strokes of this rectangle are wholly vertical or curve a little in a general downward direction, and all show the same width, about 5 mm. Quite commonly in painting these rectangles, the workman covered the top and bottom of the space with horizontal brush strokes and filled in the area between with vertical strokes. The finest brushes were required for the outlines, where the width, particularly among the hieroglyphs, was often as little as 0.5 mm.[81] There is an unusual use of brush lines 4.5 to 5.5 mm. wide to define the outlines of the figures of animals and men at the bottom of the east wall (pl. XVIII, below). The pigment is a very dark gray, and apparently the brush line was carried about the design as the first process in putting in the gray ground.[82] Nowhere else, however, in Per-nēb's decoration is it apparent that the artist began his background in this way. The black lines separating the registers are broad and were put in free-hand. The only ruled lines on the final surface are brown-red outlines defining the half loaves of bread on the offer-

[79] "Value" is the attribute of color by reason of which the normal eye perceives a particular color "as holding a position in a light-to-dark scale;" see Maerz and Paul, *Dict.*, p. 10. cf. Pope, *Painter's Terms*, pp. 12 ff., and *Munsell*, pp. 7-9. Among scientists the terms "brightness," "luminosity," and "brilliance," instead, have considerable currency.

[80] A few examples of shading, especially such emphasizing relief, have been pointed out in XIX Dynasty paintings subsequent to 1350 B.C. (Davies, *Bull. of the Met. Mus.*, 1922, December, part II, pp. 52, 54, and *Two Ramosside Tombs*, p. 18). The ʿAmarneh painting of Akh-en-Aten's daughters in the Ashmolean Museum is not shaded; see Davies, *J. E. A.*, 1921, p. 4.

[81] Dr. Soule observed under the microscope that the brown-red outline of part of a leg-hieroglyph (D 58, the letter *b*) is sharp on the outside as though trimmed off and on the inside merges irregularly into the orange-red body color.

[82] We noted a similar method in a boating scene of the tomb of Yedut.

ing tables (pl. XVII). These ruled lines average about 1.5 mm. in width, but spread or grow narrower and are thinner or heavier after the fashion of brushwork. The curved tops of the half loaves could not be ruled, and one can see where the ruled line joins on, occasionally with a heavy drop of color from the full brush.

For the most part the body colors of the final surface were put on in a single layer, but there are exceptions. Loaves of bread eventually colored brown (pls. XII, XIII) were first given a coating of deep yellow as heavy as a top pigment. This is the clearest case of a double layer of heavy pigments over entire objects and possibly is to be accounted for by a revision of the color scheme during the progress of the final painting. In the case of two other pigments, deep yellow and blue, the colors can be seen in many places to lie at two levels, the lower layer being paler. In the pale yellow we may perhaps have a stain,[83] the pigment, soluble in water, having penetrated the underlying ground; but Egyptian blue is not soluble in water, and the underlying paler and smoother blue areas are almost certainly due to the use of the pigment in a more finely ground state. We cannot say with certainty whether the pale blue ever showed on the top surface, but we incline to the opinion that it did, even though, with a magnifying glass, in our first study of these walls, we repeatedly found traces of the deeper, granular color on top of it. Our principal evidence for a pale blue on the final surface is a detached fragment with very regular oval spots of deep blue upon the lighter tint,[84] such as would hardly result from the falling away of parts of an upper layer, but seem like intentional patterning of dark on light to represent some object. In the great majority of its occurrences, however, the pale blue was once completely hidden, and its purpose may possibly have been to aid in binding in the coarser-grained, more beautiful top pigment.

The various colors named on page 25 as present on the final surface were not in every instance of one uniform tone. Several slightly differing yellows are found which may well represent as many natural ochers.[85] Two reds occur which we refer to as

[83] cf. p. 24, note 15.

[84] Equivalent to Maerz and Paul, *Dict.*, pl. 33, D 2.

[85] Of these the darkest is the shade to which the term "ocher" is often applied as a color name, but which we have called deep yellow to avoid confusion with ocher as a material; *Munsell*, YR-Y, 7-8/6, and Maerz and Paul, *Dict.*, pl. 11, G 6, well represent it. Other yellow tones are those of Maerz and Paul, *op. cit.*, pl. 9, F 4, pl. 10, E 3, F 5, and G 5. These and other color notations have had the benefit of revisions kindly made by Mrs. Grace R. Dean of Toledo.

brown-red[86] and orange-red,[87] the latter being approximately rendered in plate XIII. Microscopical examination of one sample of the orange-red[88] was not favorable to the theory that red ocher was painted over yellow ocher on the wall to produce it,[89] or that red and yellow ochers were mixed on the palette, for magnified one hundred times the particles are very small, not revealing definite forms. This finely divided pigment was probably of a hue that, thinly laid over whitewash, impresses the observer as orange-red; the Munsell notation (note 87, below) shows that the red greatly predominates over the yellow; the color is somewhat streaked with light and dark, according as the brush left more or less of the pigment. The most interesting question concerns the darker and lighter greens. Perhaps the difference is due only to a less plentiful use of malachite in the lighter green, but Dr. Soule's discovery of particles of Egyptian blue with malachite[90] suggests the bare possibility that their presence was intentional, not accidental,[91] and that they were used in order to darken the green.[92]

Thus far in our study of the painter's work we have been concerned with the main chamber. The unsculptured walls of the passage and outer room were also painted, but in very slovenly fashion and less completely than the principal room. The best attention was given to the figure of Per-nēb in his carrying chair (pl. VI). Here the brown-red flesh tones were once about as heavy as in the main chamber, and here a little green and blue were afforded for the dignitary's bead collar. Elsewhere on these walls only thin washes of the cheaper ochers and of white and gray are to be seen, their purpose being to give a semblance of finish, even though time did not suffice to sculpture and paint the walls in the regular way. Although technically crude, the colors in their distribution show regard for aesthetic effect.[93]

[86] *Munsell*, R-YR, 4-5/6; Maerz and Paul, *Dict.*, pl. 5, I 10.

[87] *Munsell*, 1 R-YR, 6/6.

[88] Made by Dr. Soule.

[89] When we first examined Per-nēb's walls, we were constantly on the lookout for places where thin brown-red might have peeled, revealing an under yellow color, but we found no such place.

[90] See above, p. 26, note 24.

[91] If accidental, we may suppose that the painter used the same instrument in applying, polishing, and trimming both pigments.

[92] Spurrell reported blue laid on top of green (*Archaeol. Journ.*, 1895, p. 228).

[93] cf. Ransom, in *Perneb*, pp. 62-63.

II. THE COLOR CONVENTIONS

The degree of confidence to be placed in color when interpreting doubtful details in scenes is of great interest to the Egyptologist.[1] And a kindred question of high importance is whether, in the study of unidentified objects among the hieroglyphs, color may be given equal weight with the two other criteria commonly employed — form and philology. That it is less often used is a natural consequence of its frequent loss, but even when known it has not always been considered.[2] Much of the color in Egyptian wall paintings having been placed with consistent and understandable intention, one would like to believe that in its day all of it had dependable cognitive significance, and that when we are at a loss to interpret it our own ignorance is at fault.[3] Yet at the best we should expect occasional stylization in color parallel to that frequent in form which would render the understanding of a given detail difficult. We propose in the following pages to examine in turn some of the clear and some of the perplexing uses of color and to essay a few general statements which we hope may prove an aid to a better knowledge of the conventions followed in painting maṣṭabeh reliefs.

The pioneer effort to utilize color in connection with form in analyzing the pictures contained in Egyptian scenes and hieroglyphs was made in 1892 by Petrie, whose chapter on the hieroglyphs in *Medum*[4] was followed by Griffith's series of studies in successive volumes of the Archaeological Survey of the Egypt Exploration Fund.[5] Of

[1] The importance of color for interpretation has often been recognized; see Griffith, *Ptah-hetep*, p. 25, and *Hieroglyphs*, p. 2; Steindorff, *Ti*, p. 2; Montet, *Scènes*, p. 250; Junker, *Anzeiger*, 1928, pp. 176-177. On the other hand, distrust of the truth of colors has also been expressed by Egyptologists and others, e.g., Whymper, *Anc. Eg.*, 1915, p. 1; Griffith, *Beni Hasan*, III, pp. 1-2; Spearing, *Childhood of Art* (2d edition), I, p. 242; Junker, *Gîza I*, p. 155: ". . . die Fälle, in denen bei erhabenem Relief mehr auf Farbenwirkung denn auf Naturtreue gesehen wurde, sind nicht selten, wie auf unserem Felde bei *N-śdr-kꜣj*, *Ḥnj.t* usw."

[2] No one seems to have asked why the supposed Pharaoh's placenta (Aa 1) should be green in color (cf. Sethe, in *Saꜣḥu-reꜥ*, II, p. 77, and A. M. Blackman, *J. E. A.*, 1916, p. 237, who comments on the yellow color of early examples and leaves out of account the usual green) or why the letter *ḳ* (N 29) should generally be colored black or blue and only by exception present the colors proper to a sandy hillslope (cf. Gardiner, *Gram.*, p. 478).

[3] We do not, for instance, understand the wavy, vertical, white streak on the mud seals of storage jars among Per-nēb's offerings (pls. XIII, XIX). Dr. Ludwig Keimer in a letter to the writer also expressed uncertainty, suggesting tentatively that it represents a cord of linen or other material, used in some way in the construction of the sealing. A white band passing spirally around sealings is often represented in Egyptian art (e.g., Winlock, *Bull. of the Met. Mus.*, 1920, December, part II, p. 19, fig. 9; Schäfer, *Priestergr.*, pl. 10, B), and we now incline to associate it with W. S. Blackman's account of the modern practice of winding cord spirally about pots to support them while they are drying in the sun (*Fellāhīn*, pp. 150, 151, figs. 77, 78).

[4] Chapter IV.

[5] *Beni Hasan*, III; *Hieroglyphs*; *Beni Hasan*, IV; in *Ptahhetep*, I, chap. III.

later date are scattered references to color by various scholars interpreting particular objects. Miss Murray included in the first volume of *Saqqara Mastabas*[6] a section on the colors of the hieroglyphs of the Old Kingdom. Lacau interspersed his record of the colors on polychrome coffins[7] with occasional suggestions as to the significance of the colors, and Quibell made statements about the colors used in the tomb of Ḥesy-Rēʿ which are of special interest because of the early date of the tomb.[8]

All previous discussions of color have been more or less limited by the lack of reproductions adequate in quality and number,[9] and this difficulty is as yet by no means removed. The greatest caution must be exercised in employing older colored plates such as those in Lepsius's *Denkmäler* illustrating the tombs of Mer-yeb and Ma-nofre.[10] Among publications, one's mainstay for the Old Kingdom must be the colored plates in *Medum* and *Ptaḥhetep*, part I, the records of color on the plates and figures of the Abusīr volumes of the German Oriental Society,[11] the records of color on certain of Davies's plates,[12] and Miss Murray's list of colors found on the hieroglyphs of a series of Old Kingdom tombs,[13] although the records and list often fail one when it comes to the finer details and precise distribution of colors. In the use of the foregoing sources two pitfalls especially are to be avoided, a white indicating merely the loss of color in the original, not the presence of white pigment, and a red which is part of a sketch from which the significant top color has peeled (cf. pp. 22-25).[14]

In addition to the publications cited above and the colors preserved in Per-nēb's tomb, we have made use of evidence culled in the cemeteries at Gīzeh and Ṣaḳḳāreh, in the Cairo Museum, and of other Old Kingdom reliefs beside those of Per-nēb in the

[6] Pages 45-46.

[7] *Sarcophages.*

[8] *Hesy*; on the date, see p. 3.

[9] A fact mentioned in Griffith, *Hieroglyphs*, p. 2.

[10] II, pls. 19-22 (Mer-yeb); pls. 65-70 (Ma-nofre). Still others wholly or partially colored and reproducing Old Kingdom walls are plates 55, 57, 58, 83, 90, 96.

[11] Borchardt, *Ne-user-reʿ*; *Nefer-ȧr-keȧ-reʿ*; *Saḥu-reʿ*, II.

[12] In particular in *Deir el Gebrâwi*, I, II. Mention should be made, too, of data about colors dispersed through the text of von Bissing, *Gem-ni-kai*, II.

[13] *Saq. Mast.*, I, pls. XLI-XLV. Of late color notes and colored plates have appeared in Lutz, *Steles*, and Junker, *Gîza I*. The colored plate III in Meinertzhagen, *Nicoll's Birds*, I, representing the famous Meidūm geese of the Cairo Museum, supplies a long-felt want. And we will not omit from this enumeration of better colored plates in Fisher, *Minor Cem.*, pls. 53-55, although they represent preliminary sketches and therefore have yielded little for the present chapter.

[14] See also the occasional possibility of a present green having been originally blue, suggested above on page 30.

Metropolitan Museum. In plates I, II, and XIX of this book, new details of ancient color and sketches are published in facsimile, and in the restoration of plate XIII a visual aid to the discussion of color is offered. The reader may control the restoration in part by reference to plate XII, giving the actual remains of color in the same wall area; details not retaining their color just here were in a large number of cases found uninjured in other places in Per-nēb's decoration, but to some extent contemporary and even later evidence has been used.[15]

Leaving aside for the moment the aesthetic impulse, we may say that the ancient Egyptians in their wall decorations used pigments principally for two purposes, as a medium with which (a) to draw and (b) to render the details of scenes and inscriptions more readily recognizable. In the one instance the paint was put on in line, and its color for the most part had no significance with respect to the color and identity of the object depicted; and in the other instance the paint was laid on in broad masses in accordance with well-understood conventions and did generally give a suggestion of the color of the object,[16] although seldom rendering it precisely. Confusion may easily arise in modern interpretations of Egyptian color by not distinguishing clearly between these two usages.

The lines of preliminary sketches and the contours and inner drawing of the final surface, as has been stated,[17] were nearly always either black or red, although a certain number of examples of yellow sketches have been noted. In choosing pigments for drawing, the availability and abundance of ocherous clays and the readiness with which pigments could be prepared from them were probably the determining factors in the case of red and yellow sketches.[18] The black pigment, in addition to being inexpensive, may have had the special quality of running easily in fine lines suitable for

[15] See further in later references to plate XIII, listed on the tissue covering the plate.

[16] Except in the case of long inscriptions, when, to save labor, the pictorial individuality of the signs was often disregarded, and all alike were painted a solid color to contrast with the background; frequently then, blue was employed on limestone (e.g., the Pyramid Texts in the sarcophagus chamber of King Unis) and green on rose hornblende granite (e.g., Borchardt, Ne-user-reᶜ, p. 36; cf. ibid., p. 65). The question of intentional departures from fidelity for the sake of aesthetic composition in the case of polychrome hieroglyphs will have attention presently (p. 72).

[17] See above, pp. 5-6, 22.

[18] Miss Murray offers a different explanation: " . . . the first sketch was made in red, as this was the colour which showed less than others" (Sculpture, p. 16). But theoretically at least the sketch was to be completely and forever hidden by opaque top colors.

the corrections and details of final sketches.[19] Also on the top surface the decorators may have found that after a certain amount of drawing had been executed in red line, some final details could be put in best in black pigment.[20] But when the decorators came to drawing on the top surface, conscious aesthetic considerations as well played a part in the choice among these common pigments. There can be no question that the decorator in Per-nēb's tomb sought to secure a pleasing effect in outlining green and blue with black, orange-red and yellow with brown-red; and the same combinations of colors were carried out in the inner drawing, also in the outlines and inner drawing of the reliefs of Ne-kau-Ḥor and Ka-em-snēw.[21] With white, either red or black looked well, and the decorator often suited the drawing to its surroundings; about a man's kilt, a brown-red outline echoing the masses of the same color in the flesh tones was more harmonious; about a mottled stone vase done in a network of black lines on white, a black outline was preferable (pl. xiii). Available colored plates do not enable one to judge how generally the practice observed in the Old Kingdom reliefs in the Metropolitan Museum was carried out; probably, however, it was part of the usage of many companies of wall decorators of the Fifth and Sixth Dynasties. Variations in the total effect of the outlines there sometimes were, nevertheless, necessitated by differences in the scheme of body colors. As an illustration, we cite a Fifth Dynasty relief in Boston, in which brown-red, instead of orange-red, is used for the body color of pottery and consequently could not be employed here for outlines — the pots, like the flesh tones of men, being left in silhouette.[22] In later times, to judge by Davies's copies of the paintings in the tomb of Nakhte, we again find red outlines about yellow, and black about green and blue.[23] On the other hand, Gardiner, describing another tomb of

[19] We have seen above (p. 25, with note 19) that soot was much used as a black pigment in ancient Egypt and probably was employed for drawing in Per-nēb's tomb; this finely divided and comparatively pure form of carbon lent itself to delicate work as charcoal with its content of silica could not.

[20] In this suggestion we have in mind especially IV Dynasty examples of the owl-hieroglyph (G 17), the one reproduced in Petrie, *Medum*, frontispiece, 2, and two examples on the stela of Wep-em-nofret which we once examined carefully on the original. The V Dynasty example of the sign in Davies, *Ptahhetep*, I, pl. xviii, 409, looks more schematic, as if composed with a view to balance in color.

[21] See plate i, especially the middle sign (D 39) of "g," where the outline, black around the blue pot, passes at once into brown-red when it reaches the supporting fingers, which, like the forearm in this sign, were originally colored yellow.

[22] Museum of Fine Arts, no. 13.3101, a and b. High on the east wall of Per-nēb's tomb in the detail of plate xix an approach to the silhouette is seen, for here the red of the pots is darker than on the side walls and the outlines, though traceable on close inspection, merge into the body color.

[23] *Nakht.*

the Eighteenth Dynasty, speaks only of red outlines throughout the decoration; apparently in this tomb there were no black outlines.[24]

In monochrome sketches, the mind readily accepts the yellow, the red, or the black lines merely as drawing. In the drawing of objects on the final surface, a fine line, if black, is also naturally interpreted as being without color significance, showing simply details of form; so the blackness of the handle of the basket-sign,[25] in its main part green, and of the cord attached to the harpoon[26] (pl. XIII) would not by most observers be understood to indicate a black handle and a black cord; one instinctively sees that these two details were drawn by means of black pigment, and that their actual color is not rendered. One of the most striking and splendidly decorative combinations of black drawing lines and significant color is to be seen in the Sixth Dynasty sarcophagus chamber of Ka-em-ꜥonekh, where the black lines indicating the rigging of a number of sailing vessels cross the white expanse of the respective sails.[27] But where on the final surface drawing was done in red line, in association with red and other colors laid on in masses, the attitude of the modern observer is not always the correct one. Frequently, for instance, in citations of color from Lacau's *Sarcophages,* when the interest is in the nature of the object depicted rather than in the decorative color scheme of the coffin, not merely the body color, which alone has point, will be given, but also the item "rayé de rouge" or "avec le trait rouge."[28] One should bear in mind that red inner lines, like black inner lines, are much more apt to be drawing lines than to have color significance — to indicate the folds of a cloth headdress, the graining of wood, the structure of an object of yellow basketry or wood (pl. I, a, below), the distribution of the erectile feathers on an owl's head (sign G 17, pl. I, b).[29]

[24] In *Amenemhēt,* p. 12.

[25] V 31.

[26] T 21.

[27] Reproduced in part in Junker, *Anzeiger,* 1926, pl. v.

[28] We refer here not to Lacau's original record, but only to the uncritical use of it. The record, because of its very completeness, is invaluable in enabling one to see what rules of polychromy held good on the coffins.

[29] We speak of other examples in the following notes 81 and 84. A diverting demonstration of the abstractness of red line is found in the XVIII Dynasty tomb of Menena in a scene of measuring grain (published in monochrome in Wreszinski, *Atlas,* pl. 231). Here the coil of rope held by the leader of the operation is painted yellow, the uncoiled length in use, red. Again in the case of the IV Dynasty queen, Ḥetep-ḥer-es II, whose hair, painted yellow, is crossed by fine red lines, both Reisner and Junker at times hesitate to decide whether she had yellow or red hair; Reisner, *Bull. of the Mus. of Fine Arts,* 1927, p. 66: "It seems clear that this lady was blonde or red-haired;" Junker, *Giza I,* p. 65 (cf. p. 9): ". . . die Prinzessin war also blond oder rothaarig . . . ." We submit that her hair or wig was blond, and that the red lines indicate the manner of its arrangement.

Perhaps in the last example, the reader will think that the red lines against the yellow were intended in part to suggest the mottled color of the owl's feathers. We reason in this case that if the contrasting colors, rather than the pattern, had been uppermost in the artist's consciousness, he would probably have used brown or gray lines on the yellow of the bird's head. The subject is not altogether simple, however. We must bear in mind that if the artist wished to render actual color which would appear as mere line in its distribution and in the scale of its reproduction — so for instance the eyebrows, eyelashes, and cosmetic line at the outer corner of the eyes of smaller human figures and the writing on the lector's open roll [30] — he had no other medium of expression than a line of color, which, if it happened to be black or red, the pigments used abstractly for drawing, would result in ambiguity for the modern observer. Critical consideration and knowledge of the actual colors of everyday objects in ancient Egypt are necessary in order to determine how generally the artist disregarded actual color when it would be reduced to lines in his work and contented himself from the point of view of representation with painting form.[31] Thus in Per-nēb's tomb the black along the back of the quail-chick-hieroglyph [32] and the same hieroglyph's black inner markings may well have color significance, being a very good schematization of the dark lines present on the fledgling of *Coturnix coturnix*, L. Our own impression is that in the Old Kingdom the decorator seldom if ever used with color significance lines as narrow as the abstract outlines and inner drawing lines. In the case cited a slight difference is perceptible between the black lines rendering the bird's dark markings and the abstract red outline of its yellow underparts.[33] But we should ask ourselves also whether lines broader than those usual for contours and inner drawing in a given painting ever were used abstractly. An illustration of this question is to be seen in the yellow receptacle resting on a red pottery stand to the right in plate XIII. The writer is not in a position to decide whether

[30] All black in Per-nēb's decoration. So little of the writing on the open rolls survives that it is impossible to say whether it was originally legible, and whether any part of it was red, suggesting glosses.

[31] Actually there is a limit to the visibility of the hue of lines at a distance, but we are dealing with an art that recorded what the decorator knew about objects, not their varied and transitory visual appearances. So we theorize, following for color a view widely held in respect to primitive drawing. But certain of the Egyptian color conventions give pause, especially the blue convention for water (cf. p. 63, note 154).

[32] G 43. We have Dr. J. Van Tyne of the University of Michigan to thank for kindly allowing us to examine specimens of the European quail in the University's collection. See on this bird and the identity with it of the hieroglyph in question, Keimer, *Annales*, 1930, p. 6, with note 5, and, with reservations, Meinertzhagen, *Nicoll's Birds*, I, pp. 71 (44), 72-73.

[33] This is even more noticeable in Davies, *Ptahhetep*, I, pl. XVIII, 411.

the red lines here represent only structure or — if the object depicted is a basket — red-dyed strands interplaited with preponderating yellow ones. In the case of various white loaves and cakes, however, which are represented in plates XIII and XIX, it seems plausible to assume that the yellow lines and spots indicate schematically harder baked indentations and ridges and therefore signify actual color as well as form. The finer red and black lines of other receptacles here and in many other sections of Per-nēb's decoration (pl. XIX) should probably be regarded as mere drawing lines, the broader, green stripes — hardly to be termed lines — as having color significance.

The colors put on in masses to render objects more readily recognizable accomplished their purpose in the main by suggesting the actual local color of the objects, unaffected by atmosphere or cast shadow, and, incidentally, through the color, also the material. In another way, however, not represented in Per-nēb's decoration, Old Kingdom painters occasionally made use of masses of color to contribute to clarity. We refer to the painting of overlapping figures of men or animals in alternately higher and lower values of the same color or in successively various colors.[34] The respective conventions were not altered, but within them the difference in value or color made evident the limits of each body. We have never noticed this practice in the case of inanimate objects. The shapes of the various joints of meat and trussed fowl included in plates XI to XIII were indicated only by the modeling and the outlines, and even where the pieces partially hid one another, all were painted the same shade of red or yellow.

The relation of the body colors in the decoration to the actual appearance of the objects depicted is very often obvious. Examples in point in Per-nēb's decoration are white for the linen kilts of men, for the corona of the eyes, for the white hair of animals such as black and white cattle, and for the lighter underparts of certain creatures;[35] black for the hair of men and animals,[36] for the horns of certain animals,[37] and for the

[34] Examples may be found in Petrie, *Medum*, pls. XII, XVIII, XXVIII, 4, 7; Borchardt, *Saḥu-reʿ*, II, pp. 15, 17; compare the later examples of A. M. Blackman, *Meir*, I, p. 26; Newberry, *Beni Hasan*, II, pl. VIII; Davies, *Nakht*, pl. XX. Contrast the confusion to the eye in Petrie, *op. cit.*, pl. XVII, where the overlapping figures of three animals have all the same color scheme.

[35] Among the offerings and in the case of hieroglyphs G 1 (vulture), G 17 (owl), G 40 (duck), I 9 (viper?), and I 10 (snake).

[36] Not only in the case of Per-nēb and subordinate figures, but also in hieroglyphs A 1, D 1, D 2, F 4 (once for the mane, generally for the tuft at the elbow), F 22 (tuft of the tail), and 𝄃. The coloring of the mane in sign F 4 must have an origin in one of the black-maned species of lions of which specimens are sometimes observed today in Tanganyika; see *Times Weekly Edition*, June 4, 1931, p. 720.

[37] e.g., *Gazella dorcas*, L., north wall, sixth register from the top, carried by the third offering bearer; south wall, fifth register from the top, carried by the last man; for mention of a hieroglyph with black horns, see p. 23, note 13.

iris of the eye; black veined with yellow for wood; red for pottery vessels,[38] for men's skin, for animal's flesh and hair,[39] for the bare skin of the head and legs of some birds,[40] and for wood;[41] yellow for the gold ceremonial vessel from which a priest pours a libation, for the papyrus from which a lector reads the service, for the tawny hair of feline animals,[42] for several kinds of grain,[43] for loaves of bread,[44] for the horns of various animals,[45] for parts of the plumage of several birds,[46] for the bare skin of other birds,[47] for the lower end of the corolla of the blue water lily, and for wood;[48] green for growing or freshly cut plants and parts of plants,[49] for green eye paint,[50] for one kind of grain,[51] for the *Cucumis melo*, L.,[52] and for amazon stone and turquoise,[53] or their substitutes, in jewelry; blue for water, for the bluish petals of *Nymphaea caerulea*, for

[38] Among the offerings and in the case of hieroglyphs W 24 and 𝄇.

[39] e.g., the joints of meat among the offerings, the hieroglyph of a shred of flesh (F 51), and the red and white oxen of the east wall, one in each of the two lowest registers. Whether the leg joint where cut from the body should be red in our restoration (pl. XIII) is uncertain, although the skinned part of the leg and the other joints were without doubt that color. We noted examples of the leg joint in Yedut's decoration with pale red where the joint was severed, with a deeper brown-red elsewhere.

[40] e.g., G 1 (vulture), the feet; G 47 (open-mouthed chick), the legs.

[41] e.g., M 43 (grape trellis), with the stalks of the vine as well as the supports red, but bunches of grapes, blue and their stems, green; O 29 and O 34.

[42] The skins worn by Per-nēb, the hieroglyphs of the fore part and hind quarters of a lion (F 4 and F 22); on the coloring of the mane of sign F 4 and of the tuft of the tail of F 22, see the preceding note 36 and the following notes 130 and 145.

[43] In the case of hieroglyph M 33, as a determinative in the offering lists.

[44] Among the offerings and in the case of hieroglyphs R 4, X 3, X 4*, X 6 (without fingers), and X 7.

[45] Well preserved in the case of oxen of the east wall; also in hieroglyphs F 1 and F 13*.

[46] e.g., among the offerings and in the case of hieroglyphs G 17 (owl), G 43 (quail chick), and 𝄇, the determinative of *mnw.t* (pigeon?) in the offering lists.

[47] Especially trussed and plucked fowl among the offerings.

[48] The staff held by the standing figures of Per-nēb on the west wall and the following hieroglyphs: D 45 (scepter), G 26 (lower part of perch), M 41, S 43, T 9, and Z 11.

[49] The leaves of lettuce (*Lactuca sativa*, L.), the leaves and sepals of the water lily (*Nymphaea caerulea*, L.), the stems of onions, the stems and filaments of papyrus, the stems of figs, and hieroglyphs M 1, M 12 (leaf only), M 17, and M 23; the green shrubs in the road-hieroglyph (N 31), of which an example from Ka-em-snēw's tomb is given in plate 1, e, and the hank of flax fiber (V 28; compare the example to the left in plate 1, f). On the other hand, the significance of the green in the sign to the right (Q 7) in plate 1, f, is not obvious.

[50] In the case of hieroglyph D 7.

[51] The *bꜣ.t*-grain, if such it is, among the offerings (cf. the following note 85) and the determinative of *bꜣt* (M 33) in the offering lists.

[52] Shown entire and striped longitudinally, not cut in two as later; see Keimer, *Bull. de l'Inst. franç.*, 1929, pp. 92-93, and *Rev. de l'Ég. anc.*, 1930, pp. 42-50.

[53] Sinaitic turquoise is apt to have a greenish cast.

grapes, for lapis lazuli or imitation lapis lazuli in jewels.[54] That the colors in their inception depended on close observation and accurate memory is seen in the regularity with which the stems of the blue water lily are painted red,[55] those of other common plants, such as onions,[56] green and in the frequent use of a tinge of red applied to the corners of the eyes.[57]

Besides conventions so close to the color experiences of most persons as to leave no doubt of the correct interpretation, there are others about which we may make plausible inferences. One is the use of black for what must surely be mud-brick walls and mud seals. Thus among the hieroglyphs we have the simple house on plan,[58] the battlemented inclosure,[59] the seals on the papyrus roll[60] and the pot θ of the offering lists, very often painted black. Among offerings, certain vessels have black tops representing the mud seal built up over an inverted saucer closing the mouth of the vessel (pl. XIX). Having chosen dark gray for the background, the Fifth Dynasty colorist could not use it also for dark gray objects. But clay seals and mud-brick structures appear black in a number of earlier paintings from Meidūm where dark gray is not the background color,[61] and where the artist could perfectly well have painted them gray had he so conceived them. We suppose therefore that the Egyptian's color concept for these objects was often of blackness rather than of grayness.[62] He was not consciously imitat-

[54] Compare blue for the flowers of growing flax as depicted on an Old Kingdom relief in the Cleveland Museum of Art (Howard, *Bulletin*, 1930, p. 189). Another example is mentioned in A. M. Blackman, *Meir*, IV, p. 38.

[55] In the case of hieroglyph M 12, as well as of the water lilies in bowls among the offerings.

[56] The coloring of the bulbs (white) and the stems (green) is of special importance for the identification of this plant, inasmuch as Miss Murray endeavored to establish that "lotus roots" and not onions are represented in it (*Saq. Mast.*, I, p. 30), although the tubers of the lotus are dark and its stems reddish.

[57] Petrie, *Medum*, pls. XI, XXVIII, 1, and often later, but not in Per-nēb's decoration, so far as preserved.

[58] O 1. Black once only in Per-nēb's tomb, on the north wall, but other examples of the sign now devoid of color may once have been black.

[59] A sign combining the battlemented inclosure of O 13 with W 10 and X 1.

[60] Y 2.

[61] We do not know how far back the dark gray background may be traced. The Cairo Museum contains at least one such background in a painting from Meidūm certainly antedating the V Dynasty, and Petrie indicates that others were found there (*Medum*, p. 29). The still earlier paintings of Ḥesy-Rēꜥ and the prehistoric paintings at Hierakonpolis do not furnish examples. But even if one could show that gray backgrounds were the older, one must believe that a strong color sensation of gray felt by the master artist in respect to an object to be painted would assert itself in representation whenever a suitable background permitted. Further, one should recall that models of sealed jars, where no question of background is involved, often have black seals; e.g., Junker, *Anzeiger*, 1928, p. 185.

[62] We can cite one example of presumable mud-brick structures painted gray, namely, granaries depicted in the tomb of Ṭi (Montet, *Scènes*, p. 231; our own notes confirm the correctness of Montet's statement, but we failed to

ing visual appearances in color any more than in form; rather, his color was determined by memory pictures which tended to become fixed in color formulae very restricted in number as compared with the actual look of things.

Exceptional or apparently false colors may sometimes be explained as having a secondary origin. Substitutes for real things of course often repeated the colors of the originals, but by no means always. When built up of materials of lovely color and texture, the natural colors of the materials would be retained. The hieroglyph representing a mace[63] is painted solid yellow in Per-nēb's tomb,[64] but generally it has a white head to represent a limestone original and a handle of any one of the colors for wood — yellow for common wood,[65] red for the coniferous wood usually spoken of as "cedar,"[66] black for "ebony."[67] Frequently the thong or cord with which the stone macehead and the wooden handle were securely united is rendered in line.[68] But in the three examples of this sign within the field of plates XI to XIII, we believe that a gold-covered ceremonial object, not an actual usable mace, is depicted.[69] To take another case, the black color of the recumbent dog or jackal[70] may be due to the imitation of a cult image fashioned of fine black wood; it certainly is not to be attributed to imitation of the usual tawny live animal.[71] As Sethe has pointed out,[72] cult images seem assured when ac-

record the color of the background, perhaps now flaked off; there is no obligation to think it was so dark as Per-nēb's; compare in this respect pl. 1). Among Middle Kingdom models, certain ones which we may suppose to represent mud-brick buildings are often gray in color (Quibell and Hayter, *Teti Pyr.*, N. Side, p. 40, pl. 24, 1, p. 42, pl. 26, 1). On the other hand, as Mr. Winlock has pointed out to us, yellow paint on models of brick structures, too, may be faithful to reality, for, especially in Upper Egypt, bricks were often made of yellowish marl obtained on the desert's edge (Quibell and Hayter, *op. cit.*, p. 41, pl. 25, 1). Compare Griffith on the desert material of which bricks were made at El ꜥAmarneh (*J. E. A.*, 1924, p. 301).

[63] T 3.

[64] So also in the tomb of Ka-ḥi-ef, in the offering list of the west wall.

[65] Petrie, *Medum*, p. 31; Lepsius, *Denkmäler*, II, pl. 69; Griffith, in *Ptaḥḥetep*, I, p. 33; cf. Steindorff, *Grabfunde*, I, pl. III, for maces with yellow handles in the pictured equipment of the dead.

[66] Steindorff, *op. cit.*, II, pl. II.

[67] Murray, *Saq. Mast.*, I, pl. XLV.

[68] A. M. Blackman, *Meir*, II, p. 36; see also Petrie, *Medum*, p. 31.

[69] Such as the heavily gilt maces carried by the statues of Tut-ꜥankh-Amūn reproduced in colors in *Illustr. London News*, December 15, 1923, pp. 1116-1117. Yellow color may also indicate wood, but in the Metropolitan Museum's collection, a funerary mace (acc. no. 11.150.20 c) of this common material is painted to simulate a mace of actual use, white paint surviving on its head.

[70] As a hieroglyph, E 15.

[71] cf. Murray, *Saq. Mast.*, I, p. 46.

[72] *Urg. u. älteste Rel.*, § 10.

cessories such as feathers, perches, and fillets are represented. The present writer thinks possible that some signs which in form suggest living animals may not really represent such but may be distinguishable as cult images by their coloring alone. And even when the living animal deity gave rise to a hieroglyphic sign, a reinterpretation as the cult image might conceivably take place later. In the instance under discussion, however, Mr. Winlock has drawn our attention to another explanation of the color, one proposed by Howard Carter, who has observed on the desert on two occasions jackals of exceptional, black color and thinks that such animals may in antiquity have been especially venerated, being sought out and kept in temple inclosures as the embodiment of Anubis. The black of the recumbent figures, whether hieroglyphs or late statuettes, would then imitate the actual appearance of these archanimals.[73]

The use of a limited number of flat colors, after all, gave little opportunity to distinguish different objects having the same color, and ambiguity was inevitable. For the ancient observer this was of less consequence than for us. He knew whether red, the usual color of the letter $\acute{s}$,[74] indicated in that sign red-dyed cloth[75] or red-dyed yarn;[76] he knew in the case of the bottom hieroglyph of "a" in our plate I whether yellow stood for wood or for wickerwork. He could tell whether the various blue dishes among Per-nēb's offerings were of copper, glazed ware, or dark stone. And he was able to decide whether the boat-shaped receptacles and the trays of like color scheme (pls. XIII, XIX) must be interpreted as actual baskets of plaited rushes or perchance could be composed of silver chased with a basketry pattern and inlaid with amazon stone.[77]

Our plates XIII and XIX present still other cases of ambiguity, among the most important the yellow fig-shaped fruits with a green stem and a spot at the outer end. The coloring of these figs is rarely as well preserved as in the detail of plate XIX.[78] The chief authority on the sycamore figs of Egypt, Ludwig Keimer, whose forthcoming book on

[73] We print the statement above with Dr. Carter's most kind permission.

[74] S 29.

[75] Borchardt, *Zeitschr. für ägypt. Spr.*, 1907, pp. 76-77.

[76] A. M. Blackman, *Meir*, II, p. 35.

[77] Presumably white was at this time as later the convention for silver. Unfortunately the color of the vessels in Borchardt, *Saḥu-reꜥ*, II, pl. 61, according to the ancient legend conceived as of silver, is not preserved. The chief objections to supposing Per-nēb's receptacles to be of silver are the high value of the metal during the Old Kingdom and the great number of the containers in question. Especially for a private tomb, we consider an interpretation as baskets more probable.

[78] We saw them, however, with colors surviving in the tomb of Ṭi, high up on the south wall of the main decorated chamber, again in the sarcophagus chamber of Ka-em-ꜥonekh on the south wall, and in the tomb of Yedut.

the subject will doubtless much enlighten us, has kindly considered the question of Per-nēb's pictured figs. Dr. Keimer confirmed by letter what we had supposed, on the evidence of his published articles,[79] to be true, namely, that the smaller, red, fig-shaped fruits with crescent-like marks, which are represented again and again among Per-nēb's offerings, are undoubtedly a common variety of sycamore fig in a fully ripe state. Both the red color and the form of the incisions—still made in Egypt a few days before the ripening of the fruit to bring about the destruction of insects within the figs—determine beyond question the identity of these fruits of *Ficus sycomorus*, L. But in form and coloring the somewhat larger and equally numerous yellow figs of Per-nēb's decoration might be either another kind of *Ficus sycomorus,* of which there are many varieties, some more palatable than others, or the fruit of *Ficus carica,* L. Dr. Keimer, although emphasizing the difficulty of identification in the case of the yellow figs,[80] suggests that incisions made to eliminate insects are perhaps more likely to be prominently represented as spots than are the ostioles of true figs, and he therefore on the whole inclines to an interpretation of Per-nēb's yellow fruits as a variety of sycamore fig.[81]

Even more difficult is the question of the bunches of vegetables wrapped and tied together in matting of Egyptian "halfa grass"[82] or rushes.[83] In our restoration, the red color on the tubers in one case is based on the preserved color shown in plate XIX, the brown color in another case imitates the flakes of brown extant on the tubers of a similar bunch of vegetables on the north wall, in the fourth register from the top, to the right of the limits of plates XI to XIII. An excellent parallel to the brown vegetables is to be seen on the walls of Deshi's burial chamber. There, the tubers are of elongated form

---

[79] *Anc. Eg.,* 1928, pp. 65-66; *Bull. de l'Inst. franç.,* 1929, pp. 49-96.

[80] The determinative of *dȝb* (fig) in Per-nēb's offering lists is a fig-shaped fruit, yellow in color but not sufficiently well preserved to show whether the outer end had a spot; none is indicated in the sculpture, but often the crescents of red sycamore figs appear in the painted surface alone and only exceptionally are they also sculptured (e.g., Steindorff, *Ti,* pls. 64, 67), hence the absence of a spot in the sculptured determinative does not prove its absence from the painted top surface. Dr. Keimer has kindly given us a number of reasons for his belief that the word *dȝb* denotes the true fig, among them the nature of the determinative in some occurrences of the word, such as that in Firth and Gunn, *Teti Pyr. Cem.,* II, pl. 3; here the usual single fig-shaped fruit is replaced by a string of what are certainly dried true figs, sycamore figs never being so strung.

[81] In the representation of figs in Per-nēb's decoration, we regard the red and black marks as without color significance. Red pigment would show on yellow, but on red body color, drawing in black would be advisable.

[82] *Eragrostis cynosuroides,* R. S.,=*Leptochloa bipinnata,* L., Hochst.; see Keimer, *Oriental. Literaturz.,* 1927, col. 153.

[83] In a recent letter to the writer, Dr. Keimer refers to the wrappings as being probably for the most part of *Juncus maritimus,* Lam.

and light brown color with crosswise markings indicated in the sculpture; those vegetables are without rootlets, are wrapped, and have chocolate-brown stems protruding from their wrappings. Deshi's decoration includes some half dozen bunches of wrapped onions of normal mature shape with white bulbs and the indication, in line, of rootlets. In the present state of Per-nēb's walls it is impossible to say whether any of the smaller bunches of wrapped vegetables had rootlets and white bulbs; if they had, according to a suggestion of Dr. Keimer's, examples so painted may possibly represent young onions (*Allium cepa*, L.) in which the bulbs have not yet assumed the more rounded form of matured onions.[84] But so far as in the final surface Per-nēb's vegetables were brown in color and without indication of rootlets, Dr. Keimer would consider them bunches of *Cyperus esculentes*, L.; as he has kindly written us, the tubers of this particular *Cyperus* are eaten by the poor of Egypt today, and he has seen them on regular sale in the native markets in Cairo and Ṭanṭa. The form of the wrapped vegetables Dr. Keimer regards as possible also for leeks (*Allium porrum*, L.), but on the ground that leeks are usually cooked, and that ancient offerings to the dead of fruit and vegetables generally comprise those eaten raw,[85] he would exclude leeks from the suggestions to be made here.

Let us now look more particularly into the question of Per-nēb's vases. In the decoration of the main chamber, excluding the hieroglyphs, vessels of fourteen different shapes are painted blue (pl. xx); only four forms have the yellow of gold, three the red of pottery, one the black proper to dark gray pottery or a dark stone such as basalt, and two the white patterned in line indicative probably of a light stone with darker inclusions or veinings — a diorite,[86] a breccia, or most likely of all at this period Oriental alabaster.[87] The spouted vessel colored blue is certainly meant to be con-

---

[84] We would speak here of an inadvertence in the restoration of the green stems of the full-grown onions thrown across the red pottery stand above on the right in plate xiii. A comparison with plate xi makes clear that the stems were omitted in the sculpture; probably they were supplied in the painted surface now lost, but our restoration should show all of them outlined in black, not with shading — the means necessarily used by us to indicate the modeling of the relief. Again in the case of the full-grown onions of Per-nēb's walls and in such representations as given by Steindorff, *Grabfunde*, I, pl. ii, and Davies, *Nakht*, pl. x, we believe that the red lines on the bulbs are used abstractly to indicate the pattern of the rootlets, not in anywise to tell the color of these bulbs, the edible portions of which are white as painted.

[85] In this connection we draw attention to the bowls with green contents, wishing to know whether these are filled with *bꜣt*-grain, and if so in what form it was consumed.

[86] See the actual diorite support found by Junker at Gīzeh and now in the Cairo Museum; *Anzeiger*, 1926, p. 104, pl. ix, a. This might well be the kind of support indicated in our plate xx, 9.

[87] cf. pp. 52-53.

sidered copper, for its shape denotes a metal original; and gold would be yellow, and silver, white. Moreover, blue is proved to be a convention for copper by its frequent occurrence on the blades of tools and weapons.[88] And indeed such copper ewers and basins for pouring water over the hands at meals have survived to modern times. The Metropolitan Museum possesses excellent examples from the Sixth Dynasty.[89] We do not know of assured examples of blue-glazed[90] or dark stone vessels' being represented in tomb paintings of the Old Kingdom by blue color, but an interpretation of the open bowls with waved edge as of dark stone is favored by the occurrence in the extant reliefs of the Saḥu-Rēᶜ temple of one such vessel with the legend *mnt.t*, a kind of stone,[91] and the blue convention for stone is unmistakable in one case in Per-nēb's decoration, that of the whetstones of the east wall.[92] The vases painted blue are very

[88] In Per-nēb's tomb in the case of hieroglyphs T 21 (harpoon), U 21 (adze), and U 23 (chisel), as preserved on the west wall.

[89] Acc. nos. 26.2.12-15, from Ṣaḳḳāreh, published in line in Firth and Gunn, *Teti Pyr. Cem.*, I, fig. 31.

[90] Petrie has stated that "the general colour of the early glaze is greenish-blue or blue-green" (*Arts and Crafts*, p. 109). Its most splendid example is the tiles of the Step Pyramid, now so indubitably dated and abundantly preserved (Firth, *Annales*, 1925, p. 154, 1927, pp. 106, 108-110, pls. I, II, 1928, p. 84; reproduced in color in *Illustr. London News*, January 7, 1928). For glazed vessels, we should expect the color convention to be blue, if it was not green; and a later bowl painted blue with a cover of basketry pattern, evidently a survival — in art, if not in contemporary use — of a sort portrayed in Per-nēb's tomb (pl. xx, 19), was thought by Griffith to be of glazed ware (*Beni Hasan*, IV, p. 8, pl. xxvi, 3). This is the form known from inscriptional evidence to have been used as a wine bowl (Jéquier, *Frises*, p. 291), although not exclusively for wine, inasmuch as other specimens, probably of cheap pottery, are shown with joints of meat sticking out of them, the covers being raised (Jéquier, *Tombeaux*, pls. vi, xi). The position of covered bowls on tables in Per-nēb's decoration indicates that they were of valuable material and of fine use.

[91] Sethe, in *Saḥu-reᶜ*, II, pp. 68, 125, pl. 61; Erman and Grapow, *Wörterbuch*, II, p. 91; unfortunately the color of this vase is not preserved. Dr. Keimer has kindly called our attention to the alabaster bowl, only 6 in. (15.8 cm.) across, published by von Bissing (*Rec. de trav.*, 1904, p. 178); this is number 18718 of the Cairo collection. Whether it is to be considered a model vase in reduced size or a normal vase intended for small flowers, it presents in its scalloped edge an interesting parallel to some of Per-nēb's deeper flower bowls (pl. xx, 8). Such bowls of water lilies, in which the lilies are conceived as actual plants in water resting in the indentations of the vessel's rim, are represented often on monuments of the Old and Middle Kingdoms and, as Schäfer has shown, are not to be confused with New Kingdom vases having upright floral ornaments of metal along their rims (*Prunkgefässe*, pp. 10-13). In the Metropolitan Museum's collection, an example of the XII Dynasty may be cited (acc. no. 09.180.13 A), from the funerary temple of Sesostris I (Lythgoe, *Bull. of the Met. Mus.*, 1909, p. 123, fig. 6; Mace, in *Handb. of the Eg. Rooms*, fig. 37). Here the well-preserved painted surface indicates that a bowl of variegated stone is intended. Not all of Per-nēb's bowls filled with water lilies, however, have the scalloped edge. Compare those shown in plates xiv and xviii above.

[92] One in use in a slaughtering scene and another as a hieroglyph (T 33) in the legend accompanying the scene. But the blue color on the offering stone — if it is a stone and not a mound of earth — over which a priest pours water, both in the scene and in the accompanying hieroglyphic legend (south and north walls, pl. IX) is ambiguous, for it may have reference to the object itself or to the water which bathes it; compare on the nature of the object washed, Jéquier, *Frises*, p. 307. We should note that the tables in front of the seated figures of Per-nēb on the west, north, and south walls are painted blue. Now supports and round tops of dark stone have been found in tombs of the Old Kingdom; here, though we cannot prove it, we favor an interpretation of blue as indicative of dark gray stone.

51

numerous here, and unless glazed and dark stone vessels are included among them, these are probably not present among Per-nēb's pictured offerings.[93] In our opinion, at least the majority of these vases were conceived as of copper. We think so because of the great variety of shapes found among small model vases of copper from tombs of the Old Kingdom.[94] Copper vessels, full sized or represented by models, are often found in the funerary equipment of the later part of the Old Kingdom and presumably would have been prominent among the pictured offerings, whereas the heyday of fine stone vessels was past, and glazed vases had not yet come into their own, either in technical development or in popularity.

The ambiguity of blue is still further augmented if we must suppose with Miss Murray that the tall storage jars bear "basket-work flaps."[95] In every case in Per-nēb's tomb, whatever the color and presumable material of the jars, the flaps, or wraps, are blue in color.[96] In many instances they are fluted plastically in a vertical or horizontal direction or in both directions; in other cases the construction of the wraps is left to the painter to indicate in line. Occasionally an opening is shown (pl. xx, 14), but usually in the side of the vessel turned toward the spectator none is indicated. Inasmuch as wraps of matting or basketry have a known employment in the Near East in preventing breakable storage jars from knocking together,[97] and as the markings on the blue accessories of the jars in question could well represent basketry construction, we consider Miss Murray's suggestion the most reasonable that has been offered. We do not understand what Gunn had in mind in calling them "cooling wraps," since they cover the vessels only partially.[98] The theory of protective wraps, however, carries with it the supposition that vessels bearing such wraps would be readily broken, and we regard as unfavorable to it the occurrence of these blue accessories on white ves-

[93] We regard the black-painted storage jars with narrow openings and mud seals as far more likely to be of dark gray pottery than of stone (pls. xiii; xx, 18), for they are about as numerous as the open-mouthed, red-pottery storage vessels with huge mud seals (pls. xix; xx, 16).

[94] Reisner, *Bull. of the Mus. of Fine Arts*, 1913, pp. 60-61; Firth and Gunn, *Teti Pyr. Cem.*, I, figs. 17, 24, 27, 37.

[95] *Saq. Mast.*, I, pp. 21, 44.

[96] They occur black, however, elsewhere; see Murray, *op. cit.*, p. 21.

[97] Mentioned by Dr. Keimer, who, kindly responding to our inquiry, characterized the blue convention as understandable, on the ground that Egyptian rushes often verge from dark green into dark blue. Keimer also mentioned the effective position of the supposed basketry protectors, always at the widest part of the vessel.

[98] So Dr. Keimer expressed himself. See for Gunn's designation *Teti Pyr. Cem.*, I, p. 163.

sels patterned in line, most likely to have been intended to represent stone[99] and on other tall spouted vessels painted yellow, almost certainly intended for gold.[100]

That one color could and must represent more than one material is too evident to require demonstration. But we need to inquire whether the converse was true, that one material might be represented in the decoration by several color conventions. This, too, is quite obviously true in some cases, such as that of different kinds of woods, which varied in color among themselves. But granted, for instance, that blue very often represents copper, must we assume that copper objects always were painted blue[101] in Egyptian art, or was the appearance of a new, highly polished vessel or implement of copper ever approximately caught by Egyptian decorators? The convention in such a case would naturally be red, and this color seems to have been adopted for the copper or bronze disks of mirrors. The Egyptian wished for himself in the next life mirrors made of precious metals, and accordingly the mirrors on polychrome coffins of the Sixth Dynasty and later are most commonly white or yellow, often accompanied by legends giving the material, "silver" or "gold." But occasionally a brown or brown-red mirror disk is pictured, and one of the published examples has the material *bi3*, "base metal," named.[102] The present writer does not know of a demonstrable instance of green for a copper object which had acquired a green patina.

Continuing the study of that most disconcerting of Egyptian colors, blue, let us consider its occurrence on the pin-tailed duck (*Dafila acuta*, L.), a bird of dull plumage, which displays in part through much of the year a beautiful bronze brown color and markings of black on pale gray, but never blue color. Some Egyptian paintings show this bird with naturalistic coloring,[103] others with considerable markings of blue;

[99] Junker found at Gîzeh dating from the IV Dynasty actual pottery vessels covered with a white slip (*Gîza I*, p. 114, 111), and he suggests of the *nmś.t*-vessel pictured in Petrie, *Medum*, pl. XIII, as white that it may be such a white-covered pottery vessel. Pottery vessels painted to imitate fine vases of diorite or alabaster and of gold are of course possibilities, but we know of none such, and the Meidûm example we take to be a copper vessel, the picture of it together with hieroglyph Q 1 being white in the plate because it has lost its color.

[100] One example is preserved on Per-nēb's south wall in the third register from the top.

[101] Or black, see the following pages. To Wolf, discussing weapons of the New Kingdom, blue indicates iron, red, bronze (*Bewaffnung*, pp. 65, 76). Miss Murray, too, takes red to mean copper (*Saq. Mast.*, I, p. 46). The blue convention for copper was recognized long ago in Petrie, *Medum*, p. 31; cf. Lutz, *Steles*, p. 19, no. 45.

[102] Lacau, *Sarcophages*, no. 28024, 13, pl. XXXVII, 136; cf. *op. cit.*, no. 28083, 56, pl. XXXVII, 145, without ancient indication of material, stated to be "brun clair." Examples of red mirror disks are cited in Lutz, *Steles*, p. 16, no. 28; p. 18, no. 36.

[103] Petrie, *Medum*, pl. XXVIII, 2 (in part); wholly naturalistic on the stela of Wep-em-nofret even to dark gray feet.

and blue is frequent in paintings of other birds totally devoid of blue plumage in nature.[104] One's first impulse is to pronounce Egyptian coloring an unreliable aid. We think that the crux of the matter here lies in a peculiarity of blue, which, as we have seen,[105] was the last of the pigments for primary colors to be acquired by the Egyptians. Not only was it employed at once for things which impress the modern beholder as blue in color, but also for others which to most eyes do not look blue. From their first employment of blue pigment, the ancient Egyptians certainly used it as a frequent alternative for black. The hair of human beings and of animals was painted not only black, but sometimes blue, a convention which was perpetuated down through the centuries into archaic Greek art. Every hieroglyph representing a mud-brick structure or patch of alluvial ground could be, and often was, painted blue,[106] the letter *t* was now black, now blue,[107] so were the metal blades of the chisel[108] and the adze[109] and the points of harpoons.[110] The trapped ducks represented in a Meidūm painting have the legs, closed wings, back of neck, bill, and eyes painted solid black, the front of the neck, the breast, and the underpart of the body painted white.[111] The present-day observer readily accepts this scheme as differentiating the parts of the bird which were dark-hued, if not actually black as in some ducks, from those of lighter color. With the substitution of blue for black in many an Egyptian painting, he is immediately puzzled, expecting blue to indicate blue in the object represented; blue bills

[104] Examples published only in monochrome, or not at all, occur in the VI Dynasty burial chambers of Deshi and Ka-kher-Ptaḥ; recorded in Murray, *Saq. Mast.*, I, pl. XLII; cf. Griffith, in *Ptahhetep*, I, p. 19, figs. 80, 103; also preserved in Per-nēb's tomb in the case of hieroglyphs G 1 (vulture), G 5 (falcon), G 36 (sand martin), G 40 (duck), and G 47 (open-mouthed chick).

[105] Pages 29-31.

[106] In Per-nēb's tomb, hieroglyphs N 17, O 2, O 49, and U 30, in whole or in part. In our opinion, sign N 29 and perhaps Q 1, when painted blue as in Per-nēb's decoration, belong here.

[107] In Per-nēb's decoration the letter (X 1) is everywhere blue. On Ka-em-snēw's false door, some person in authority ordered all the *t*-signs, which were originally black, repainted blue; cf. p. 33, note 71. The case for the interpretation of this sign as a loaf of bread has been most fully set forth by Sethe, taking into consideration the evidence of color as well as philology (*Nachrichten*, 1922, pp. 219-220, *Urspr. d. Alphabets*, p. 156, *Pyramidentexte*, IV, § 132).

[108] U 23, black in one example, blue in another on Per-nēb's west wall; cf. pl. XIII, left.

[109] U 21, preserved once blue on Per-nēb's west wall.

[110] T 21, preserved both blue and black on Per-nēb's west and north walls.

[111] Petrie, *Medum*, pl. XVIII. The closer the actual mottling of the bird's plumage, the more likely that in rapid and unskilled decoration masses of unbroken color would be used. But the finest of Old Kingdom work included beautifully rendered plumage of dark gray or brown color with formalized pattern of feathers in line.

and blue feet[112] for birds seem to him unaccountable, and only when he understands that their color is a substitute for black can they appear rational.

To say that the Egyptian artist used blue as a substitute for black is to avoid coming to grips with the real problem. Our minds require some explanation of why he did so. One possible position is to assume that he liked his blue pigment especially well, that when it had the novelty and fascination of a recent acquisition and the conventions in its use were developing, the number of elements entering into his designs which were actually blue in the world about him was not sufficient to satisfy his craving to use the new pigment liberally, and that therefore he introduced it where blue did not to his eyes exist in nature.[113] By this path we arrive at a purely aesthetic and, from the point of view of representation, arbitrary basis for much of the blue present in Egyptian wall decorations.

Schäfer has hinted at another explanation in suggesting that the blueness of hair had a symbolic meaning.[114] He refers to the subject only incidentally and vaguely, and a discussion with precise illustrations is needed when someone has the time and interest to undertake it. But in passing we wish to propose that many of the apparent examples of blue hair in later Egyptian art may be susceptible of a different interpretation. The various divinities and the dead — both kings and private people — in their rôles of identification with Osiris were frequently depicted wearing an archaic headdress blue in color. We think that in these cases the uncovered natural hair or wig was not represented, but instead the hair was conceived as protected by a blue kerchief. If this is so, they do not illustrate the blue convention for hair; rather, the blueness is that of blue-dyed linen. Actual head kerchiefs of the Eighteenth Dynasty, three in number, are preserved in the Metropolitan Museum's collection, and these were discussed by Winlock some years ago in a valuable essay in which he offered for the first time patterns showing the cut of various styles of linen wig covers worn by the ancient Egyptians.[115] Important for our point is the fact that one of the ex-

---

[112] See plate 1, d, for an ibis bill originally black repainted blue. Per-nēb's decoration presents many examples of blue on the bills and feet of birds; on his walls the blue-black interchange for plumage is found in the quail-chick-hieroglyph (G 43) of which the markings are blue in some examples, black in others.

[113] This statement grew out of a conversation with Mr. Lansing, although we would not convey the impression that it is a final and settled conviction of his.

[114] *Von ägypt. Kunst* (3d edition), p. 73, referring in a general way to the hair of gods, kings, and deceased persons.

[115] *Bull. of the Met. Mus.*, 1916, pp. 238-242; acc. nos. 09.184.217-219, of which numbers 218 and 219 are white, and number 217 is blue in color. In such a scene as that given in Davies, *Two Ramesside Tombs*, pl. xiv, the God-

tant head kerchiefs is deep blue in color. We should note that Schäfer's suggestion of symbolism in blue color, like that of the preceding paragraph, involves the abandonment of a theory of would-be fidelity in representation. For our own part we should be better satisfied with a hypothesis that did not set apart blue as in intention used differently from other colors. The psychology of the blue-black practice would seem to us to be analogous to that suggested above for the use of black where we should employ dark gray (pp. 46-47), namely, to originate in mental pictures of certain things carried in memory now as blue, now as black.

Let us see where a working theory that the Egyptian artist in his use of blue and black was expressing what he saw about him will lead us. The differences between his rendering of the objective world and what appears to us typical and natural are the immediate difficulty, as we have set forth above. Two lines of inquiry deserve consideration. The first may be introduced by a remark of Koldewey as quoted by Miss Swindler when writing of blue hair in archaic Greek sculpture: "Koldewey calls attention to the fact that in the East the hair of men and animals always has a touch of blue. Where we think black, they thought blue."[116] Here the cause of the blue convention is placed in the object of vision. If this is true of hair, then in early Egypt so also must mud-brick walls, fields ploughed but not yet verdant with crops, mud seals, and the black to gray plumage of birds all have had a touch of blue in them. One modern example of such a color impression is found in Bengt Berg's description of what the migratory birds flying above the Delta of the Nile see: "The first glimpse of Egypt that the birds-of-passage behold consists of the blue-gray earth and the green fields. . . ."[117] The question at this point is whether inherent and reflected blues under the conditions of light in Mediterranean lands would be strong enough to occasion the blue interchange for black and gray in the case of the objects mentioned.

A second inquiry is suggested by various observations about the vision of present-day Egyptian peasants, who are believed to have retained many of the physical char-

dess of the West appears in the blue archaic headdress, the deceased is represented in the garb of the living with a contemporary style of wig painted black. The representation of deified human beings is always, that of gods, very often, anthropomorphic, but the iconography was established in early times and remained thereafter fairly static. Contemporary fashions in dress are seen chiefly in the case of human beings depicted as living, and even though wig covers had a use in the XVIII Dynasty, as these extant specimens prove, the dignitaries of the later age did not, so far as we have noted, choose to be portrayed wearing them. Thus a distinct difference is noticeable in the headgear of the gods and of living men and women which does not necessarily find its explanation in symbolism.

[116] *Painting*, p. 139.

[117] *To Africa with the Migratory Birds*, p. 86.

acteristics and habits of their remote ancestors. Mackay inclines to attribute the blue convention for hair to a lack of visual perception of a difference between blue and black, and says that the modern fellāḥ cannot readily distinguish between these two colors.[118] Further, Miss Blackman has pointed out an analogy between modern and ancient practice in the use of blue for mourning,[119] the meager ancient evidence having first been made known by Gardiner.[120] But of greater bearing on the question are the investigations made early in the present century by W. H. R. Rivers with the assistance of Randall-MacIver. These two scholars, the first versed in medicine, the second in Egyptology, examined the color terminology and vision of eighty Upper Egyptian peasants[121] and found a limited vocabulary resulting, for instance, in talk about "blue and green donkeys," and a tendency to match wools according to their similarity in saturation[122] rather than according to their similarity in hue.[123] The "specific threshold"[124] for blue of these peasants was found to be high as compared to that of north Europeans; in other words, they were less sensitive to blue. We ourselves often find it difficult to distinguish a very dark blue from black, and we should suppose that, if ancient Egyptian eyes were less sensitive to blue than ours, the range of stimuli, which might seem in the case of different artists fairly well represented now by blue, now by black, or again by dark gray paint, would thereby be increased.

Rivers has shown that what he observed of the Egyptian peasants is not an isolated phenomenon, but characterizes other peoples undeveloped culturally. Of a tribe in southern India, he wrote: "In its present state the colour-vocabulary of the Todas has reached very much the same degree of development as that of the Egyptian peasant or the native of the Torres Straits. There are definite words for red and yellow,

[118] *J. E. A.*, 1918, p. 113.

[119] *Fellāḥīn*, pp. 286, 295.

[120] *Zeitschr. für ägypt. Spr.*, 1910, pp. 162-163.

[121] Rivers, *Journ. of the Anthr. Inst.*, 1901, pp. 229-247, summarized in Parsons, *Colour Vision* (2d edition), pp. 159-160.

[122] In other terminologies called variously "color intensity," "chroma," "chromaticity," "purity." "It is that attribute of color by which the normal eye perceives, in addition to hue, the presence or absence of gray" (Maerz and Paul, *Dict.*, p. 10).

[123] Almost universally used for that one of the three attributes of color by which red, yellow, blue, etc., are differentiated one from another.

[124] Parsons, *Colour Vision* (2d edition), pp. 22, 66. When light is gradually admitted to a dark room, the moment when the eye distinguishes between dark and light, perceiving white and tones of gray in addition to black, is called the "general threshold." With more light the eye sees the different hues, each one of which has its "specific threshold."

less definite nomenclature for green and blue; blue and black are often given the same name, and there are no definite terms for brown or violet. . . . The Todas confirm the conclusion reached in my previous papers, that the defective nomenclature for blue which is so generally found among races of low culture is associated with a certain degree of defective sensibility for this colour."[125] In this connection, it is of interest to recall the controversy ranging back through the decades to the time of Gladstone, who in 1858 propounded the theory that the vision of the Homeric Greeks was still in an undeveloped state.[126] The question of vision in Homeric times has recently been examined anew, and the author summarized her results as follows: "I under-took the study of the use of color in Homer with the conviction that its peculiarities were caused by shortcomings in the vision of the Homeric Greeks. But further study of both Homer and modern scientific theories of color have failed to reveal grounds for this idea. . . . The only trace of a perception of colors in Homer different from our own is the preponderance of black, gray, and white words over those expressing hue."[127] No such study as that carried out by Miss Wallace in respect to the Homeric poems has yet been undertaken of terms for color in ancient Egyptian literature.[128] Such an investigation, although interesting in itself, would have no vital importance for us, in-asmuch as poverty of color terms in antiquity if established for Egypt would not nec-essarily imply limited color sensations. One may perceive more than he has need to differentiate by a special name. Color vocabulary is indicative of the level of culture but is not, we believe, a safe criterion of actual color experiences. The question now before us is whether the blue, black, and gray conventions in ancient Egyptian paint-ing had their basis in a physiological equipment for vision similar to that of the Up-per Egyptians as studied by Rivers, one not pathological or even undeveloped, since the ancient Egyptian was able, as his paintings well prove, to perceive and utilize all the primary pigments, much less a condition of color blindness, but a vision differing slightly from that of men of more northern climes and more favorable to occasional blue-black-gray confusion.[129] This theory places the cause of the conventions in the

[125] *Brit. Journ. of Psychology,* 1904-1905, pp. 321-396, in particular, pp. 327, 331.

[126] *Studies on Homer,* III, pp. 483-484, 488.

[127] Wallace, *Color in Homer,* pp. 82-83.

[128] See, however, Grapow, *Bildl. Ausdrücke des Aegyptischen,* pp. 54-57, 106.

[129] Whether or not the high threshold for blue postulated for the Egyptians under this theory could be due to greater macular pigmentation, as Rivers once suggested (see Parsons, *Colour Vision* [2d edition], p. 160), or possi-bly to climatic or housing conditions with a constant strain on the eyes for dark and light adaptation is outside our province to judge.

organ of vision rather than in the object of vision. We think this subject should have further examination. Since scientific theories of color vision and methods of research have been advancing rapidly in the last years, probably new tests of the peasants' vision are now advisable.

A number of blue-black alternatives persisted from the time of the introduction of blue pigment throughout Pharaonic Egyptian art, but certain preferences developed among them to which we should now give attention. Although the convention of blue for hair was never lost, in a large majority of cases the conception of hair as black prevailed.[130] On the other hand, the blue concept for water was generally preferred. The rightness according to Egyptian standards of these two choices is amusingly illustrated in some of the hieroglyphs; that of the streaming eye[131] has the lids with their lashes black, the tears blue;[132] the sign ⟨glyph⟩ has the man's hair black, the water issuing from the pot usually blue, although in Per-nēb's south offering list it is black.[133] In still other hieroglyphs which include a dash of water, the water is commonly blue in color.[134] And this statement is not contradicted by the common hieroglyphs for *n* and *mw*,[135] nearly always black.[136] These signs represent ripples of water, stylized just as are the ripples on blue bodies of water in scenes of sport and of other activities involving water and in the pool- and well-signs.[137] The blackness is here the abstract blackness of drawing lines, not the black of the older rendering of water,[138] and in these

---

[130] In Per-nēb's decoration, as far as its present condition permits one to judge, the blue convention occurred only for the mane of the lion in hieroglyph F 4. Human hair and wigs are everywhere black. Occasionally in Old Kingdom art the two conventions appear together, as when in Per-nēb's tomb hieroglyph F 4 has the mane blue and the tuft of hair at the elbow black (pl. XIII), and when on the stela of Nen-khefty-ka sign D 2 has the hair black and the beard blue. Compare the more usual coloring of the last-mentioned sign given in plate I, i.

[131] D 9.

[132] We observed an example so painted in the tomb of Yedu on the north wall to the east of the entrance.

[133] Blue, however, on his north wall.

[134] e.g., A 6, D 60, W 15 (in Per-nēb's tomb with the addition of a spout), and W 16. cf. Griffith, *Beni Hasan*, III, p. 18, fig. 48 (W 16), "contrary to the usual practice, the water is coloured black." The monogram ⟨glyph⟩ , the older scheme of which with stream black is reproduced in Petrie, *Medum*, pl. XXIV, occurs on Per-nēb's north and south walls with spittle blue, and the same coloring is to be seen in the burial chamber of Ka-kher-Ptaḥ.

[135] N 35 and N (35).

[136] See Lutz, *Steles*, p. 17, no. 31, a provincial stela, not earlier than the close of the Old Kingdom, with *n* blue.

[137] N 39 and N 41.

[138] As in another form of the pool-sign, N 37, solid black in Petrie, *Medum*, pls. XVIII, XXIII, XXIV. We are not in a position to say whether the artists here thought of water as black or only painted it so for lack of a blue pigment. cf. the following note 149.

zigzags, whether drawn on bodies of water or separately placed, movement, not the water itself, is the underlying conception. We must not omit to note, too, that blue for the sky early took its place among the favored Egyptian color concepts. The variable blue and black in the granary-sign (pl. I, j) [139] and in another common hieroglyph, X 8,[140] have yet to be cleared up.

Obviously what the ancient Egyptian artist was capable of seeing and carrying as color memories and what he could express in pigments are two very different things, the latter being far more limited.[141] So the blue-black interchanges may well be more crass on his walls than they ever were in his color concepts. He had as his most available blue pigment one of very intense and nearly pure hue, and this must usually do duty for mere tints of blue in nature, such as the "heavenly" blue petals of *Nymphaea caerulea*,[142] and for shades of blue so dark that even we should readily confuse them with black. There seem to be some indications that when the Egyptian artist employed both black and blue on a single object, he used black for the darker parts; thus eyelashes surely appear blacker than tears,[143] the hair of the head is sometimes darker than a beard,[144] the tufts of hair at a lion's elbows are often darker than the mane,[145] and in some birds, notably the *Neophron percnopterus*, L., or Egyptian vulture, the primary and tail feathers, painted black by the Egyptians (pl. XIII),[146] look

[139] O 51, usually with blue and black together but in variable distribution. See Junker's discussion of the sign (*Gîza I*, p. 178) and the example given in colors in Davies, *Ptahhetep*, I, pl. XVIII, 401; we noted an unpublished example of the sign in Ka-em-nofret's decoration painted as the one just cited from Ptaḥ-ḥotpe's tomb.

[140] In Per-nēb's tomb this sign, except for its free interior, was black; in Ka-em-ʿonekh's burial chamber, the bottom of the frame is black, the inner pyramidal mark is blue, and the sloping sides are black. cf. Griffith, *Beni Hasan*, III, p. 32, and *Hieroglyphs*, p. 64.

[141] We conceive of the ancient Egyptian artists as having (1) manifold sensations or perceptions of color; (2) a selection of the foregoing carried in memory as color concepts for particular things; (3) far less numerous conventions, the last being limited in part by the nature of the foregoing categories 1 and 2, in part by the number of available pigments, the degree of experience attained to in utilizing pigments, and other conditions controlling artistic practice in ancient Egypt.

[142] Pale blue was used very little, if at all, on the top surface; certainly not, just where one might expect it, on the petals of the blue water lily.

[143] cf. above, p. 59.

[144] cf. p. 59, note 130.

[145] This is true of a magnificent male lion in the Toledo Zoölogical Garden, whose tufts are wholly deep black and whose mane is in part black, in part yellow.

[146] Second sign, second rectangle from left, third from top of plate. For the correct raptorial beak and form of head, which have unfortunately been lost in plate XIII, compare plate XI. The distribution of blue and black in our restoration is in large part guaranteed by bits of color on various examples of the sign in Per-nēb's tomb, but in the white area with inner spots marked off on the wing, we were guided (as we now suspect, wrongly) by Griffith, *Beni Hasan*, III, pl. II, 13.

darker than the secondary feathers, which were painted blue.[147] This consideration may well have value for the interpretation of puzzling hieroglyphs painted in part black, in part blue, such as those mentioned at the close of the preceding paragraph.

We are greatly obliged to Dr. John F. Shepard, Professor of Psychology in the University of Michigan, for reading and discussing with us the foregoing paragraphs on gray-black-blue interchanges. Dr Shepard reminds us that gray-black interchanges may be fully accounted for by differences in surroundings, one observer regarding as black what another, under other lighting or environment, would see as gray. He suggests that in the substitution of blue for black — or for gray — some influence of color contrast may at the outset have been the determining factor. Blue sensations are readily induced in the laboratory by means of juxtaposing yellow and gray or yellow and black, blue color being complementary to yellow. Natural conditions in historical times would seem to the present writer probably always to have been favorable to promoting induced blues in the vision of the inhabitants of Egypt. This is particularly true now in Upper Egypt because of the inclosing cliffs and strips of desert, which are prevailingly yellow in tone and are generally in view, near by or in the distance. In such an agricultural country much yellow must have been visible, too, in the fields, in the past as it is now, at the time of the ripening and the harvesting of grain. And at all seasons of the year, in the almost rainless climate, the yellow of diffuse sunlight is, and undoubtedly was in ancient times, especially strong and abundant.[148] In judging the matter, one must recall that the European or American visitor to Egypt today is bound by many visual habits acquired in a different environment, and that the ancient Egyptians seldom experienced other conditions for vision than those of their own land. On the other hand, in Dr. Shepard's opinion, the substitution of a black concept for a blue one[149] might well be accounted for by a high threshold

---

[147] See the description of this bird by Whymper in *Anc. Eg.*, 1915, p. 2. We are indebted to Dr. Frank M. Chapman of the American Museum of Natural History for opportunity to examine specimens of *Neophron percnopterus* in the Museum's collection.

[148] Hering regarded diffuse sunlight as distinctly yellow (thus quoted in Parsons, *Colour Vision* [2d edition], p. 28).

[149] It is a question how many blue-black interchanges of ancient Egyptian painting may be so classified; usually one is concerned with a blue pigment used for black as seen by most persons, and one is uncertain finding both blue and black in use for an object of vision such as water, which we commonly regard as blue, whether the black was not a hold-over from a time when artists had no blue pigment, when their only green pigment (crushed malachite) was costly, and they perhaps used black as their nearest practical approach to recording in painting what they saw as blue.

for blue, if this was really characteristic of the ancient Egyptians. The tests used by Rivers, however, he regards as inadequate to prove the conclusion Rivers reached, and he suggests that the lesser sensitiveness to blue of present-day Egyptian peasants may be attributable to color ignorance, akin to that exhibited by untrained observers of color everywhere, though conceivably greater in degree.

Miss Murray noted among color interchanges in the painting of birds not only a blue-black, but also a green-blue, interchange.[150] The green-blue interchange is comparatively rare, if not questionable, in the Old Kingdom and therefore concerns us in this book far less than the blue-black alternation. We would record the occurrence in Per-nēb's tomb of green on the handle and front projection of the hieroglyph supposed to represent a stone jug,[151] the remainder of its color being lost; the corresponding parts of this sign in Ptaḥ-ḥotpe's decoration are blue. In this case possibly the respective artists had in mind different materials for the jug. We are on surer ground in taking the Old Kingdom conventions for the plumage of definite birds and for water. The green alternative for blue in such cases does not once occur in Per-nēb's chambers; one must look for it chiefly in the Meidūm and Abusīr decorations,[152] and the small number of examples as compared with the preponderance of blue in the same signs and details elsewhere renders the green when it occurs open to the suspicion of not being original, but being due to chemical change.[153] These cases then require further examination. If really to be trusted, they present interesting questions as to the organization of the controlling artists and the perturbations through which color

[150] Saq. Mast., I, p. 46; Miss Murray, loc. cit., refers also to a red-yellow interchange in the coloring of birds; this has not come under our observation.

[151] W 9.

[152] See the colored plates of Petrie, Medum, and the records of colors in Borchardt, Saˀḥu-reᶜ, II, Nefer-ir-keˀ-reᶜ, and Ne-user-reᶜ, also scattered examples given in Murray, Saq. Mast., I, pl. XLII. In view of the existence of a blue-black interchange, an occasional apparent green-black interchange is in nowise surprising. In the Saḥu-Rēᶜ funerary temple the signs for house and court, O 1 and O 4, appear one black, the other green (Borchardt, op. cit., II, pls. 34, 55), and the letter t (X 1) is noted only once as blue (Borchardt, op. cit., II, pl. 17), everywhere else it is black or green.

[153] cf. above, pp. 30 and 39 with note 14. Azurite blue being an unstable color and Egyptian blue exceptionally dependable, we should not look for a chemical change from original blue to green after Egyptian blue had completely superseded the earlier pigment — that is, assuming that azurite blue was considerably used on earlier monuments and was only gradually replaced by the artificial blue pigment. The only change taking place in the latter is a slight graying of the surface, probably to be attributed in part to alteration in the vehicle or varnish used with it, in part to surface accumulation of finely divided extraneous matter (cf. pp. 32-33). Griffith's conjecture of a green being due to the use of a "compound colour from which the vegetable element has disappeared" (Hieroglyphs, p. 19) is obsolete, for today Pharaonic Egyptian pigments are not believed ever to have had a vegetable origin.

conventions passed before a generally accepted system was worked out. On the other hand, a substitution at times in later Egyptian decorations of green for blue is undeniable, the instances being too numerous and too consistently carried out to be accidental. Thus we find occasionally a two-color scheme formerly black and blue transposed as it were into a higher key of blue and green. This applies to the Metropolitan Museum's fragment (acc. no. 15.2.4), part of a door jamb dating from the Eighteenth Dynasty (around 1500 B.C.), in which certain signs have blue earth and green water[154] instead of black earth and blue water as so often in the Old Kingdom.[155] Again the blackish collar of the Egyptian cobra (*Naja haje*, Linn.), represented in sign I 10, is rendered now by blue,[156] now by green.[157] It is given sometimes as a band of pigment from edge to edge of the sign, but in the Old Kingdom more often by a rounded spot suggesting its under blacker part.[158]

The green-blue interchanges so far as they are genuinely of ancient date seem less puzzling than the interchanges of blue and black, in that they may well have their origin in color sensations which we have all experienced. Besides the unitary green

[154] The sea the Egyptian conceived as green, for he called it "the Great Green," but the green convention for water is comparatively infrequent in his art, blue prevailing in the New Kingdom as earlier. The fact is interesting that the blue convention for water goes back to the pyramid age. Nothing could be less true of the Nile and the irrigation canals of Egypt in most of their appearances, but of all their changing aspects, blue, like the sky above, was the one which impressed itself on the artist's memory and became his usual color concept for water.

[155] We refer for the XVIII Dynasty door jamb to signs N 36, N 39, and N 41; Per-nēb's decoration has the blue-black combination preserved in signs N 37, N 40, and N 41. Also of interest here is the later introduction of blue in the sign of the flowering reed (M 17), which in the V Dynasty was entirely green. The examples of this sign on the private shrine found by Frankfort at El ʿAmarneh and published by him in monochrome in *J. E. A.*, 1927, pls. XLV, 2, 3, and XLVII, as we noted on the original in Cairo, have a blue stem and rib, continuous to the end of the drooping top, and green only on the branches. That this is not an erratic example is proved by a XII Dynasty occurrence of the same color scheme for M 17 (A. M. Blackman, *Meir*, I, pl. XXXI, 1) and by others of the New Kingdom (e.g., Davies, *Two Sculptors*, pl. VIII). We recall both blue and green on the sign in the temple of Medīnet Habu. Here, it looks as if green were used for the part of the flowering reed which is lighter in color, blue for the darker part.

[156] e.g., in the decorations of Ka-ḥi-ef, Nen-khefty-ka, and Yedut; black, however, in Lepsius, *Denkmäler*, II, pl. 96.

[157] Examples of the Old Kingdom recorded in Murray, *Saq. Mast.*, I, pl. XLII, one of the XVIII Dynasty reproduced in Griffith, *Hieroglyphs*, pl. II, 16.

[158] See the description of the cobra's coloring in Anderson, *Reptilia and Batrachia*, p. 313. The yellow above and streak of white below, which characterize the creature — aside from its markings — in sign I 10 of Egyptian art, correspond about as closely as one expects in conventions to the natural, somewhat variable, coloring, brown above, yellowish below. Gardiner, *Gram.*, p. 466, cautiously interprets sign I 10 only as a "snake." The colors and patterning of the sign in the more careful ancient paintings (so far as we have been able to get to them) seem to us to speak for its identification with the cobra. Sethe so identifies it (*Urspr. d. Alphabets*, p. 157), but we cannot follow him in supposing the cobra goddess's name to mean "die Grünliche," or in his later translation "die Papyrusfarbene" (*Urg. u. älteste Rel.*, § 52).

and blue sensations, many green-blue blends are felt by normal eyes which are only to be correctly described by the use of both color names, for neither color loses its identity in the union, as do red and green when they unite to make yellow. It would seem that a transition from unitary blue to a green-blue blend might easily arise in the preparation of pigments,[159] and might readily be followed by another transition from the blend to unitary green. When the color is not unitary, and even when it is, the modern observer often has difficulty with nomenclature. This is true of one of the colors appearing in the representation of wall hangings in the tomb of Ḥesy-Rēᶜ which is called green by Quibell[160] and blue by Miss Murray.[161] Likewise the Egyptian vulture (G 1. *Neophron percnopterus*) in a painting at Beni Ḥasan is described by Griffith as having green color,[162] whereas Whymper calls the color blue.[163] We need hardly wonder that the passage from blue through green-blue to green was made by the ancient colorist. But though the green-blue interchanges may have been fortuitous in origin, they were afterwards deliberately cultivated, possibly having a connection with a tendency in later painting to depart from the full strong colors of the earlier age and to use tones higher in the scale of values. The acquisition of a cheap artificial green pigment, which was probably unknown in the time of the Old Kingdom, would have facilitated their cultivation. In the first examples mentioned on page 63, namely, signs depicting earth and water, the later color schemes do not violate known Egyptian conventions; in the case of the cobra's markings, we must at least consider whether cult images could be back of the coloring.[164] An interchange of green and blue in this and numerous other possible cases of temple apparatus and royal regalia might get started as representing respectively inlays of amazon stone or turquoise and inlays of lapis lazuli.[165] If our theory is right, these are not true interchanges, in the sense

[159] See Russell's account of the preparation of green and blue frits in *Medum*, pp. 45-46. The Egyptians had the green-blue blend in glazes before they acquired Egyptian blue frit, but they developed green frit for use as a pigment from blue frit.

[160] *Hesy*, p. 6, colored pls. VIII, IX. We hope that the tomb will one day be re-excavated, and that a chemical examination will be made of this pigment, which in the plates, however, as defined in the Munsell notation (G 7/2) is not a blend, but a green.

[161] *Sculpture*, p. 44.

[162] *Beni Hasan*, III, fig. 13, commented on in *Hieroglyphs*, p. 19.

[163] *Anc. Eg.*, 1915, p. 2.

[164] A cobra divinity was worshiped in early times in the X nome of Upper Egypt and is pictured in the nome-sign in the form of hieroglyph I 10 plus a feather and carried on a standard; cf. Sethe, *Urg. u. älteste Rel.*, § 52.

[165] They would then fall under the secondary colors referred to on our pages 47-48.

in which we wish to employ the term. In the former case we had alternating conventions for objects which do not change their essential appearance, but here in the postulated cobra-statues' collar and like examples, alternating colors in the object itself.

Certain other alternations of color invite an examination, among them the yellow and red conventions for the skin of men and women. At Meidūm, there is clear and abundant evidence for both yellow and red as conventions for men's flesh color,[166] but none for red for women's skin. The red convention for women is found, however, in later times.[167] By the Fifth Dynasty, the Egyptians had an almost fixed convention of red for the hieroglyphs depicting human members, and these we may believe would generally be considered masculine even when not demonstrably so. Only in a sign or two does the alternation continue, as in that of the forearm stretched forth holding an offering pot,[168] the arm being yellow on Ka-em-snēw's wall (pl. I, a, g), likewise in Per-nēb's tomb,[169] but elsewhere occasionally red.[170] Red by the late Fifth Dynasty definitely belonged to men,[171] yellow to women; and these conventions prevailed gen-

[166] Hieroglyphs A 20, D 58, and V 15, yellow in Petrie, *Medum*, pls. XI, XIII, red in pls. XII, XIII, XVII, XXIII, XXIV, XXVIII, must be regarded as derived from men's figures; in the scenes the men's figures range in color through several shades of red and pale brown-red to one almost yellow in the scene of boat making depicted in plate XI. Other signs for parts of the human body painted now red, now yellow, are D 21, D 28, D 36, and D 46, and probably mere chance has preserved at Meidūm the seated shepherd (A 47) only yellow and the negating arms (D 35), the arms with a shield and a weapon (D 34*), and the legs supporting a pot (W 25) only red. An alternation of red and yellow for hieroglyphs representing parts of the body is indicated, too, for certain reliefs of early date in the Cairo Museum, where sign D 36 has been observed red, and the hieroglyphs of the open mouth (D 21), the hand (D 46), and the leg (D 58), yellow (Murray, *Saq. Mast.*, I, pl. XLI). Compare the yellow flesh tones of the statue of King Djoser mentioned in Firth, *Annales*, 1925, p. 150, and Murray, *Sculpture*, p. 33.

[167] See Lepsius, *Denkmäler*, Text, III, p. 222; Davies, *El Amarna*, I, p. 14, note 1. On the stela of Nen-waf (Metropolitan Museum, acc. no. 12.182.3; Ransom, *Bull. of the Met. Mus.*, 1913, p. 74, fig. 5), the skin of women is painted with a red only slightly higher in value than that used for men.

[168] D 39.

[169] It is yellow also in Ka-ne-nesut II's decoration.

[170] Murray, *Saq. Mast.*, I, pl. XLI. In Ka-em-ꜥonekh's tomb, the sign of the forearm with palm downward (D 41) is yellow above a group of musicians in the upper chamber, red in the burial chamber. Wholly regular, however, is the yellow skin of the figure leaning on a forked staff (corresponding to A 20) in the title ꜥmꜥy.t of En-sedjer-ka, for the hieroglyph is assimilated to the sex of the tomb owner, the dress too being feminine.

[171] Very cautiously and tentatively we would suggest that the early lighter convention for men's skin may have had its basis in the influx of lighter-skinned people into the lower Nile Valley, which is believed greatly to have strengthened the Egyptian race in the Early Dynastic period just when the hieroglyphs were multiplying (Smith, *Anc. Egyptians*, pp. 95 ff.). Coming from the north, the new people were of lighter complexion than those already long established in Egypt. As Mr. Winlock has reminded us, the inhabitants of the Delta have at all times been somewhat lighter of complexion than Upper Egyptians. In the Meidūm paintings we should then have the waning yellow and the waxing red conventions, the latter being influenced by the more southerly darker-skinned population. On the IV Dynasty stela of Wep-em-nofret — which is without blue color — the red convention is already completely in the ascendency, there being no yellow hieroglyphs on it which represent parts of the body.

erally in wall scenes from the Fifth Dynasty on, although the alternative for each sex occasionally manifested itself.[172]

The hieroglyph of the human head in front view[173] seems to belong in a different class; it undoubtedly represents a male head, inasmuch as it is bearded, and early and late alike, as far as evidence shows,[174] it is invariably of yellow complexion (pls. 1, i, XIII). For the yellow convention in this case some special meaning now lost to us may be responsible. In this connection, we remind the reader of the yellow convention in the Saḥu-Rēᶜ reliefs for the god Sopdu and the demi-god Magic, possibly conceived as Asiatics, and for the demi-god Napri (Grain), for whom, of course, yellow was fitting.[175] Although we prefer the hypothesis just stated, we wish to mention Mr. Winlock's suggestion that yellow was used here merely to facilitate the painting of the eyes, nose, and mouth, dependent in a front view on a good contrast between the pigment of the complexion and those used for the features. We ourselves attribute the use of orange-red instead of brown-red for hieroglyphs representing parts of the body to a desire for greater legibility, no difference of significance being discernible between the two reds as used in Per-nēb's decoration. We should, however, expect a difference in the meaning of red and yellow as colors for the skin in the late Fifth Dynasty.

Certain early changes from a yellow to a green convention must also be given consideration. This is a matter principally of hieroglyphs representing baskets, ropes, plant fibers, and the like. All of these hieroglyphs which occur in Per-nēb's main chamber are green in color.[176] We must go farther back, to Meidūm and scattered monu-

---

[172] Yellow has been reported in a representation of a statue of a tomb owner, but Junker suggested that the intention was to render the color of the material of the statue rather than that of a man's skin (*Anzeiger*, 1929, p. 112). Yellow for living men in reliefs of the XII Dynasty is noted in A. M. Blackman, *Meir*, I, p. 17. Compare also a figure in the round of Meket-Rēᶜ presiding at the counting of cattle (Winlock, *Bull. of the Met. Mus.*, 1920, December, part II, p. 18, fig. 8), to the yellowness of which Mr. Winlock once called our attention, attributing it to Meket-Rēᶜ's high station and consequent protection from exposure to the sun in field labor; compare also the yellow-skinned male rowers of a boat model belonging to the Toledo Museum of Art (no. 27.138). Several references for red as the flesh color of women have been given in note 167.

[173] D 2.

[174] The white of this sign in Petrie, *Medum*, pl. XI, we suppose to indicate loss of color, for the beard would not have been painted white.

[175] Borchardt, *Saʾḥu-reᶜ*, II, pp. 19, 38, 41, pls. 5, 20, 25, 30. The yellow skin of the god "Grain" is interesting as an example of symbolism rather than representation in Egyptian color. But here we have to do with a being that had no objective existence. Even here, however, some will see an element of representation in that the god's figure is anthropomorphic and covered over with tiny ovals as if clad in grain or tattooed with it.

[176] We refer to signs M 17, Q 3, V 4, V 13, V 16, V 28, V 30, V 31, and Aa 1.

ments of the Fourth Dynasty, to find them generally yellow, although the yellow convention in their case seems to have persisted somewhat longer than the common use of yellow for men's skin, occurring as it does on certain reliefs which have the hieroglyphs of the parts of the body red.[177] In the past, the supposition has been that the early yellow color stood for dry rushes,[178] but no one has explained why green should have been substituted for it. As papyrus, rushes, flax, or palm fibers, surely would not long have remained green when worked into baskets and cords, we should think that the convention altered perhaps during the progress of the basket industry, in which more and more dyed materials may have been used, green-dyed rushes suggesting the color of the fresh materials and being especially liked.[179] This idea is more plausible for baskets than for ropes, and perhaps we should do better to entertain the theory that the color concept green, involving a knowledge of the original color of baskets and ropes before they had dried out, in some unknown way came largely to supersede the earlier convention yellow.[180]

But we have further to consider a suggestion by which, if it is right, the early yellow convention for basketry and ropes becomes nonexistent. Junker, discussing the inlaid colors of the hieroglyphs on the pedestal of a statue of Prince Ḥem-Ōny, a contemporary of Khufu, noted a large amount of yellow, which seemed to him hardly naturalistic in the case of the flowering-reed- and basket-signs;[181] and he suggested that the depressions for signs having inner drawing, but no cells to receive the contrasting pigments, were first filled with a "neutral" mass[182] and then topped with thin layers of the proper colors. He called attention, further, to a certain all-yellow group in the maṣṭabeh of Nūfer-maꜥet as probably once having had top color which

---

[177] Junker, *Giza I*, pl. xxiii, and the stela of Wep-em-nofret. In Meidūm sometimes associated with red for parts of the body as in sign V 15; see Petrie, *Medum*, pls. xii, xxiv.

[178] Griffith, *Hieroglyphs*, p. 47, apropos of V 30. We should note here that in the New Kingdom the yellow convention for rope occurs in some scenes (e.g., Davies, *Puyemrê*, I, pls. xviii, xix; cf. above, p. 42, note 29), but the green convention for rope-hieroglyphs established in the Old Kingdom is generally retained (e.g., Davies, *Two Sculptors*, pl. viii).

[179] Hangings, presumably of matting, very often exhibit a yellow-green design. Such a one was projected behind Per-nēb's litter in the outer chamber, and another is to be seen behind a seated figure on Ka-ḥi-ef's west wall; still another in Yasen's tomb. The coloring of the mat in hieroglyph R 4 is green and yellow on Per-nēb's west wall. The matting over the back of a hornless bull on Kai's north wall is yellow in color, at Deir el Gebrâwi a similar covering is striped green and yellow (Davies, *Deir el Gebrâwi*, II, pl. xix).

[180] In a scene of rope making in Ka-ḥi-ef's tomb, the rope is green in color (Junker, *Anzeiger*, 1913, p. 27).

[181] M 17 and V 30.

[182] Junker uses this term, surely an inadvertence in the case of yellow.

has peeled away.[183] If we understand him rightly, he would account not only for a frequent absence of inner drawing, but also for the presence of what he deems false yellow color, by the peeling away of the upper surface.[184] First, we must note that yellow on basket-, fiber-, and rope-signs is not confined to inscriptions incised in stone and filled with color, as are those which were the subject of Junker's discussion. If we were to suppose that inlaid signs when yellow had lost an upper layer of green, we should have to suppose that in bas-relief, too, green in early times customarily had a foundation of yellow. Now, as a matter of fact, green is a somewhat fugitive pigment, easily peeling cleanly enough to leave no record of its one-time presence; moreover, we have observed a few examples in bas-relief of green above yellow which might seem to support a theory that yellow when occurring on rope- and basket-signs was only a foundation, not a top, pigment.[185] Yet this explanation does not satisfy the conditions as regards inner drawing. Again and again inner drawing is preserved at Meidūm, and we have complete signs, yellow in color, with the drawing and outlines normal to them in red or black line.[186] We do not think it likely that green was ever present, covering and hiding these drawing lines, except where a deliberate change was made during the progress of the decoration, and a sign originally yellow was overpainted green.[187] We attribute the rare cases of both yellow and green occurring in the

[183] Petrie, *Medum*, pl. xxiv, in the case of the successive signs F 25, G 43, V 31. In this Junker followed the opinion expressed by Petrie, *op. cit.*, p. 29, at the end of chapter III, under Green (see reference, note 184).

[184] *Gîza I*, p. 155.

[185] The stela of Wep-em-nofret, in bas-relief, as we examined it in 1915, had the following signs yellow: Q 3, V 4, V 13, V 31, Aa 1. In the case of M 17, one example was yellow, two were green, and of the latter, one had the green clearly above yellow. Two signs, M 23 and M 28, showed green on top of yellow, while M 30 was part green, part yellow.

[186] See especially the basket-signs, V 30 and V 31, in Petrie, *Medum*, pl. xvii, bottom register at right, pl. xviii at left, and the letter ẖ (Aa 1), pl. xxiii, bottom register, all of which show the normal inner drawing in red line which presumably has been lost from the solid yellow signs under modern vicissitudes and abuse; cf. Petrie, *op. cit.*, p. 25.

[187] The hieroglyphs on Wep-em-nofret's stela which show green above yellow (M 17 and M 28) are everywhere at Meidūm green, as we should expect of signs representing living plants. The flowering reed (M 17), which might be used fresh or dried, and which fluctuates on the stela, does so also at Meidūm. In the tomb of Kai, signs M 17, V 28, V 30, and Aa 1 occur both green and yellow, M 23 occurs only green; Q 3, V 13, and V 31 are only yellow there, as far as we observed. In the tomb of Nesut-nofre we noted V 4, V 13, V 16, and Aa 1 only yellow, and M 17, M 23, Q 3, and V 28 only green; the basket-sign V 30 is here elaborately checkered in black and green. The burial chamber of Ka-em-ᶜonekh has an example of sign M 17 painted yellow, so also has the stela of Nen-khefty-ka. Junker's other Gîzeh volumes will no doubt greatly enrich our knowledge of Old Kingdom polychromy, but in the meantime we are availing ourselves of his most kind and generous permission to make free use of the color notes we took in the tombs of his concession.

same decoration for one or another of the basket- and rope-signs[188] to a fluctuation between two possible conventions similar to that seen in Per-nēb's tomb in the case of the hieroglyph of a house (O 1), appearing at least once black, but usually blue, and in the case of the quail-chick-hieroglyph (G 43) with inner markings sometimes black sometimes blue. We should record here, too, that in the painted but unsculptured inscription on the round lintel of Per-nēb's entrance, one of the basket-signs[189] and parts of the scepter- and chisel-hieroglyphs,[190] customarily green in the later Fifth Dynasty, are painted yellow, whether as a survival of an older convention or as a foundation for green subsequently lost or never added; we suspect here that parsimony in the use of malachite prevented the employment of green.

We continue the subject of the preceding paragraph in turning to the color conventions of cartouches, for, when detailed, cartouches appear to represent a piece of rope whose ends are lashed together, and are very often painted green.[191] We are not acquainted with any polychrome decoration containing them which certainly antedates the Fifth Dynasty, but in the tomb of Mer-yeb of the earlier part of the dynasty,[192] the cartouches are blue, and so they are very often.[193] We venture to think that the green convention is significant of rope, the blue, a mere abstract substitute for black drawing pigment; we have never noted black cartouches, but presume that they existed in the Third and Fourth Dynasties, if not later. A like condition is to be observed in the ground lines separating registers. These occur rarely green[194] and blue,[195] generally black in color, as in Per-nēb's decoration. The occurrence of green suggests that

---

[188] See the examples cited in the preceding note. On the stela of Ḥem-Mīn, one basket-sign (V 31) is yellow, another (V 30) green.

[189] V 30. The yellow signs W 10 of the offering lists (pl. XIII) are probably conceived as baskets, rather than as gold vessels, for on the stela of Nūfer, where they are green, the reeding of the baskets is indicated in the modeling.

[190] S 42 and U 23. Perhaps the handles of the objects represented by these signs were wound with rushes to cushion them. Or again, they may have been conceived as ceremonial objects with colored inlays, alternate blue and green stripes characterizing the signs on Nen-khefty-ka's stela, alternate yellow and green an example of U 23 on the west wall of Per-nēb's main chamber; under the second interpretation, yellow is more likely to represent gold than merely common wood, and even under the first suggestion, the fact that the handles of the signs on Per-nēb's lintel are striped horizontally, as sketch lines indicate, is against yellow meaning wood here.

[191] e.g., in Ka-em-snēw's tomb, on the stela of Tep-em-ꜥonekh, and in the tombs of Yedut, Nesut-nofre, and Seshem-nofre; see also Borchardt, Saꜣḫu-reꜥ, II, pls. 12, 38, 52, 69.

[192] See Junker, Gîza I, p. 9, for the date.

[193] Lepsius, Denkmäler, II, pls. 21, 22, for Mer-yeb; Davies, Deir el Gebrâwi, II, pl. v. Also in the tomb of Yedut and on the stela of Ḥem-Mīn.

[194] e.g., in the tombs of Nesut-nofre, Seshem-nofre, and En-sedjer-ka.

[195] e.g., in the tomb of En-sedjer-ka.

in the beginning these lines may have had color significance, being thought of as the cultivated land, black before vegetation appeared, green after the crops made verdant the land;[196] blue would then be an occasional alternative for black.[197] The frequency of these register divisions and their long-stretched character would very quickly result in their being felt more as lines than as ground, and their color therefore would take on an abstract quality, to which also the need for vertical division lines would contribute. Another interesting speculation concerns the gray background, whether, as some authorities have suggested,[198] it is reminiscent of mud-brick walls. Whether or not, we may be confident that its value as a neutral, knitting together and harmonizing all parts of the color scheme, contributed to its long popularity.

A few other color conventions found in Per-nēb's decoration should go on record, although we cannot take the space to discuss them in detail. The hieroglyph of the sun is painted red with a white rim,[199] that of the star has yellow rays, the center being lost.[200] The side supports of the booth-hieroglyph, yellow in the main like the roof, are blue at the bottom, whether to represent earth into which they are sunk or which is banked up about them, copper sheathing, a binding with different rushes, or what not.[201] The single stroke (pl. XIII) is found both blue and black, the color probably being abstract here, if it was not in origin.[202] The pellet-sign occurs now black, now blue, now green, now red, in part with apparent appropriateness to the several words determined.[203] The shoots of the rush-hieroglyph are blue.[204] The flint teeth of the sickle-sign are white,

[196] Compare the green line frequent at the base of hieroglyphs N 25 and N 26; see Petrie, *Medum*, pl. XIV, and Griffith, *Hieroglyphs*, p. 31.

[197] Compare the alternating blue and black conventions for the land-hieroglyphs, N 16, N 17, N 20, N 21, and N 22; in Per-nēb's decoration, the land-sign N 17 is blue.

[198] Recently in conversation with the writer, Mr. Winlock, and in print, Miss Swindler (*Painting*, p. 39). Another opinion is represented in Davies, *Ḳen-Amūn*, I, p. 60.

[199] N 5.

[200] N 14.

[201] O 22, in which, following Griffith (in *Hieroglyphs*, p. 36), we suppose yellow to be the color of bundles of reeds bound together. A similar color scheme with blue near the ground is to be seen in hieroglyph O 11 on the stela of Nen-khefty-ka; in Per-nēb's tomb, however, this sign is yellow (for wood, or for reeds of a primitive structure?) with black at the bottom; the grains within, which belong to the Old Kingdom form of the sign, are yellow in both cases. Compare the coloring — red above, black below — of the column-sign (O 28) on the pedestal of Ḥem-Ōny's statue, which Junker interprets as "eine in Nilschlamm gesetzte Holzbündelsäule" (*Gîza I*, p. 155).

[202] Z 1.

[203] N 33*.

[204] M 22; so also in the tomb of Ptaḥ-ḥotpe.

individually suggested in line, the handle and frame are the usual and still unexplained green.[205] The supposed baker's instrument is preserved only black.[206] The black top of the beer jar, which is in the main red, may possibly hark back to predynastic black-topped ware, although the form does not favor this view.[207] The horns of the supposed viper are black (pl. XIII), we cannot say whether with color significance or not; the body is yellow with a white streak below.[208] The bivalve shell is in part green.[209] Here we may mention that the color of lettuce roots is not preserved in Per-nēb's tomb, and the yellow given to them in plate XIII is based on their color in the tombs of Deshi and Ṭetu.

In the Egyptian artist's distribution of his colors, balance and rhythm are often to be observed parallel to the same qualities in the representation of form, whether in smaller details or in the composition of larger sections of the decoration. We have referred above (p. 44) to the overlapping figures of men and animals; as drawn, they please the aesthetic sense with their rhythm; as colored, they satisfy a liking for order by their regular sequence of two or more color units. The absence of differentiating tones in the case of overlapping cuts of meat and trussed fowl (pl. XIII) may be due to the artist's instinct that where the arrangement of the elements of the design was heterogeneous, accentuation of it in the color would not be agreeable. In Per-nēb's decoration the designer was ingenious in the ordering of his numerous small red pottery or blue bowls and their contents of green b3.t-grain(?) or blue grapes. In all, four combinations of these colors were possible: (a) blue bowl with blue contents; (b) blue bowl with green contents; (c) red bowl with blue contents; (d) red bowl with green contents. The bowls were variously placed, singly and in groups of two, three, and four, and the available combinations of pigments were manipulated to produce attractive interplays of color. For aesthetic enjoyment, the fidelity of the colors to the colors of the original objects which composed such designs is immaterial. For our inquiry it is of much consequence.

[205] U 1; the handle and frame are always solid green, not horizontally striped in part green, as is the rule with the handle in signs S 42 and U 23.

[206] U 31.

[207] W 22; for the exact form here, see plate XIII, upper left corner; in Per-nēb's decoration the several hieroglyphs W 18 have the top black, sign W 14 has the top blue.

[208] I 9. This creature has been discussed anew by Miss Murray, who makes the identification with *Cerastes cornutus*, Hasselq., appear rather improbable (*Anc. Eg.*, 1929, p. 18).

[209] L 6*.

Let us look for a moment at details "a" and "g" of plate I, in particular at the groups of three round-bottomed bowls in each one.[210] In "a" the color composition of the group is that of three repeating blue units, in "g" in the same group, the opportunity for a central color, green, and two balancing blues was seized. The blue, as we have seen (p. 51), may well be indicative of copper, and we want to know whether the green also is significant — of copper with a green patina, of glazed ware? — or whether we must reckon with the possibility that it is arbitrary, chosen only to make a pretty color group. A like situation exists in the case of the hieroglyph supposed on etymological grounds to represent a seat;[211] although, if it is an indoor seat in side view, its proportions, as far as we can tell from our knowledge of Egyptian furniture, are distorted. In Ka-em-snew's decoration, this sign when occurring singly is green, but in groups of three there, the central one is yellow, the flanking signs are green. In Per-nēb's tomb, all examples of the sign which have retained color are blue. In the tomb of Ptaḥ-ḥotpe, Mr. Gunn kindly pointed out to us one group of three with the outside signs blue and the central one green, and another group with the outside signs green and the central one blue.[212] One example at Meidūm appears to have been white,[213] if it was not found devoid of color.[214] Studied such color groupings unquestionably were, but we have yet to determine whether the artist restrained his choice to the colors natural to the objects depicted or sometimes dressed them up to fit into a color scheme. Perhaps the reader will inquire whether all this is interesting as regards the color interchanges previously discussed. We do not think so; as we understand the interchanges, they represent in origin, in most cases,[215] different color concepts for the same unvarying object of vision, according as it impressed different artists, and in this paragraph we are undoubtedly concerned with designs made by a single artist who with intention used different colors, either falsifying facts or manipulating actual colors to produce a color composition.

[210] W 24.

[211] Q 1.

[212] Similar balanced or rhythmical groups are observable on the stela of Nen-khefty-ka.

[213] Petrie, *Medum*, pl. XIII.

[214] See Griffith's explanation of the colors in *Hieroglyphs*, p. 54, which, however, does not take account of green. The complete absence of inner drawing from all examples of the sign is also of importance for its interpretation.

[215] Ignorance of many details of the ancient Egyptian's surroundings often renders quite tentative any classification of the conventions under the principles we have tried to define.

THE DECORATION OF THE TOMB OF PER-NĒB

Without question the Egyptian practice of enriching cult objects and articles for the king's use with colorful inlays and appliqués of precious materials gave legitimate occasion for a bright array of colors in many wall scenes. But we do not agree with Borchardt's view that the blue convention for hair in statues arose from the conception that the gods had hair of lapis lazuli.[216] Rather, the conception that hair was blue preceded the choice of the dark blue stone lapis lazuli in poetry and occasionally in fact (in the case of statues) to represent hair. We need, however, to ask ourselves whether Egyptian art furnishes parallels to the literary imagery in the well-known description of the beneficent serpent whose body was overlaid with gold and whose eyebrows were of real lapis lazuli.[217] Whether the artists painted only such splendid things as did or could exist about them, or created on occasions shapes and colorings purely imaginative, makes much difference to our interpretations. Such fantastic creatures as those depicted on early ceremonial palettes, the king as sphinx in literature and art, the human-headed bird for the soul (b3) are imaginative motives that come to mind at once. But our impression is that during earlier Pharaonic times, in the tomb paintings representing equipment for the deceased, the attitude of the designer was a sober one, that not until the Nineteenth Dynasty, when he began to picture an unseen Nether World, did he really allow his imagination to run riot in the creation of multitudinous genii, minor gods, and the paraphernalia of their shadowy existence.

The present writer's study of Old Kingdom color, although far from yielding a convincing explanation for every color puzzle, has given her confidence that the colors in wall decorations are to be taken seriously, that there is no compelling reason to suppose the artist allowed a desire for aesthetic effect or flights of fancy to control his choice of pigments to the exclusion of truth, and that when colors were not faithful to the ultimate original of a hieroglyph or of an object in a scene, it was because knowledge of that original had become confused or was entirely lost, painters often turning to other decorations rather than directly to nature for their inspiration. The presumption of truth within the conventions adopted by Egyptian colorists accords with the belief generally held that the decoration in tombs had utility for the deceased, enabling him to enjoy in the next life the environment and possessions which

---

[216] *Porträts*, p. 6, note 2.

[217] *Shipwrecked Sailor*, lines 64-65. An English translation is available in Erman, *Egyptian Literature*, pp. 30-35.

had been his on earth. In judging the conventions and in using them as evidence allowance must be made for inadvertence on the part of the ancient decorator, and attention must be paid to the quality of a decoration and the amount of detail in it. In the present state of Egyptological science, we are able to understand the meaning of colors for the most part only when we already know what the painted object is, and we wish to use the colors to help interpretation. But more and more, as the study of extant colors continues, they should, we believe, prove useful in conjunction with other evidence in ferreting out the unknown.

LIST OF
REFERENCES CITED

LIST OF REFERENCES CITED

Anderson, J. *Reptilia and Batrachia* (*Zoology of Egypt,* vol. I). London, 1898.

Barron, T., and W. F. Hume. *Topography and Geology of the Eastern Desert of Egypt. Central Portion* (*Geological Survey Report*). Cairo, 1902.

Belzoni, G. *Narrative of the Operations and Recent Discoveries . . . in Egypt and Nubia and of a Journey to the Coast of the Red Sea . . . and Another to the Oasis of Jupiter Ammon.* 3d edition. 2 vols. London, 1822.

Berg, B. *To Africa with the Migratory Birds.* New York and London, 1930.

Berlin, Königliche Museen zu. *Ausführliches Verzeichnis der aegyptischen Altertümer und Gipsabgüsse.* 2d edition. Berlin, 1899.

Bissing, F. W. von. "Un Autre Vase à fleurs égyptien." *Recueil de travaux relatifs à la philologie et à l'archéologie égyptiennes et assyriennes,* 1904, vol. XXVI, p. 178.

—— *Die Mastaba des Gem-ni-kai,* vol. II. Leipzig, 1911.

Bissing F. W. von, and M. Reach. "Bericht über die malerische Technik der Hawata Fresken im Museum von Kairo." *Annales du Service des antiquités de l'Égypte,* 1906, vol. VII, pp. 64-70.

Blackman, A. M. *The Rock Tombs of Meir,* parts I-IV (*Archaeological Survey of Egypt,* Memoirs XXII-XXV). London, 1914, 1915, 1924.

—— "The Pharaoh's Placenta and the Moon-God Khons." *The Journal of Egyptian Archaeology,* 1916, vol. III, pp. 235-249.

Blackman, Winifred S. *The Fellāhīn of Upper Egypt, Their Religious, Social, and Industrial Life To-Day with Special Reference to Survivals from Ancient Times.* London, 1927.

Borchardt, L. "Drei Hieroglyphenzeichen." *Zeitschrift für ägyptische Sprache und Altertumskunde,* 1907, vol. 44, pp. 75-79.

—— *Das Grabdenkmal des Königs Ne-user-reꜥ* (*Ausgrabungen der Deutschen Orient-Gesellschaft in Abusir, 1902-1904,* vol. I = 7. wissenschaftliche Veröffentlichung der D. O.-G.). Leipzig, 1907.

—— *Das Grabdenkmal des Königs Nefer-ir-keꜣ-reꜥ* (*ibid., 1902-1908,* vol. V = 11. wissenschaftliche Veröffentlichung der D. O.-G.). Leipzig, 1909.

—— *Porträts der Königin Nofret-ete* (*Ausgrabungen der Deutschen Orient-Gesellschaft in Tell el-Amarna,* vol. III = 44. wissenschaftliche Veröffentlichung der D. O.-G.). Leipzig, 1923.

Borchardt, L., with the collaboration of E. Assmann, A. Bollacher, O. Heinroth, M. Hilzheimer, and K. Sethe. *Das Grabdenkmal des Königs Śaḥu-reꜥ,* vol. II (*Ausgrabungen der Deutschen Orient-Gesellschaft in Abusir, 1902-1908,* vol. VII = 26. wissenschaftliche Veröffentlichung der D. O.-G.). Leipzig, 1913.

British Museum. *Hieroglyphic Texts from Egyptian Stelae, &c., in the British Museum,* part I. London, 1911.

Budge, E. A. Wallis. *Egyptian Sculptures in the British Museum.* London, 1914.

Burton, W. "Ancient Egyptian Ceramics." *Journal of the Royal Society of Arts,* 1911-1912, vol. LX, pp. 594-602.

Capart, J., with the collaboration of Marcelle Werbrouck. *Memphis à l'ombre des pyramides* (*Fondation égyptologique Reine Élisabeth*). Brussels, 1930.

Clarke, Somers, and R. Engelbach. *Ancient Egyptian Masonry. The Building Craft.* Oxford and London, 1930.

Crow, J. K. "Report on Samples of Colours Scraped from the Monuments." *Annales du Service des antiquités de l'Égypte,* 1903, vol. IV, pp. 242-243.

Daressy, G. *Ostraca* (*Catalogue général des antiquités égyptiennes du Musée du Caire*). Cairo, 1901.

Davies, N. de Garis. *The Mastaba of Ptahhetep and Akhethetep at Saqqareh,* parts I, II (*Archaeological Survey of Egypt,* Memoirs VIII, IX). London, 1900, 1901.

—— *The Rock Tombs of Deir el Gebrâwi,* parts I, II (*ibid.,* Memoirs XI, XII). London, 1902.

—— *The Rock Tombs of el Amarna,* parts I, IV (*ibid.,* Memoirs XIII, XVI). London, 1903, 1906.

—— *Five Theban Tombs* (*ibid.,* Memoir XXI). London, 1913.

—— *The Tomb of Nakht at Thebes* (*Publications of the Metropolitan Museum of Art. Robb de Peyster Tytus Memorial Series,* vol. I). New York, 1917.

—— "Mural Paintings in the City of Akhetaten." *The Journal of Egyptian Archaeology,* 1921, vol. VII, pp. 1-7.

—— "The Graphic Work of the Expedition." *Bulletin of the Metropolitan Museum of Art,* 1922, vol. XVII, December, part II, pp. 50-56.

—— *The Tomb of Puyemrê at Thebes,* vol. I (*Publications of the Metropolitan Museum of Art. Robb de Peyster Tytus Memorial Series,* vol. II). New York, 1922.

—— *The Tomb of Two Sculptors at Thebes* (*ibid.,* vol. IV). New York, 1925.

77

LIST OF REFERENCES CITED

——— *Two Ramesside Tombs at Thebes* (ibid., vol. V). New York, 1927.

——— *The Tomb of Ķen-Amūn at Thebes*, vol. I (*Publications of the Metropolitan Museum of Art Egyptian Expedition*). New York, 1930.

Davis, T. M., Sir G. Maspero, and G. Daressy. *The Tombs of Harmhabi and Touatânkhamanou (Theodore M. Davis' Excavations. Bibân el Molûk).* London, 1912.

Edgar, C. C. "Remarks on Egyptian 'Sculptors' Models.'" *Recueil de travaux relatifs à la philologie et à l'archéologie égyptiennes et assyriennes*, 1905, vol. XXVII, pp. 137-150.

——— *Sculptors' Studies and Unfinished Works (Catalogue général des antiquités égyptiennes du Musée du Caire).* Cairo, 1906.

Eibner, A. *Entwicklung und Werkstoffe der Wandmalerei vom Altertum bis zur Neuzeit.* Munich, 1926.

Engelbach, R. "Evidence for the Use of a Mason's Pick in Ancient Egypt." *Annales du Service des antiquités de l'Égypte*, 1929, vol. XXIX, pp. 19-24.

See also Clarke, Somers, and R. Engelbach.

Erman, A. *The Literature of the Egyptians.* . . . Translated by A. M. Blackman. London, 1927.

——— *Ägyptische Grammatik mit Schrifttafel, Paradigmen, und Übungsstücken.* . . . 4th edition. Berlin, 1928, 1929.

Erman, A., and H. Grapow. *Wörterbuch der aegyptischen Sprache*, vol. II. Leipzig, 1928.

Fechheimer, Hedwig. *Die Plastik der Ägypter.* Berlin, 1914.

Firth, C. M. "Excavations of the Department of Antiquities at the Step Pyramid, Saqqara (1924-1925)." *Annales du Service des antiquités de l'Égypte*, 1925, vol. XXV, pp. 149-159.

——— "Excavations of the Service des antiquités at Saqqara (November 1926-April 1927)." *ibid.*, 1927, vol. XXVII, pp. 105-111.

——— "Excavations of the Service des antiquités at Saqqara (October 1927-April 1928)." *ibid.*, 1928, vol. XXVIII, pp. 81-88.

Firth, C. M., and B. Gunn. *Teti Pyramid Cemeteries (Service des antiquités de l'Égypte. Excavations at Saqqara).* 2 vols. Cairo, 1926.

Fisher, C. S. *The Minor Cemetery at Giza (The Eckley B. Coxe, Jr., Foundation*, n. s., vol. I). Philadelphia, 1924.

Fouqué, F. "Sur le bleu égyptien ou vestorien." *Bulletin de la Société française de minéralogie*, 1889, vol. XII, pp. 36-38.

——— "Sur le bleu égyptien ou vestorien." *Comptes rendus hebdomadaires des séances de l'Académie des sciences*, 1889, vol. CVIII, pp. 325-327.

Frankfort, H. "Preliminary Report on the Excavations at Tell El-ᶜAmarnah, 1926-7." *The Journal of Egyptian Archaeology*, 1927, vol. XIII, pp. 209-218.

Gardiner, A. H. "The Colour of Mourning." *Zeitschrift für ägyptische Sprache und Altertumskunde*, 1910, vol. 47, pp. 162-163.

——— *The Tomb of Amenemhēt (The Theban Tomb Series*, Memoir I). Copied in line and color by Nina de Garis Davies. London, 1915.

——— *Egyptian Grammar.* . . . Oxford, 1927.

——— *Catalogue of the Egyptian Hieroglyphic Printing Type.* . . . Oxford, 1928.

Gladstone, W. E. *Studies on Homer and the Homeric Age.* 3 vols. Oxford, 1858.

Glanville, S. R. K. Review of Lucas, *Materials*, and H. Garland and C. O. Bannister, *Ancient Egyptian Metallurgy. The Journal of Egyptian Archaeology*, 1928, vol. XIV, pp. 188-191.

Grapow, H. *Die bildlichen Ausdrücke des Aegyptischen.* Leipzig, 1924.

See also Erman, A., and H. Grapow.

Griffith, F. Ll. *Beni Hasan*, parts III, IV (*Archaeological Survey of Egypt*, Memoirs V, VII). London, 1896, 1900.

——— *The Tomb of Ptah-hetep (Egyptian Research Account, 1896).* Copied by R. F. E. Paget and A. A. Pirie. London, 1898.

——— *A Collection of Hieroglyphs.* . . . (*Archaeological Survey of Egypt*, Memoir VI). London, 1898.

——— "The Hieroglyphs of Ptahhetep and Akhethetep." In Davies, *Ptahhetep*, I, chap. III, pp. 12-38.

——— "Excavations at El-ᶜAmarnah, 1923-24." *The Journal of Egyptian Archaeology*, 1924, vol. X, pp. 299-305.

Gunn, B. "The Inscriptions." In *Teti Pyramid Cemeteries*, by C. M. Firth and B. Gunn, vol. I, pp. 85-289.

Hall, H. R. *Royal Scarabs (Catalogue of Egyptian Scarabs, etc., in the British Museum*, vol. I). London, 1913.

Hofmann, K. B. "Über die Schmelzfarben von Tell el Jehûdîje. Offener Brief an Dr. E. Ritter v. Bergmann." *Zeitschrift für ägyptische Sprache und Altertumskunde*, 1885, vol. 23, pp. 62-68.

Holwerda, A. E. J., P. A. A. Boeser, and J. H. Holwerda. *Die Denkmäler des alten Reiches (Beschreibung der aegyptischen Sammlung des niederländischen Reichsmuseums der Altertümer in Leiden).* The Hague, 1908.

H[oward], R. "Old Kingdom Reliefs of Ancient Egypt." *The Bulletin of the Cleveland Museum of Art*, 1930, vol. 17, pp. 185-190, 195.

Hussey, C. *Tait McKenzie. A Sculptor of Youth.* Philadelphia, 1930.

Illustrated London News, The, December, 1923, pp. 1116-1117; November 12, 1927, p. 861; January 7, 1928; April 19, 1930, p. 688.

Jéquier, G. *Les Frises d'objets des sarcophages du Moyen Empire (Mémoires publiés par les membres de l'Institut français d'archéologie orientale du Caire*, vol. 47). Cairo, 1921.

——— *La Pyramide d'Oudjebten (Service des antiquités de l'Égypte. Fouilles à Saqqarah).* Cairo, 1928.

——— *Tombeaux de particuliers contemporains de Pepi II (ibid.).* Cairo, 1929.

Jéquier, G., with the collaboration of D. Dunham. *Le Mastabat Faraoun (ibid.).* Cairo, 1928.

78

Junker, H. "Vorbericht über die zweite Grabung bei den Pyramiden von Gizeh. . . ." *Anzeiger der philosophisch-historischen Klasse der kais. Akademie der Wissenschaften,* June 11, 1913, no. XIV.

—— "Vorläufiger Bericht über die vierte Grabung bei den Pyramiden von Gizeh. . . ." *ibid.,* May 19, 1926, no. XII.

—— "Vorläufiger Bericht über die fünfte Grabung . . . bei den Pyramiden von Gizeh." *ibid.,* April 27, 1927, no. XIII.

—— "Vorläufiger Bericht über die sechste Grabung . . . bei den Pyramiden von Gizeh. . . ." *ibid.,* July 4, 1928, nos. XIV-XVII.

—— "Vorläufiger Bericht über die siebente Grabung . . . bei den Pyramiden von Gîza. . . ." *ibid.,* May 27, 1929, nos. XIII-XV.

—— *Die Kultkammer des Prinzen Kanjnjswt im Wiener Kunsthistorischen Museum.* 3d edition. Vienna, 1931.

Junker, H., with the collaboration of K. Holey. *Giza I. Die Maṣṭabas der IV. Dynastie auf dem Westfriedhof (Akademie der Wissenschaften in Wien. Philosophisch-historische Klasse, Denkschriften,* vol. 69, *Abhandlung* I). Vienna and Leipzig, 1929.

Keimer, L. "Flechtwerk aus Halfagras im alten und neuen Ägypten." *Orientalistische Literaturzeitung,* 1927, vol. 30, cols. 76-85, 145-154.

—— "An Ancient Egyptian Knife in Modern Egypt." *Ancient Egypt,* 1928, pp. 65-66.

—— "Sur quelques petits fruits en faïence émaillée datant du Moyen Empire." *Bulletin de l'Institut français d'archéologie orientale,* 1929, vol. XXVIII, pp. 49-96.

—— "Sur l'ornementation d'un bracelet en ébène datant du Nouvel Empire." *Revue de l'Égypte ancienne,* 1930, vol. III, pp. 42-50.

—— "Quelques hiéroglyphes représentant des oiseaux." *Annales du Service des antiquités de l'Égypte,* 1930, vol. XXX, pp. 1-26.

Klebs, Luise. *Die Reliefs des alten Reiches (Abhandlungen der Heidelberger Akademie der Wissenschaften. . . . Philosophisch-historische Klasse,* no. 3, July 28, 1914). Heidelberg, 1915.

Lacau, P. *Sarcophages antérieurs au Nouvel Empire (Catalogue général des antiquités égyptiennes du Musée du Caire).* 2 vols. Cairo, 1904, 1906.

Lansing, A. *An Exhibition of Copies of Egyptian Wall Paintings . . . (The Metropolitan Museum of Art).* New York, 1930.

Laurie, A. P. *Greek and Roman Methods of Painting.* Cambridge, 1910.

—— *The Materials of the Painter's Craft in Europe and Egypt . . . with Some Account of Their Preparation and Use.* London and Edinburgh, 1910.

—— "Ancient Pigments and Their Identification in Works of Art." *Archaeologia, or Miscellaneous Tracts Relating to Antiquity,* 1913, vol. LXIV, pp. 315-335.

Laurie, A. P., W. F. P. McLintock, and F. D. Miles. "Egyptian Blue." *Proceedings of the Royal Society of London,* series A, 1914, vol. 89, pp. 418-429.

Reviews of, in: *The Chemical News,* 1913, vol. 108, p. 300; *Ancient Egypt,* 1914, pp. 186-188; *The Journal of Egyptian Archaeology,* 1914, vol. I, p. 73.

Lepsius, R. C. *Denkmäler aus Aegypten und Aethiopien.* VI parts, 12 vols. Berlin, 1849-1859.

—— *op. cit., Text,* edited by K. Sethe. 5 vols. Leipzig, 1897-1913.

Lucas, A. *Antiques, Their Restoration and Preservation.* London, 1924.

—— "Mistakes in Chemical Matters Frequently Made in Archaeology." *The Journal of Egyptian Archaeology,* 1924, vol. X, pp. 128-132.

—— *Ancient Egyptian Materials.* London, 1926.

—— "Problems in Connection with Ancient Egyptian Materials." *The Analyst. Journal of the Society of Public Analysts and Other Analytical Chemists,* 1926, vol. LI, pp. 435-450.

—— "The Chemistry of the Tomb." In *The Tomb of Tut·ankh·Amen,* vol. II, by Howard Carter, Appendix II, pp. 162-188. London, 1927.

Lutz, H. F. *Egyptian Tomb Steles and Offering Stones of the Museum of Anthropology and Ethnology . . . (University of California Publications. Egyptian Archaeology,* vol. IV). Leipzig, 1927.

Lythgoe, A. M. "Recent Egyptian Acquisitions." *Bulletin of the Metropolitan Museum of Art,* 1908, vol. III, pp. 217, 220-223.

—— "The Egyptian Expedition." *ibid.,* 1909, vol. IV, pp. 119-123.

—— "The History of the Tomb and the Principal Features of Its Construction." In *Perneb,* by Lythgoe and Ransom, chap. I, pp. 1-45.

Lythgoe, A. M., and Caroline L. Ransom. *The Tomb of Perneb (The Metropolitan Museum of Art).* New York, 1916.

Mace, A. C. "The Fourth and Fifth Egyptian Rooms." In *A Handbook of the Egyptian Rooms (The Metropolitan Museum of Art),* pp. 41-78. New York, 1911.

Mackay, E. "Proportion Squares on Tomb Walls in the Theban Necropolis." *The Journal of Egyptian Archaeology,* 1917, vol. IV, pp. 74-85.

—— "On the Various Methods of Representing Hair in the Wall-Paintings of the Theban Tombs." *ibid.,* 1918, vol. V, pp. 113-116.

—— "On the Use of Beeswax and Resin as Varnishes in Theban Tombs." *Ancient Egypt,* 1920, pp. 35-38.

—— "The Cutting and Preparation of Tomb-Chapels in the Theban Necropolis." *The Journal of Egyptian Archaeology,* 1921, vol. VII, pp. 154-168.

Maerz, A., and M. R. Paul. *A Dictionary of Color.* New York and London, 1930.

Mariette, A. *Les Mastabas de l'Ancien Empire.* Paris, 1889.

Meinertzhagen, R. *Nicoll's Birds of Egypt.* 2 vols. London, 1930.

Micault, V. "Couleurs anciennes obtenues par l'emploi des oxydes de cuivre." *Bulletin de la Société minéralogique de France,* 1881, vol. IV, pp. 82-84.

LIST OF REFERENCES CITED

Möller, G. "Goldschmiedearbeiten in ägyptischem Stil." In *Ägyptische Goldschmiedearbeiten (Königliche Museen zu Berlin, Mitteilungen aus der ägyptischen Sammlung*, vol. I), by H. Schäfer, with the collaboration of G. Möller and W. Schubart, pp. 11-80. Berlin, 1910.

—— *Die Metallkunst der alten Ägypter.* Berlin, 1925.

Montet, P. *Les Scènes de la vie privée dans les tombeaux égyptiens de l'Ancien Empire (Publications de la Faculté des lettres de l'Université de Strasbourg*, no. 24). Strasbourg, 1925.

Munsell Book of Color, Defining, Explaining, and Illustrating the Fundamental Characteristics of Color. Standard edition. Baltimore, 1929.

Murray, Margaret A. *Saqqara Mastabas*, part I (*Egyptian Research Account*, 1904). London, 1905.

—— "The Cerastes in Royal Names." *Ancient Egypt*, 1929, pp. 18-21.

—— *Egyptian Sculpture.* London, 1930.

Newberry, P. E. *Beni Hasan*, parts I, II (*Archaeological Survey of Egypt*, Memoirs I, II). London, 1893.

—— *The Life of Rekhmara.* Westminster, 1900.

Parsons, Sir J. H. *An Introduction to the Study of Colour Vision.* 2d edition. Cambridge, 1924.

Petrie, Sir W. M. Flinders. *Abydos*, part II (*The Egypt Exploration Fund*, Memoir XXIV). London, 1903.

—— *Arts and Crafts of Ancient Egypt* (*The World of Art Series*). Chicago and Edinburgh, 1910.

—— *Tools and Weapons* (*British School of Archaeology in Egypt and Egyptian Research Account. . . . 1916*). London, 1917.

—— *Prehistoric Egypt (ibid. 1917).* London, 1920.

Petrie, Sir W. M. Flinders, with chapters by F. Ll. Griffith, Dr. A. Wiedemann, Dr. W. J. Russell, F.R.S., and W. E. Crum. *Medum.* London, 1892.

Petrie, Sir W. M. Flinders, with chapters by A. H. Sayce, F. Ll. Griffith, and F. C. J. Spurrell. *Tell el Amarna.* London, 1894.

Petrie, Sir W. M. Flinders, E. Mackay, and G. Wainwright. *Meydum and Memphis (III)* (*British School of Archaeology in Egypt and Egyptian Research Account. . . . 1910*). London, 1910.

Petrie, Sir W. M. Flinders, G. A. Wainwright, and E. Mackay. *The Labyrinth, Gerzeh, and Mazghuneh (ibid. 1912).* London, 1912.

Pisani, F. "Substance bleue provenant d'un ancien atelier gallo-romain." *Bulletin de la Société minéralogique de France*, 1880, vol. III, pp. 197-198.

Pope, A. *The Painter's Terms (An Introduction to the Language of Drawing and Painting*, vol. I). Cambridge, Massachusetts, 1929.

Porter, Bertha, and Rosalind L. B. Moss. *Memphis . . . (Topographical Bibliography of Ancient Egyptian Hieroglyphic Texts, Reliefs, and Paintings*, vol. III). Oxford, 1931.

Quibell, J. E. *The Tomb of Hesy (Service des antiquités de l'Égypte. Excavations at Saqqara [1911-1912]).* Cairo, 1913.

Quibell, J. E., and F. W. Green. *Hierakonpolis*, part II (*Egyptian Research Account*, Memoir V). London, 1902.

Quibell, J. E., with sections by Sir H. Thompson and W. Spiegelberg. *Excavations at Saqqara (1907-1908) (Service des antiquités de l'Égypte).* Cairo, 1909.

Quibell, J. E., and A. G. K. Hayter. *Teti Pyramid, North Side (Service des antiquités de l'Égypte. Excavations at Saqqara).* Cairo, 1927.

Raehlmann, E. *Über die Maltechnik der Alten . . . nebst einer Anleitung zur mikroskopischen Untersuchung der Kunstwerke.* Berlin, 1910.

—— "Die blaue Farbe in den verschiedenen Perioden der Malerei. . . ." *Museumskunde. Zeitschrift für Verwaltung und Technik öffentlicher und privater Sammlungen*, 1913, vol. IX, pp. 224-232.

—— *Über die Farbstoffe der Malerei in den verschiedenen Kunstperioden nach mikroskopischen Untersuchungen.* Leipzig, 1914.

Ransom, Caroline L. "Egyptian Furniture and Musical Instruments." *Bulletin of the Metropolitan Museum of Art*, 1913, vol. VIII, pp. 72-79.

—— "A Study of the Decorative and Inscriptional Features of the Tomb." In *Perneb*, by Lythgoe and Ransom, chap. II, pp. 47-79.

Reisner, G. A. *The Early Dynastic Cemeteries of Naga-ed-Dêr*, part I (*University of California Publications. Egyptian Archaeology*, vol. II). Leipzig, 1908.

—— "New Acquisitions of the Egyptian Department." *Bulletin of the Museum of Fine Arts*, 1913, vol. XI, pp. 53-66.

—— "The Tomb of Meresankh, a Great-Granddaughter of Queen Hetep-Heres I and Sneferuw." *ibid.*, 1927, vol. XXV, pp. 63-79.

—— "The Empty Sarcophagus of the Mother of Cheops." *ibid.*, 1928, vol. XXVI, pp. 76-88.

Reisner, G. A., and C. S. Fisher. "Preliminary Report on the Work of the Harvard-Boston Expedition in 1911-13." *Annales du Service des antiquités de l'Égypte*, 1914, vol. XIII, pp. 227-252.

Rivers, W. H. R. "The Colour Vision of the Natives of Upper Egypt." *The Journal of the Anthropological Institute of Great Britain and Ireland*, 1901, vol. XXXI, pp. 229-247.

—— "Observations on the Senses of the Todas." *The British Journal of Psychology*, 1904-1905, vol. I, pp. 321-396.

Roeder, G. *Die Mastaba des Uhemka im Pelizaeus-Museum zu Hildesheim.* Wienhausen (Kreis Celle), 1927.

Ross, Sir E. Denison (editor). *The Art of Egypt through the Ages.* London, 1931.

Russell, W. J. "Egyptian Colours." In *Medum*, by Sir W. M. Flinders Petrie and others, chap. VIII, pp. 44-48.

Schäfer, H. *Die altägyptischen Prunkgefässe mit aufgesetzten Randverzierungen (Untersuchungen zur Geschichte und Altertumskunde Aegyptens*, vol. IV, part I). Leipzig, 1903.

LIST OF REFERENCES CITED

———— *Priestergräber und andere Grabfunde vom Ende des alten Reiches bis zur griechischen Zeit vom Totentempel des Ne-user-rê (Ausgrabungen der Deutschen Orient-Gesellschaft in Abusir, 1902-1904, vol. II = 8. wissenschaftliche Veröffentlichung der D. O.-G.).* Leipzig, 1908.

———— "Flachbild und Rundbild in der ägyptischen Kunst." *Zeitschrift für ägyptische Sprache und Altertumskunde,* 1923, vol. 58, pp. 138-149.

———— *Grundlagen der ägyptischen Rundbildnerei und ihre Verwandschaft mit denen der Flachbildnerei (Der alte Orient, vol. 23, part 4).* Leipzig, 1923.

———— *Ägyptische und heutige Kunst und Weltgebäude der alten Ägypter.* Berlin and Leipzig, 1928.

———— *Von ägyptischer Kunst: eine Grundlage.* 3d edition. Leipzig, 1930.

Sethe, K. "Die Inschriften." In *Saʒḥu-reʿ,* II, by Borchardt and others, part III, pp. 72-132.

———— *Die altaegyptischen Pyramidentexte,* vol. IV. Leipzig, 1922.

———— "Die aegyptischen Ausdrücke für rechts und links und die Hieroglyphenzeichen fur Westen und Osten." *Nachrichten der Königlichen Gesellschaft der Wissenschaften zu Göttingen. Philologisch-historische Klasse,* 1922, pp. 197-242.

———— *Der Ursprung des Alphabets. Die neuentdeckte Sinaischrift.* Berlin, 1926.

———— *Urgeschichte und älteste Religion der Ägypter (Abhandlungen für die Kunde des Morgenlandes, vol. XVIII, no. 4).* Leipzig, 1930.

Smith, G. Elliot. *The Ancient Egyptians.* London and New York, 1911.

———— "Egyptian Mummies." *The Journal of Egyptian Archaeology,* 1914, vol. I, pp. 189-196.

Spearing, H. G. *The Childhood of Art,* vol. I. 2d edition. London, 1930.

Spurrell, F. C. J. "Notes on Egyptian Colours." *The Archaeological Journal,* 1895, vol. LII, pp. 222-239.

Steindorff, G. *Grabfunde des mittleren Reichs in den königlichen Museen zu Berlin:* part I, *Das Grab des Mentuhotep;* part II, *Der Sarg des Sebk-o.—Ein Grabfund aus Gebelên (Mittheilungen aus den orientalischen Sammlungen, nos. VIII, IX).* Berlin, 1896, 1901.

———— *Das Grab des Ti (Veröffentlichungen der Ernst von Sieglin Expedition in Ägypten, vol. II).* Leipzig, 1913.

———— *Die Kunst der Ägypter.* Leipzig, 1928.

Swindler, Mary H. *Ancient Painting from the Earliest Times to the Period of Christian Art.* New Haven and London, 1929.

Times Weekly Edition, The, June 4, 1931, p. 720; March 19, 1931, p. 371.

Toch, M. "The Pigments of the Tomb of Perneb." *Journal of Industrial and Engineering Chemistry,* 1918, vol. 10, pp. 118-120.

Wallace, Florence E. *Color in Homer and in Ancient Art. Preliminary Studies (Smith College Classical Studies, no. 9).* Northampton, 1927.

Whymper, C. "Birds in Ancient Egyptian Art." *Ancient Egypt,* 1915, pp. 1-5.

Wiedemann, A. "Cobalt in Ancient Egypt." *Proceedings of the Society of Biblical Archaeology,* 1892-1893, vol. XV, pp. 113-114.

Winchell, A. N. *The Optic and Microscopic Characters of Artificial Minerals with Determinative Tables for Identifying Artificial Minerals Microscopically, Chiefly by Means of Their Optic Properties (University of Wisconsin Studies in Science, no. 4).* Madison, 1927.

Winlock, H. E. "Ancient Egyptian Kerchiefs." *Bulletin of the Metropolitan Museum of Art,* 1916, vol. XI, pp. 238-242.

———— "The Egyptian Expedition, 1918-1920. II. Excavations at Thebes, 1919-20." *ibid.,* 1920, vol. XV, December, part II, pp. 12-32.

Wolf, W. *Die Bewaffnung des altägyptischen Heeres.* Leipzig, 1926.

Wreszinski, W. *Atlas zur altaegyptischen Kulturgeschichte.* Leipzig, 1923.

———— *Bericht über die photographische Expedition von Kairo bis Wadi Halfa zwecks Abschluss der Materialsammlung für meinen Atlas zur altägyptischen Kulturgeschichte (Schriften der Königsberger Gelehrten Gesellschaft. Geisteswissenschaftliche Klasse,* Year 4, part 2). Halle a. S., 1927.

INDEXES

I. COLOR CONVENTIONS IN PER-NĒB'S DECORATION

(Incomplete because of loss of colors)

A. OBJECTS TO COLOR

Adze blade	blue, 51 n. 88, 54, 54 n. 109
Amazon stone	green, 45
Baker's instrument (?)	black, 71
Baskets	green, 42, 66
	red and yellow (?), 43-44
	white and green, 44, 48 n. 77
	yellow, 69, 69 n. 189
Birds'	
bare skin	red, 45, 45 n. 40
	yellow, 44, 45, 45 n. 47
bills and feet	blue (in some cases), 55 n. 112
plumage	
chick, open-	
mouthed	blue (in part), 54 n. 104
ducks	black, blue, and white, 44 n. 35, 54 n. 104
falcon	blue (in part), 54 n. 104
owl	white and yellow, 44 n. 35, 45 n. 46
pigeon (?)	yellow (in part), 45 n. 46
quail chick	yellow with black markings, 43, 45 n. 46, 55 n. 112, 69
	yellow with blue markings, 45 n. 46, 55 n. 112, 69
sand martin	blue (in part), 54 n. 104
vulture (the	
letter)	black, blue, and white, 44 n. 35, 54 n. 104, 60-61, 60 n. 146
Booth	yellow side supports, blue at bottom, roof yellow, 70; cf. 70 n. 201
Bread	brown, 36
	white with crusty parts yellow, 44
	yellow, 43, 45 n. 44
Brick, Mud	black, 46-47, 46 n. 58, 46 n. 59
	blue, 54 n. 106 (in part), 69
Chisel blade	black, 54 n. 108
	blue, 51 n. 88, 54 n. 108
Cloth (?), Red-dyed	red, 48
Copper tools	see Adze blade and Chisel blade
Copper vessels	blue, 48, 50-51, 52
Copper weapons	see Harpoon points
Cosmetic lines	black, 43
	green, 45
Cucumis melo	green, 45
Curtain for litter	green and yellow, 67 n. 179

Dog or jackal (Anubis)	black, 47-48
Eyebrows	black, 43
Eyelashes	black, 43
Eye paint	see Cosmetic lines
Eyes	
Corona of	white, 44
Iris of	black, 44-45
Figs	
Sycamore	red with green stems, 45 n. 49, 49
	yellow with green stems (?), 45 n. 49, 48-49
True (?)	yellow with green stems, 45 n. 49, 49, 49 n. 80
Flesh of animals	red, 45, 45 n. 39
Flint	see Sickle
Glazed vessels (?)	blue, 48, 51 n. 90, 52
Gold vessels	yellow, 45, 50, 53, 53 n. 100
Grain	green, 45, 45 n. 51, 50 n. 85, 71
	yellow, 45, 70 n. 201
Grapes	blue with green stems, 34 n. 75, 45-46, 45 n. 41, 71
Ground, Alluvial	black, 63 n. 155
	blue, 54 n. 106 (in part), 70 n. 197
Hair	
of animals	black, 44, 44 n. 36, 48 (?), 59 n. 130
	blue, 59 n. 130
	red, 45
	white, 44
	yellow, 45, 45 n. 42
of men	black, 44, 44 n. 36, 59, 59 n. 130
Harpoon points	black, 54 n. 110
	blue, 51 n. 88, 54 n. 110
Horns of animals	black, 44, 44 n. 37
	yellow, 45, 45 n. 45
Joints of meat	red, 44, 45 n. 39
Jug	green (in part), 62
Lapis lazuli	blue, 45-46
Letter *t* (bread?)	blue, 54 n. 107
Linen garments	white, 44
Leopard's skin	white and yellow spotted black, 34 n. 75, 45 n. 42
Mace	yellow all over, 47
Matting	green, 49
	green and yellow, 67 n. 179

85

INDEXES

B. COLOR TO OBJECTS

(For page references see Objects *under* A)

II. LIST OF OLD KINGDOM PRIVATE TOMBS
AND RELIEFS MENTIONED

(References given in Porter and Moss, *Memphis*, cited below as P. and M., are not repeated in this index. Attention should be drawn to the fact that the separates of Junker's "Vorläufige Berichte" for 1912 to 1914 are independently paged; those for 1925 ff. bear the same page numbers as the corresponding reports in the Vienna *Anzeiger*. In Porter and Moss, *Memphis*, the pages of the *Anzeiger* volumes are cited throughout. Professor Junker in *Giza I* uses the title "Vorbericht" and the lower page numbers of the early separates. The letter-press of this book contains a few references to the *Anzeiger* for 1913, inadvertently giving the page numbers of the separate.)

Deshi — Ṣakkāreh; burial chamber in the Egyptian Museum, Cairo, no. 1572. Dynasty VI. P. and M., p. 181 (Deshri)
Pages 49-50, 54 n. 104, 71

En-sedjer-ka — Gīzeh. Dynasty V, first half (?). P. and M., p. 25 (Nensezerka I)
Pages 65 n. 170, 69 n. 194, 69 n. 195

Ḥem-Mīn — Ṣakkāreh; stela in the Egyptian Museum, Cairo, no. 1417. Dynasty V. P. and M., p. 147 (no. 2 under Tepemʿankh II), the stela being given as 1415
Pages 69 n. 188, 69 n. 193

Ḥem-Ōny — Gīzeh; decorated walls, statues, etc., in the Pelizäus Museum, Hildesheim. Dynasty IV, early period. P. and M., p. 26 (Ḥemyunu)
Pages 67-68, 70 n. 201

Ḥeny the Black *see* Pepy-ʿonekh

Ḥesy-Rēʿ — Ṣakkāreh. Dynasty III, early period. P. and M., pp. 99-100 (Ḥesy)
Pages 6 n. 14, 17 n. 14, 29, 39, 46 n. 61, 64

Ḥetep-her-Akhty — Ṣakkāreh; decorated chamber in the Egyptian Collection, National Museum of Antiquities, Leyden. Dynasty V. P. and M., pp. 157-158 (Akhtiḥotp-ḥeri)
Pages 16, 17, 19

Ka-em-nofret — Ṣakkāreh; decorated walls in the Museum of Fine Arts, Boston, no. 04.1760. Dynasty V. Capart, *Memphis*, fig. 256; P. and M., p. 115 (Kaemnefert)
Pages 8 n. 20, 8 n. 21, 8 n. 22, 60 n. 139

Ka-em-ʿonekh — Gīzeh. Dynasty VI. P. and M., p. 29 (Kaemʿankh)
Pages 16 n. 5, 42, 48 n. 78, 60 n. 140, 65 n. 170, 68 n. 187

Ka-em-snēw — Ṣakkāreh; west wall of one chamber in the Metropolitan Museum, acc. no. 26.9.1. Dynasty VI. P. and M., p. 143 (Kaemsenu and Werzededptaḥ)
Pages v, 4 n. 4, 4 n. 5, 6 n. 13, 6 n. 15, 19 n. 17, 24 n. 16, 33 n. 71, 34 n. 74, 41, 45 n. 49, 54 n. 107, 65, 69 n. 191, 72, *and* pls. I, II

Ka-hi-ef — Gīzeh. Dynasty V, late, or VI, early period. P. and M., p. 30 (Kaḥif)
Pages 20 n. 18, 47 n. 64, 63 n. 156, 67 n. 179, 67 n. 180

Kai — Gīzeh. Dynasty V, middle period. P. and M., p. 29 (Kai)
Pages 16 n. 5, 67 n. 179, 68 n. 187

Ka-kher-Ptaḥ — Gīzeh; a fragment of the superstructure in the Egyptian Collection, Prussian State Museums, Berlin, no. 1137. Dynasty VI. Berlin, *Ausf. Verz.* (2d edition), p. 57; P. and M., p. 37 (Kakherptaḥ)
Pages 54 n. 104, 59 n. 134

Ka-ne-nesut I — Gīzeh; decorated chamber in the Art Museum, Vienna. Dynasty V, early period(?). Junker, *Giza I*, pp. 9, 36, 79; P. and M., pp. 27, 29 (Kanenesut I)
Pages 21, 21 n. 5

Ka-ne-nesut II — Gīzeh. Dynasty V, middle period. P. and M., p. 24 (4870 a)
Page 65 n. 169

Ma-nofre — Ṣakkāreh; decorated walls, etc., in the Egyptian Collection, Prussian State Museums, Berlin, no. 1108. Dynasty V. Lepsius, *Denkmäler, Text*, I, pp. 233-238; Schäfer, *Von ägypt. Kunst* (3d edition), fig. 260; P. and M., pp. 163-164 (Manūfer)
Pages 6 n. 13, 7 n. 19, 8 n. 23, 8 n. 24, 9 n. 28, 11 n. 33, 12 n. 36, 13, 16, 17, 19, 39

Mer-yeb — Gīzeh; decorated chamber in the Egyptian Collection, Prussian State Museums, Berlin, no. 1107. Dynasty V, early period(?). Berlin, *Ausf. Verz.* (2d edition), pp. 48-50; Reisner and Fisher, *Annales*,

III. LIST OF HIEROGLYPHS REFERRED TO

(Those of Per-nēb's tomb and others)

A 1   23 n. 13, 44 n. 36

A 6   59 n. 134

A 20   65 n. 166, 65 n. 170

A 40   23 n. 13

A 47   65 n. 166

D 1   23 n. 13, 44 n. 36

D 2   6 n. 15, 13 n. 38, 23 n. 13, 44 n. 36, 59 n. 130, 66

D 4   23 n. 13

D 7   45 n. 50

D 9   59 n. 131, 59 n. 132

D 21   65 n. 166

D 28   65 n. 166

D 34*   65 n. 166

D 35   65 n. 166

D 36   65 n. 166

D 39   41 n. 21, 65 n. 168, 65 n. 169, 65 n. 170

D 41   65 n. 170

D 45   45 n. 48

D 46   65 n. 166

D 58   35 n. 81, 65 n. 166

D 60   59 n. 134

E 15   23 n. 13, 47 n. 70, 48

F 1   45 n. 45

F 4   44 n. 36, 45 n. 42, 59 n. 130

F 13*   45 n. 45

F 22   44 n. 36, 45 n. 42

F 24   23

F 25   68 n. 183

F 51   45 n. 39

G 1   44 n. 35, 45 n. 40, 54 n. 104, 60 n. 146, 60-61, 64

G 5   54 n. 104

G 17   41 n. 20, 42, 43, 44 n. 35, 45 n. 46

G 26   33 n. 71, 45 n. 48

G 36   54 n. 104

G 40   44 n. 35, 54 n. 104

G 43   34 n. 74, 43, 43 n. 32, 43 n. 33, 45 n. 46, 55 n. 112, 68 n. 183, 69

G 47   45 n. 40, 54 n. 104

I 9   44 n. 35, 71 n. 208

I 10   44 n. 35, 63, 63 n. 156, 63 n. 157, 63 n. 158, 64 n. 164

L 6*   71 n. 209

M 1   45 n. 49

M 12   45 n. 49, 46 n. 55

M 17   14, 34 n. 76, 45 n. 49, 63 n. 155, 66 n. 176, 67 n. 181, 68 n. 185, 68 n. 187

M 22   70 n. 204

M 23   45 n. 49, 68 n. 185, 68 n. 187

INDEXES

Hieroglyphs not in Gardiner, *Grammar*, Sign-list, or *Catalogue of . . . Printing Type*

Abu Gurōb (Ghurāb) Sun temple, Blue pigment of, 30; Green pigment of, 26; Gypsum, carbonate of lime, both underlying pigments of, 21 n. 1

Abusīr, Green-blue interchanges at, 62

Adze, Possible use of, 16-17

Aesthetic considerations, 14, 18, 34 n. 78, 37, 41, 41 n. 20, 42, 55, 70, 71-73

Akh-en-Aten, King, Painting of daughters of, not shaded, 35 n. 80

Allium cepa, see Onions

Allium porrum, see Leeks

ᶜAmarneh, El, Crude brick at, 47 n. 62; Shrine found at, 63 n. 155; Technique of reliefs at, 16 n. 5, 20 n. 18; Wall painting from, 35 n. 80

Amazon stone, 45, 48, 64

Ambiguity in colors, 48-53, 72

Anubis animal, 47-48

Apiculture, Evidence for, 32 n. 64

Ashmolean Museum, ᶜAmarneh painting in, 35 n. 80

Autun, Egyptian blue pigment found near, 27 n. 32

Azurite, 29-30, 30 n. 50, 30 n. 51, 62 n. 153

bꜣ, 73

Background, Aesthetic importance of gray, 70; begun in broad line on east wall, 35; Grayness of, perhaps originally significant, 70, 70 n. 198; History of, 46, 46 n. 61, 46-47 n. 62; laid under color of small sign, 34 n. 74

Balance in color, Examples of, 71-72

bꜣ.t-grain, 45 n. 51, 50 n. 85, 71

Baskets in offering lists, 69 n. 189

Beard, Rare blue convention for, 59 n. 130, 60

Beeswax, 32, 32 n. 64

Beni Ḥasan, Black pigment from, 25 n. 19; Vulture-sign at, 64

Berard, Hazel de, *see* tissues of pls. XII, XIII, XIX

bḥ, 53

Binding mediums, 31-33

Black, abstract in line, 42; for blue, Question of, 61, 61 n. 149, 62

Blends, Green-blue, 63-64

Blue, Emergence of, in Egypt, 29-31, 54; for black, and its causes, 53-59, 61-62; in object of vision, 56; Induced, 61; inlay, of I Dynasty, 29; Monochrome, for inscriptions on limestone, 40 n. 16; mourning color, 57; Specific threshold of Egyptian peasants for, 57

Egyptian: Color characteristics of, 27, 27 n. 33; Composition of, 27, 27 n. 34; crystalline in form, 27, 28-29;

Earliest documented examples of, 30; IV Dynasty origin of (?), 30, 30 n. 52; Investigations of, 27-28, 28 n. 35, 28 n. 39; Pale tint of, rare, if present, on top surface, 36, 60 n. 142; paler, smoother, when finely ground, 36; present with malachite, 26 n. 24, 37; Precursors of, 29-30; principal blue pigment of antiquity, 26-27, 27 n. 29; Production of, 28-29; Revival of, proposed, 28, 28 n. 37; Stability of, 27, 28 n. 37, 62 n. 153; Synthetic production of, 28, 28 n. 36; Wide distribution of, 27, 27 n. 32

Vestorian: 26, 26 n. 28, 27, 27 n. 34, 32; *see also* Blue, Egyptian

Breasted, James H., 30

Brick, Crude: Color of, actual and as seen, 46, 56; Various color conventions for, 46-47, 46-47 n. 62, 70

British Museum, Cylinder seals of blue frit in, 31 n. 57

Brittany, Egyptian blue in, 27 n. 32

Brushes, Finest, required for outlines, 35; Nature of, 35; not used with green and blue pigments, 34, 34 n. 73; Pigments with which, were used, 35; Widths of, 35

Brushwork, 6-7, 13 n. 37, 35-36, 36-37

Bull, Ludlow, vi

Cairo, Egyptian Museum: Bowl of alabaster in, 51 n. 91; Diorite stand in, 50 n. 86; Material in, used in this book, v, 39; Ostraca in, 6 n. 14; Painting of geese in, 39 n. 13; Private shrine in, 63 n. 155; Reliefs in, 65 n. 166, *see also* Index II

Canons of Proportions, *see* Proportions, Canons of

Carbon, in black pigments, 25, 41 n. 19

Carter, Howard, 48, 48 n. 73

Cartouches, Color conventions for, 69

Cerastes cornutus, 71 n. 208

Chapman, Frank M., 61 n. 147

Charcoal, Powdered: as black pigment, 25, 41 n. 19; mixed with gypsum as gray pigment, 25 n. 19

Checks (in first sketches), as substitutes for horizontals, 11-12; for lateral measurements, 9, 9 n. 28; for position of feet, 12, 12 n. 36

Chisel, Actual, possibly for a sculptor's use, 16 n. 2; Background lowered by use of, 16; Mallet-driven (?), for cutting outlines, 15, 15 n. 2; Pointed, for dressing building blocks, 4

Chrysocolla, Powdered, as green pigment, 26, 26 n. 24, 26 n. 25

Cobalt, absent from Per-nēb's blue pigment, 27 n. 29, 27 n. 34; pigment, unknown in antiquity, 27 n. 29

INDEXES

INDEXES

Glazed vessels, 51, 51 n. 90, 52, 72

Glazes, Early Egyptian, 51 n. 90, 64 n. 159; Egyptian, laid on silicious base, 28; Ingredients of early Egyptian, 28; Powdered, make poor pigments, 28

Glazing pottery, Art of, not developed by Egyptians, 28

Glue, 31

Grain, a demi-god, *see* Napri

Greek art, Blue convention for hair in, 54, 56

Green, 25-26, 37; in predynastic times, 25, 25 n. 20; Monochrome, for inscriptions on granite, 40 n. 16; Question of yellow foundation for, 67-69

and blue, costliest of the pigments, 34, *cf.* 37; put on walls last, 33-34; Spatula, not brush, used with, 34; Special technique for, 33, 34

Guiding lines, 6, 13; dispensed with, 14; in antechamber, 9, 12-13; in main chamber, 7-11; in other Old Kingdom tombs, *see* Sketch, First: Examples of; in passage, 9, 11-12

Horizontal: defining registers, 7; Number of, within registers in V Dynasty, 7-8, 12, in VI Dynasty, 8-9, 9 n. 26; Positions of, in V Dynasty, exceptional, at top of head, 8, 8 n. 24, usual, at level of (1) knees, 7, (2) base of hips, 7, (3) lowest ribs, 8, 8 n. 20, (4) armpits, 8, 8 n. 20, (5) base of neck, 8, 8 n. 21, (6) top of forehead, 7; Positions of, in VI Dynasty, same as in V Dynasty with addition of (7) a line between knees and ground, 8-9, 9 n. 26; Positions of, in XVIII Dynasty, at top of head regular, others, few in number, irregular, 8 n. 25; replaced sometimes by dots or checks, 9 n. 28, 11-12

Perpendicular: 12-13; for human figures, 8, 8 n. 22, 9, 11-13; for jars and stands, 8, 8 n. 23; Relation of, to sketch and sculpture, 9; Vertical alignment of, rare, 10, 10 n. 29

Pigment used for, always red, 6 n. 13; ruled in Old Kingdom, 7; snapped on wall with cord in XVIII Dynasty, 7; Utility of, 10-11

Guiding squares, 9, 10, 10 n. 31

Gum arabic, 31

Gums, 31

Gunn, Battiscombe, v, 72

Gypsum, 21 n. 1, 25 n. 19; as white pigment, 25; calcined, High grade of, 20; Crude, 4-5; *cf.* Plaster of Paris

Haematite, 5 n. 11

Hair, Blue: an alternative for black hair, 54; Black convention preferred to, 59; in painting, due to blue tinge in actual hair (?), 56; in poetry and statues, 73; Lapis lazuli for, 73; Possible physiological basis for convention of, 56-59; Symbolic meaning suggested for, 55-56

Halfa grass, Egyptian, 49

Hall, Lindsley F., vi, 9, *and* tissues of pls. x, xvi, xx

Hangings for walls, Yellow-green designs for, 67 n. 179

Harkness, Edward S., v

Hering on color of diffuse sunlight, 61 n. 148

Ḥetep-ḥer-es II, Queen, Color of hair of, 42 n. 29

Hierakonpolis, Predynastic paintings at, 25, 46 n. 61

Homeric Greeks, Vision of, 58

Hue, 57, 57 n. 123

Imaginary things, Whether tomb paintings include, 73

Indigo, not identified in ancient paintings, 27 n. 29

Inner details, 34, 34 n. 75; few in number in Per-nēb's decoration, 34

Inscriptions, Monochrome, abstract in color, 40 n. 16

Isesy, King, 9 n. 26

Juncus maritimus, 49 n. 83

Junker, Hermann, v, 68 n. 187

Keimer, Ludwig, 38 n. 3, 48, 49, 49 n. 80, 49 n. 83, 50, 52 n. 97, 52 n. 98

Khufu, King, 21, 30, 67

Koldewey, 56

Lactuca sativa, *see* Lettuce

Lampblack, *see* Soot

Lansing, Ambrose, vi, 55 n. 113

Lapis lazuli, 46, 64, 73

Lateral measurements, Dots or checks for, 9; rare, 9 n. 28

Leeks, 50

Leptochloa bipinnata, 49 n. 82

Lettuce, 45 n. 49, 71

Lime ground, or wash, Question of, 19 n. 17, 20-21 n. 1, 31 n. 59

Limestone, Pore filler needed for, 22; Powdered, mixed with gypsum in fine plaster, 19, 19 n. 17; Softness of, 15 n. 2, 18

Line, black and red, Abstract use of, 42-44

Line drawing, 34-35

Lotus roots or onions, 46 n. 56

Lythgoe, Albert M., v, 16 n. 6

Mace, Coloring of, 47; Funerary, 47 n. 69; Gilt, carried by statues of Tut-ʿankh-Amūn, 47 n. 69

Magic, a demi-god, with yellow complexion, 66

Malachite, 30 n. 50, 69; Powdered, used as eye paint, 25 n. 20, used as pigment, 25-26, 37, 61 n. 149

Mallet, Sculptor's, 15, 15-16 n. 2

Maṣṭabeh tombs in Metropolitan Museum, *see* Index II; Projected volume on, v

McKenzie, R. Tait, 11 n. 32

Medīnet Habu, 63 n. 155

Meidūm, Backgrounds at, 46, 46 n. 61; Black convention for mud brick and mud seals at, 46; Blues at, do not in early IV Dynasty include Egyptian blue, 29, 29 n. 48; Color conventions at, for baskets, rope, and fibers, 66-68, for human skin, 65, 65 n. 166, 65 n. 171; Ducks in a painting at, 54; Green-blue interchanges at, 62; Hieroglyph for seat at, 72; Malachite as green pigment at, 25-26; *nmś.t*-vessel pictured at, 53 n. 99; Painting of geese from, 39 n. 13; Painting on bare stone at, 21; Pigment used on mummy from, 30, 30 n. 50; Resin as binding material at, 32; Tombs at, *see* Index II; Yellow for rope and red for men's skin in same sign at, 67 n. 177

Meir, Photographs of scenes at, 9 n. 26; Plaster reliefs at, 20 n. 18; Tomb at, *see* Index II

Meket-Rēʿ, Figure of, 66 n. 172

Memory pictures, 47, 56, 60, 63 n. 154

Menena, Scene of measuring grain in tomb of, 42 n. 29

Mer-es-ʿonekh III, Queen, 3 n. 1; Second sketch recognized in tomb of, 22 n. 11

INDEXES

"Raehlmannfirniss," 32-33

Ramesside times, Plaster reliefs in, 20 n. 18

Randall-MacIver, 57

Red, abstract in line, dots, and dabs, 42, 42 n. 29, 49 n. 81, 50 n. 84; Availability of, 40; easily prepared, 40

Reisner, G. A., v

Rekh-mi-Rēꜥ, Dressing of building stones represented in tomb of, 4 n. 3

Reliefs, of plaster, 20 n. 18; see also Modeling of reliefs

Repainting, Examples of, 33 n. 71, 54 n. 107, 55 n. 112, 68

Resins, 32, 32 n. 64

Rhythm in color, 71-72

Rivers, W. H. R., 57, 58, 58 n. 129

Roman period, Calcining of limestone first practised in Egypt in (view of Lucas), 31 n. 59; Raehlmann's studies of Egyptian, or Vestorian, blue in, 32, 32 n. 68

Rome, Egyptian blue found at, 27, 27 n. 30, 27 n. 32

Ropes, Color conventions for, 42 n. 29, 66-67, 67 n. 178, 68-69

Ruled lines, 7, 35-36

Rushes, Green to blue, 52 n. 97; Green-dyed (?), 67; Yellow for dry, 67

Saḥu-Rēꜥ, King, Reliefs in funerary temple of, 51, 62 n. 152, 66

Ṣaḳḳāreh, Carved plaster at, 16 n. 5; Evidence gathered at, used in this book, v, 33, 39; Ewers and basins from, 51 n. 89; Mortar and mason's plaster at, 5 n. 7; Plaster reliefs at, 20 n. 18; Reliefs from, see Index II; Tombs at, see Index II

Sandstone, Polisher of, see Polishing stone

Saturation, 57, 57 n. 122

Scharff, Alexander, 32 n. 68

Sculpturing the walls, Processes of: (1) cutting outlines, 15-16; (2) lowering background, 16-17; (3) modeling figures, 17-18; (4) finishing surfaces, 18; (5) repairing defects, 19-20; Sequence of, 18-19

Sea, conceived as green, 63 n. 154

Seals (the instrument), Cylinder, of Egyptian blue frit, 31, 31 n. 57

Seals (the sealings), Mud, 38 n. 3, 46, 46 n. 61, 52 n. 93, 56

Secondary colors (as regards meaning), 47-48, 64 n. 165

Sesostris I, King, Relief from temple of, 51 n. 91

Shading, almost unknown in Egypt, 35, 35 n. 80

Shepard, John F., 61-62

Silhouettes, 34, 41, 41 n. 22; Black, in first sketches, 6 n. 15

Silicate, Double, of copper and calcium, 27, 27 n. 34

Silicate of copper, see Chrysocolla

Silver, Color convention for, 48 n. 77, 51, 53

Sixth Dynasty, Guiding lines in, 8 n. 22, 8-9; Outlines in wall decorations of, 41; Pigments laid over or in plaster in, 22; Plaster reliefs numerous in, 20 n. 18; Poor grades of stone frequent in tombs of, 20 n. 18, 21

Size, 31

Sketch, First: 5-15; Degree of dependence on, 9, 13; Disappearance of last traces of, 17

Examples of, in tombs of: Ḥesy-Rēꜥ, 6 n. 14; Ka-em-nofret, 8 n. 20, 8 n. 21, 8 n. 22; Ka-em-snēw, 6 n. 13, 6 n. 15; Ma-nofre, 7 n. 19, 9 n. 28, 11 n. 33, 12 n. 36;

Minor Cemetery, Gīzeh, 8 n. 24; Ne-kau-Ḥor, 5 n. 12, 14; Nekhbu, 9 n. 26; Pepy II's queen, 6 n. 15; Pepy-ꜥonekh, 9 n. 26; Ptaḥ-ḥotpe, 8 n. 22, 10 n. 29; Raꜥ-em-ka, 5 n. 12, 15; Sen-nu-ka, 5 n. 12, 16

Inner details commoner in black than in red, 13 n. 38; laid on bare walls, 4

Lines of: brushwork, 6-7; classified, 6; ruled in part, 7; Width of, 6, 14

Pigments used for, in Old Kingdom: black, 5, 5 n. 12, 6 n. 15, 14, 15, 15 n. 1; black silhouette, 6 n. 15; red, 5; red, corrected in black, 5-6, 6 n. 13; red line, followed by black silhouette, 6 n. 15; yellow, corrected in red, 6, 6 n. 14; cf. Guiding lines, Pigment used for

Preparation of walls for, 4; where preserved in Per-nēb's tomb, 3-4

Sketch, Painter's, see Sketch, Second

Sketch, Second: 22-25; Additions in, 24; Color of, 22; Corrections in, 24, 24 n. 17; Discrepancies between, and reliefs, 24-25; Examples of, 22-23; Existence of, hitherto almost unnoted, 22, 22 n. 11; mistaken easily for top color, 39; Red wash belonging to, 23-24; Utility of, 22; Width of line of, 22

Skin, Color conventions for human, 65-66

Smalt, 27 n. 29

Soot, as black pigment, 25, 25 n. 19, 41 n. 19

Sopdu, a god, with yellow complexion, 66

Soule, B. A., 20 n. 1, 25 n. 19, 26, 26 n. 24, 26 n. 25, 28 n. 36, 35 n. 81, 37, 37 n. 88

Spatula, used for blue and green pigments, 34

Stains, Possible, from sinking in of pigments, 24 n. 15, 36

Step Pyramid, 29; Reliefs found at, 21; Tiles of, 51 n. 90

Superposing of colors in masses, Questions of, 36, 37 n. 92

Syria, Egyptian blue found in, 27 n. 32

Tears, Color convention for, 59, 60

Technique, 3-37; studied but little, 3; Three main processes of, 3

tempera, a, technical method of ancient Egyptian painting, 31, 31 n. 59, 33 n. 72

Theban tombs, Technique of, 3 n. 1, 5 n. 8, 22 n. 9

Theban wall paintings, Facsimiles of, in Metropolitan Museum, 32 n. 64

Third Dynasty, Blue color sparingly preserved from early part of, 29; Cartouches black(?) in, 69; Reliefs of, 21; Sculptor's chisel (?) from, 16 n. 2

Threshold, General, 57 n. 124; Specific, for blue, 57, 61-62

Todas, Vision and color vocabulary of, 57-58

Toledo Museum of Art, Boat model in, 66 n. 172

Toledo Zoölogical Garden, Lion in, 60 n. 145

Tools, see Adze, Brushes, Chisel, Mallet, Sculptor's, Polishing stone, and Spatula

Turquoise, 45, 45 n. 53, 64

Tut-ꜥankh-Amūn, King, Mace held by statues of, 47 n. 69

Twelfth Dynasty, Flowering-reed-sign blue and green in, 63 n. 155; Guiding squares of, 10 n. 31; Pigments of (bibliography), 25 n. 19; Plaster reliefs in, 20 n. 18; Second sketch absent from certain sculptures of, 22 n. 11; Vase of water lilies in a decoration of, 51 n. 91; Yellow convention for men's skin in, 66 n. 172

INDEXES

PLATES

PLATE II

Details of plaster, first sketches, and unfinished carving. Tomb of Ka-em-snēw. Metropolitan Museum. Scale 2:3. See pp. 40, 88.

a. From fourth vertical line to left of main false door. See pp. 4 n. 4, 4 n. 5, 6 n. 13.

b. From same line as "a," lower down. See p. 6 n. 13.

c. From smaller false door, left inner jamb, line 2. See p. 19 n. 17.

d. From smaller false door, lower flat lintel. See pp. 4 n. 4, 4 n. 5, 19 n. 17.

e. From third vertical line to left of main door. See pp. 4 n. 4, 4 n. 5, 6 n. 13, 6 n. 15.

f. From the smaller door, left outer jamb. See pp. 6 n. 15, 13 n. 38.

PLATE II

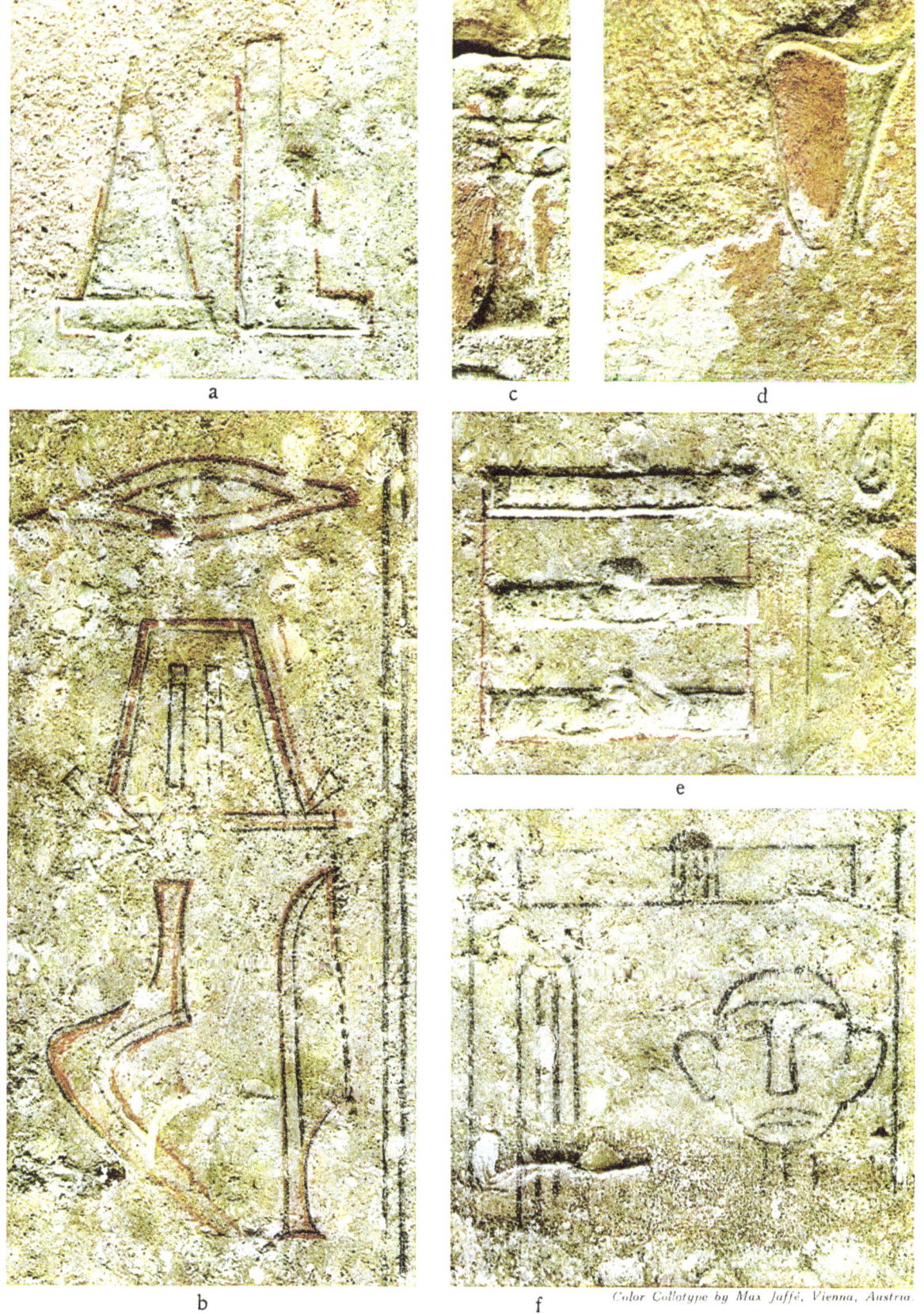

a

c   d

b   e

f

Color Collotype by Max Jaffé, Vienna, Austria.

PLATE III

First sketch, preliminary to sculpture, hastily
finished with washes. Tomb of Ne-kau-Ḥor.
Metropolitan Museum. Scale 1:6. See pp.
5 n. 12, 14, 15, 89.

PLATE III

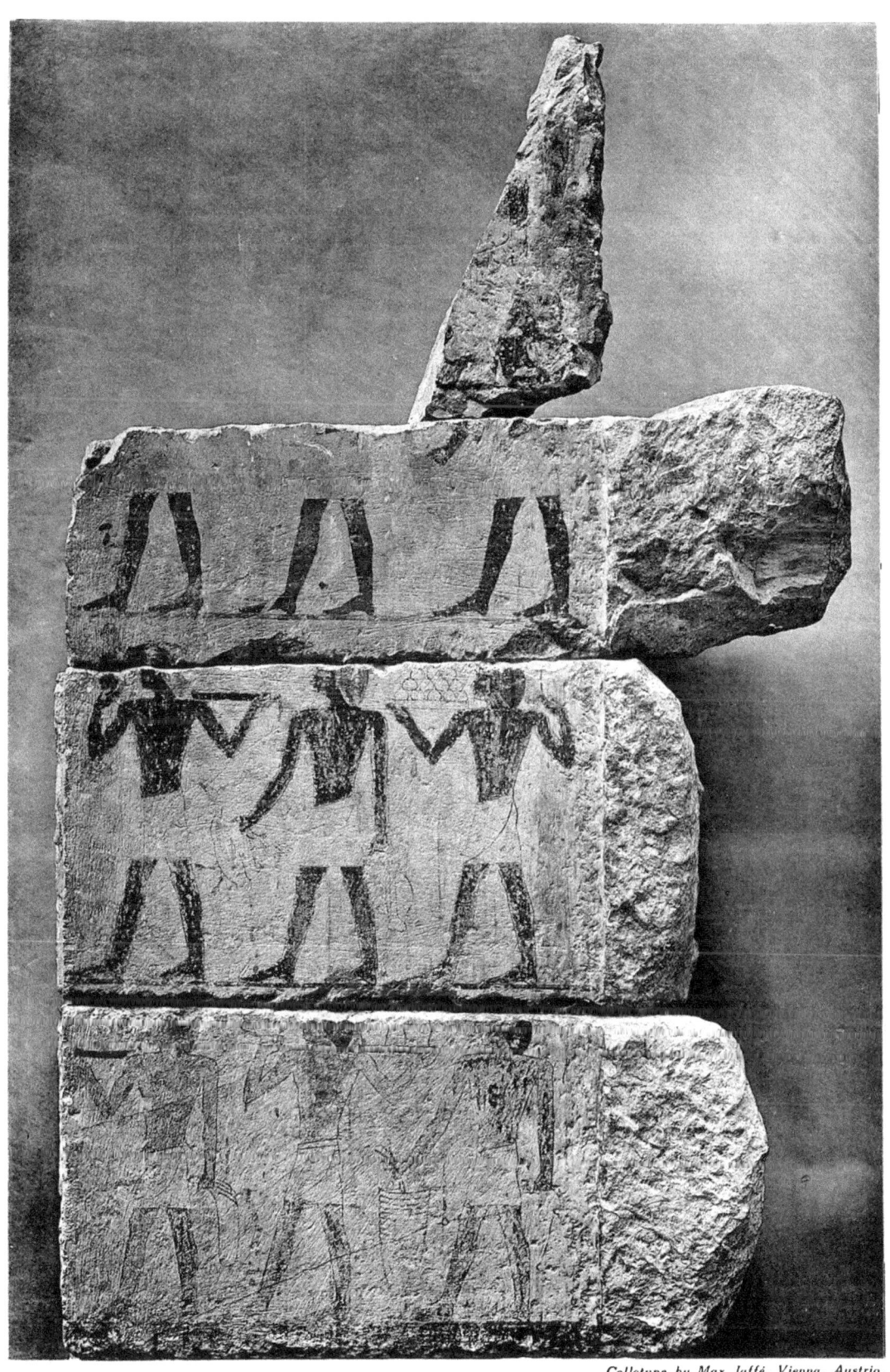

Collotype by Max Jaffé, Vienna, Austria.

PLATE IV

Beginning of sculptor's work following lines of first sketch now nearly
obliterated. Tomb of Raᶜ-em-ka. Metropolitan Museum. Scale 1:4.
See pp. 5 n. 12, 15-16, 15 n. 1, 18, 19, 89.

PLATE IV

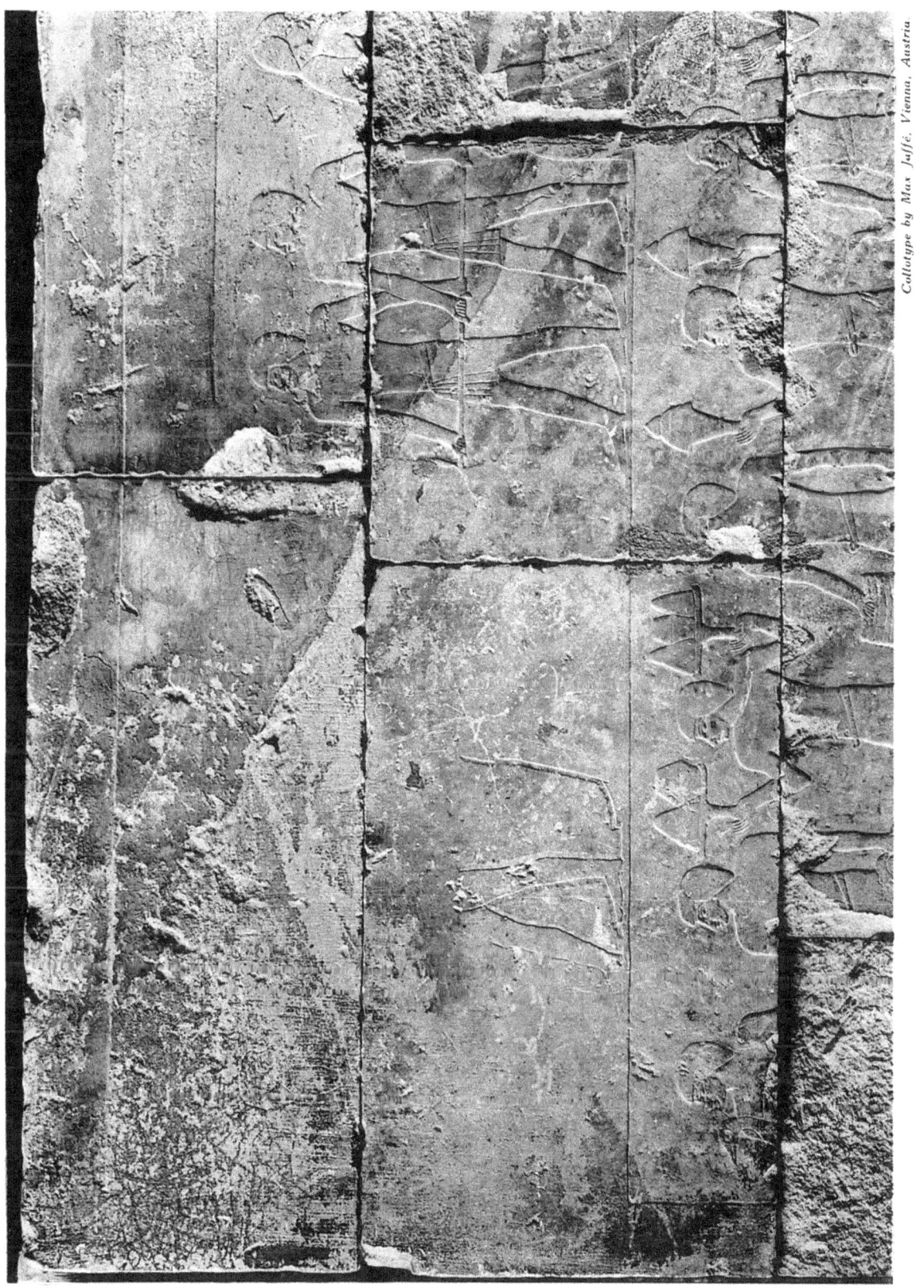

Collotype by Max Jaffé, Vienna, Austria.

PLATE V

Unfinished sculptured figure with remains of
first sketch. Tomb of Sen-nu-ka. Museum of
Fine Arts, Boston. Not to a determined scale.
See pp. 5 n. 12, 16-17, 16 n. 6, 18, 89.

PLATE V

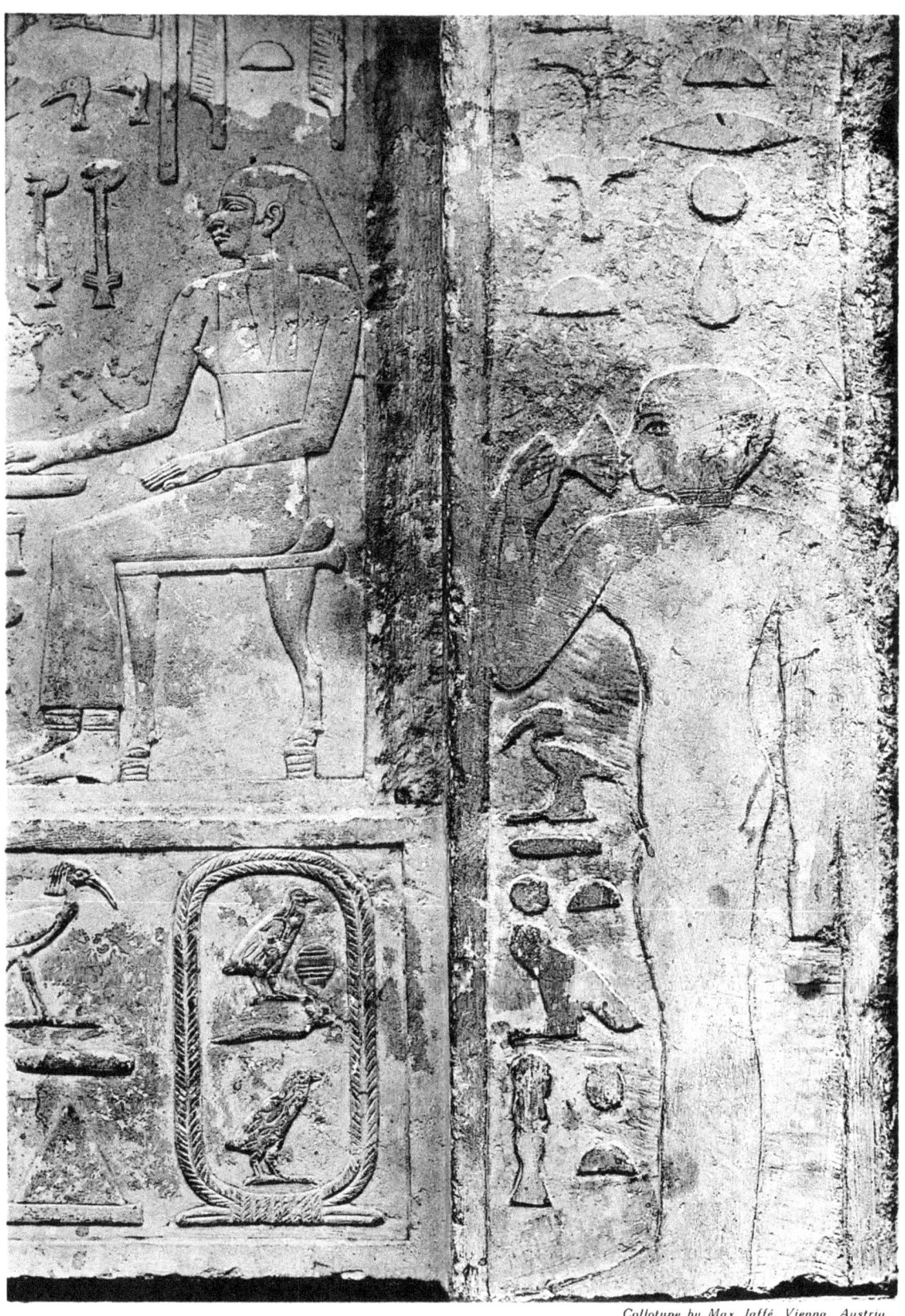

PLATE VI

Perpendicular guiding lines and first sketch
with later addition of washes. Tomb of Per-
nēb, outer chamber, west wall. Metropolitan
Museum. Scale 1 : 11. See pp. 3, 4, 9, 12-13,
13 n. 38, 14, 15, 17, 24, 37.

PLATE VI

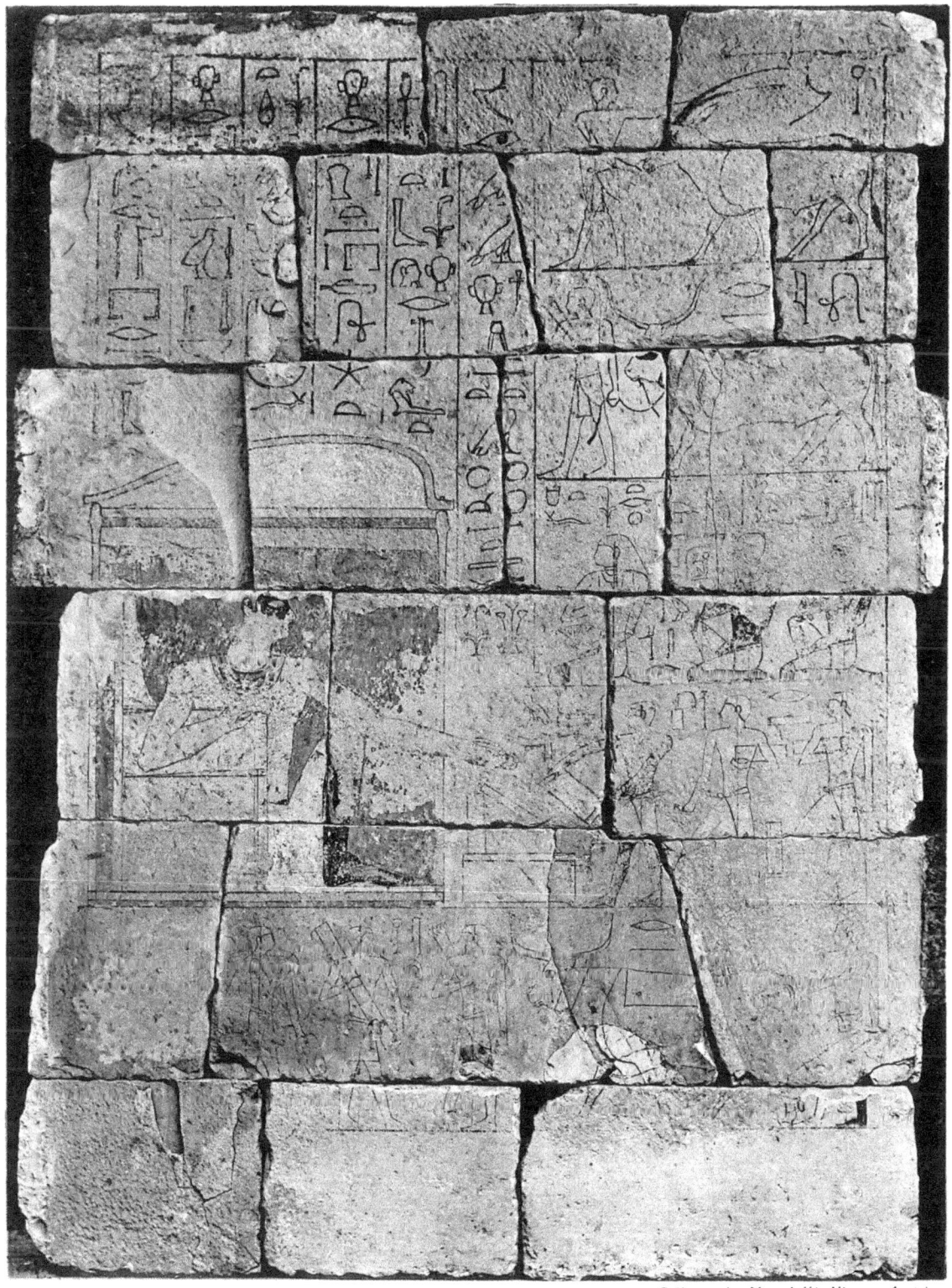

PLATE VII

Perpendicular guiding lines, guiding checks, and first sketch, with later washes. Tomb of Per-nēb, east wall of the passage. Scale 1:7. See pp. 4, 9, 11-12, 37.

PLATE VII

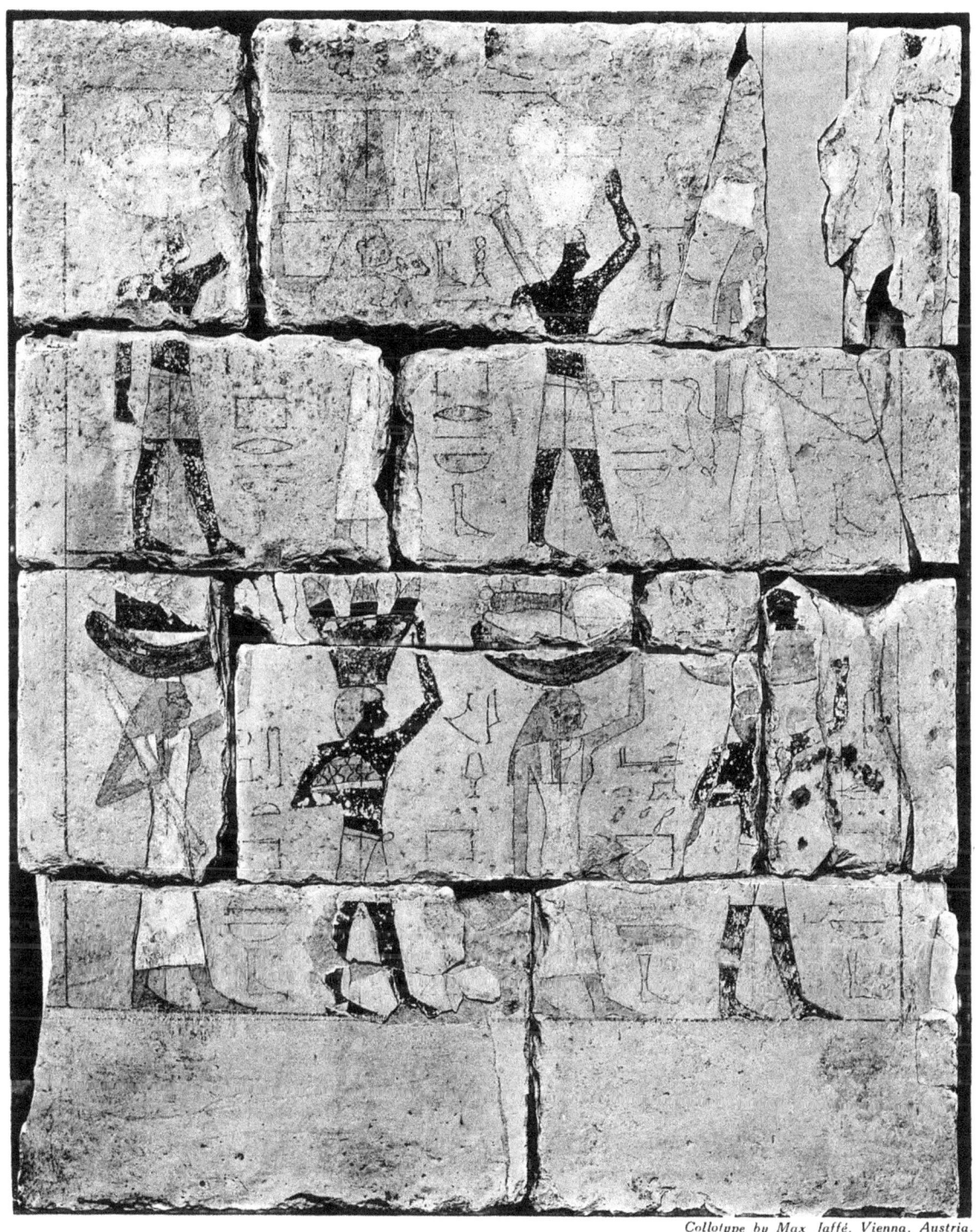

PLATE VIII

Perpendicular guiding lines, guiding checks, and first sketch, with later washes. Tomb of Per-nĕb, west wall of the passage. Scale 1:7. See pp. 4, 9, 12, 37.

PLATE VIII

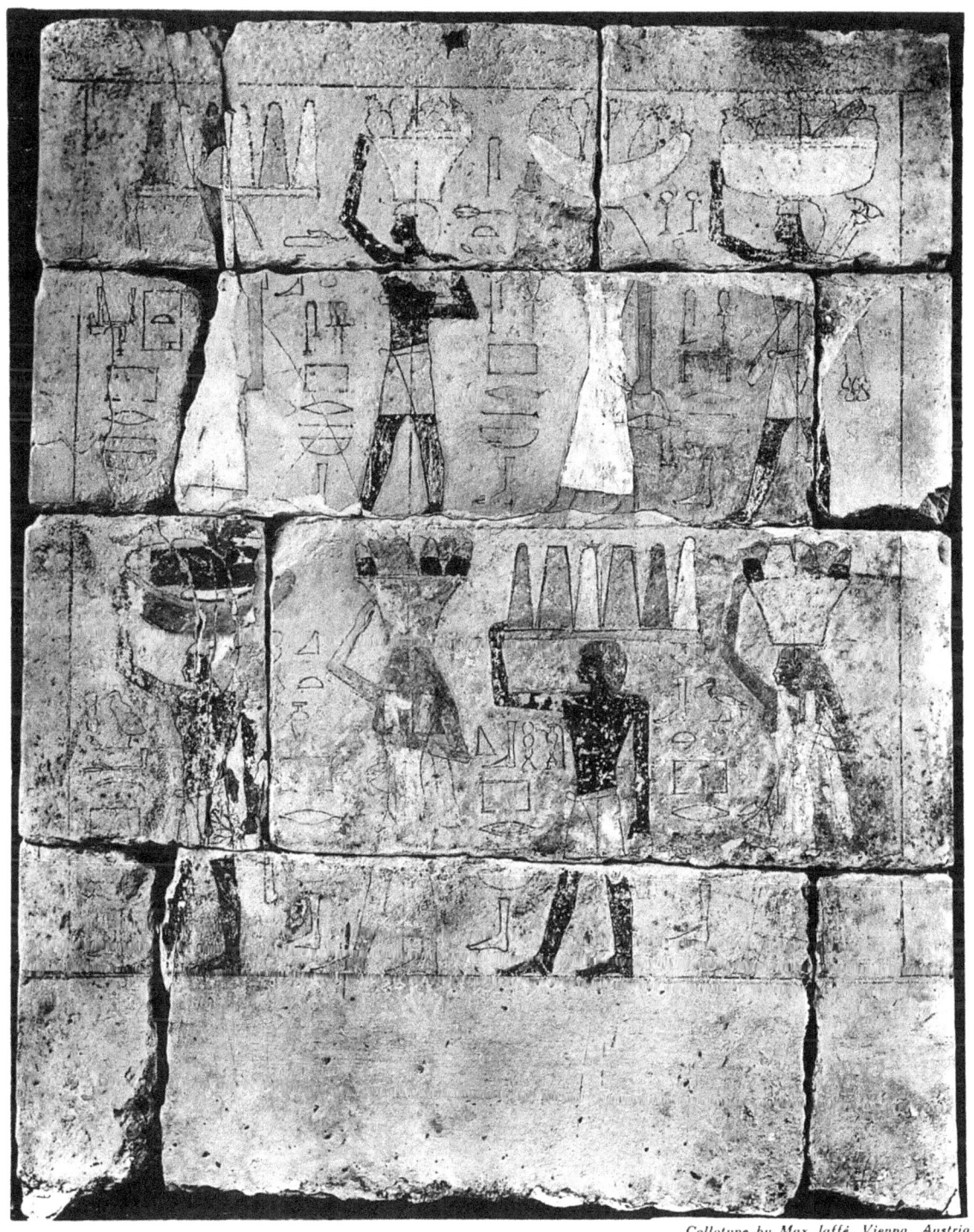

PLATE IX

Remains of horizontal guiding lines for first sketch where background was not lowered. Tomb of Per-nēb, main chamber, north wall, parts of registers 4, 5, and 6 from top. Compare pl. x. Scale 1 : 5. See pp. 4, 7, 7 n. 18, 10 n. 30, 17, 18, 51 n. 92.

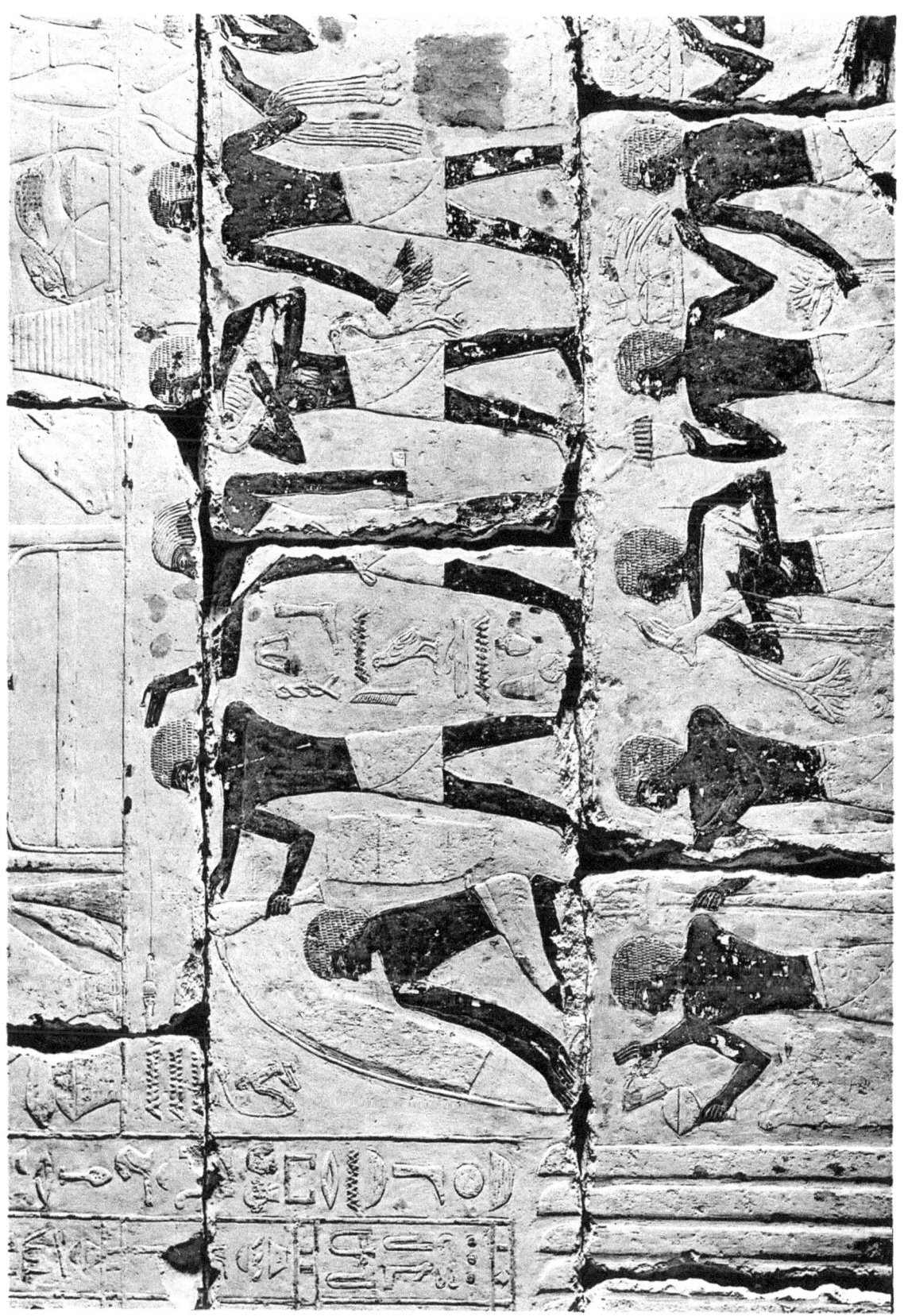

PLATE IX

Collotype by Max Jaffé, Vienna, Austria.

PLATE X

Restoration of guiding lines (in red) shown in relation to extant sculpture. Tomb of Pernēb, main chamber, north wall, parts of registers 3, 4, 5, 6, and 7 from top. Compare pl. ix. Drawn by Lindsley F. Hall. To no determined scale. See pp. 9-10, 12, 13.

PLATE X

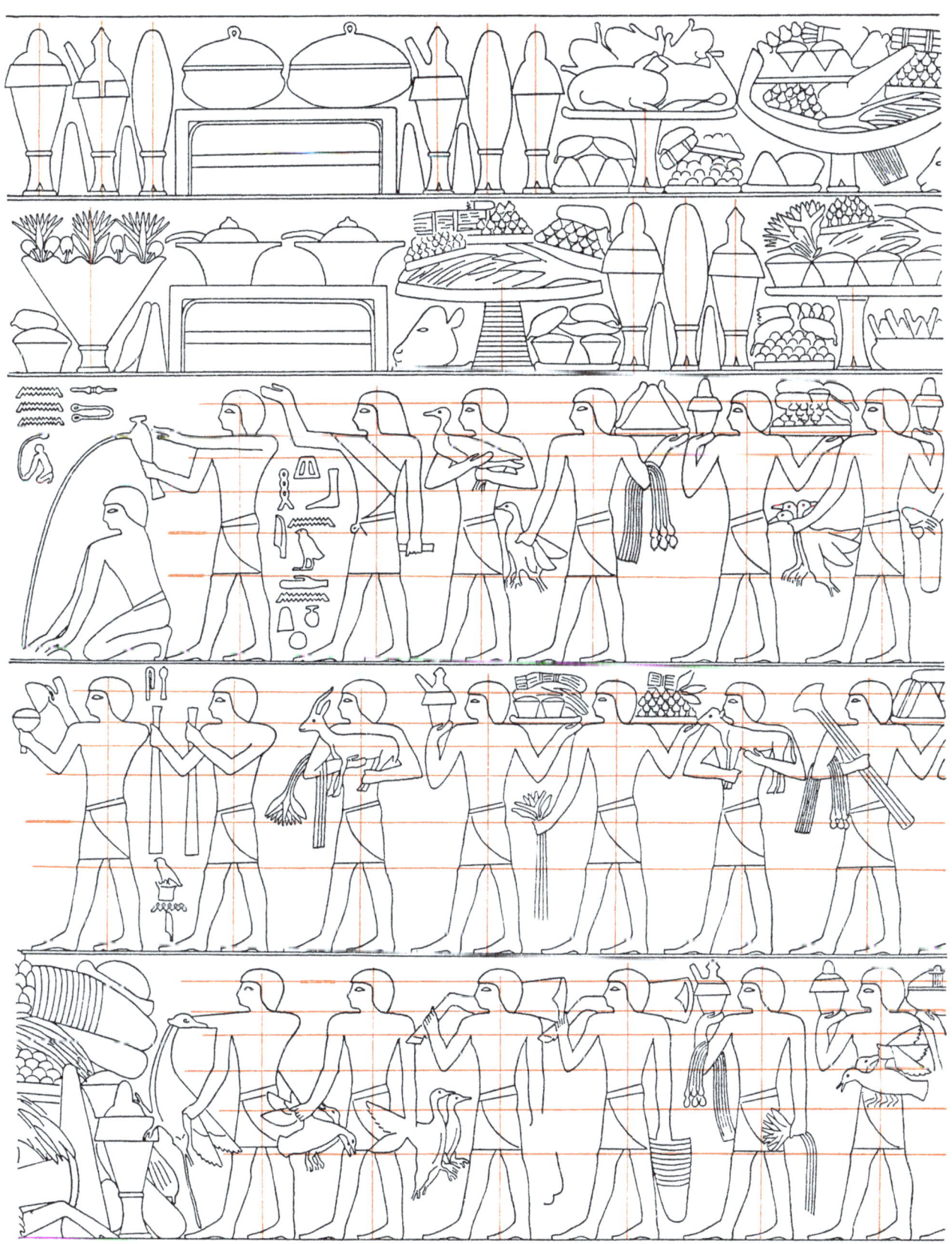

PLATE XI

Section of decoration, present condition. Tomb of Per-nēb, main chamber, north wall, parts of registers 1, 2, 3, and 4 from top. Compare pls. XII, XIII. Scale 1 : 5. See pp. 7 n. 18, 10 n. 30, 24, 44, 47, 50 n. 84, 52-53, 60 n. 146.

PLATE XI

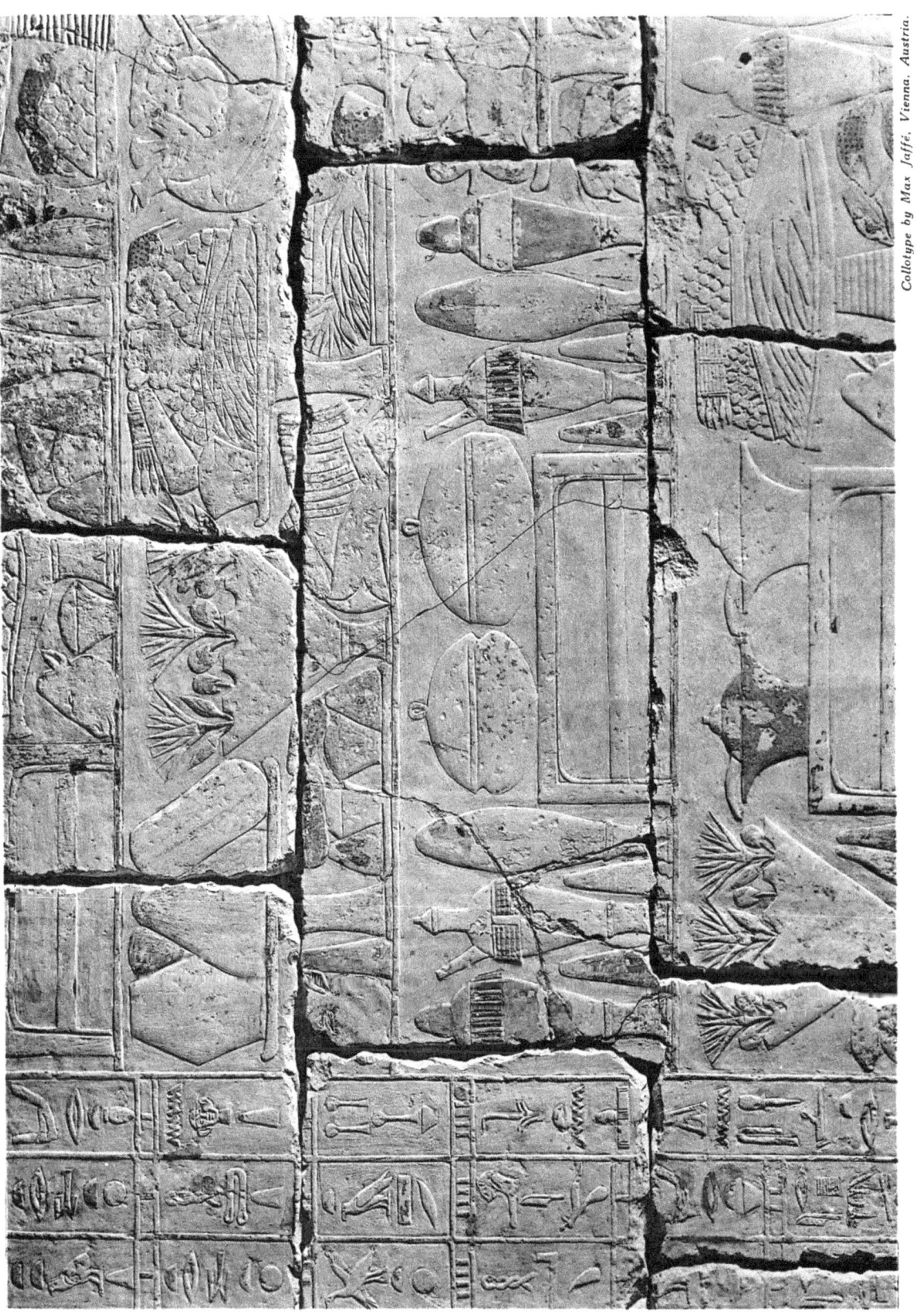

PLATE XII

Section of decoration with extant colors. Tomb of Per-nēb, main chamber, north wall, parts of registers 1, 2, 3, and 4 from top. Compare pls. XI, XIII. Copied by Hazel de Berard. Scale 1 : 5. See pp. 10 n. 30, 24, 34 n. 75, 36, 40, 44, 47, 50-53.

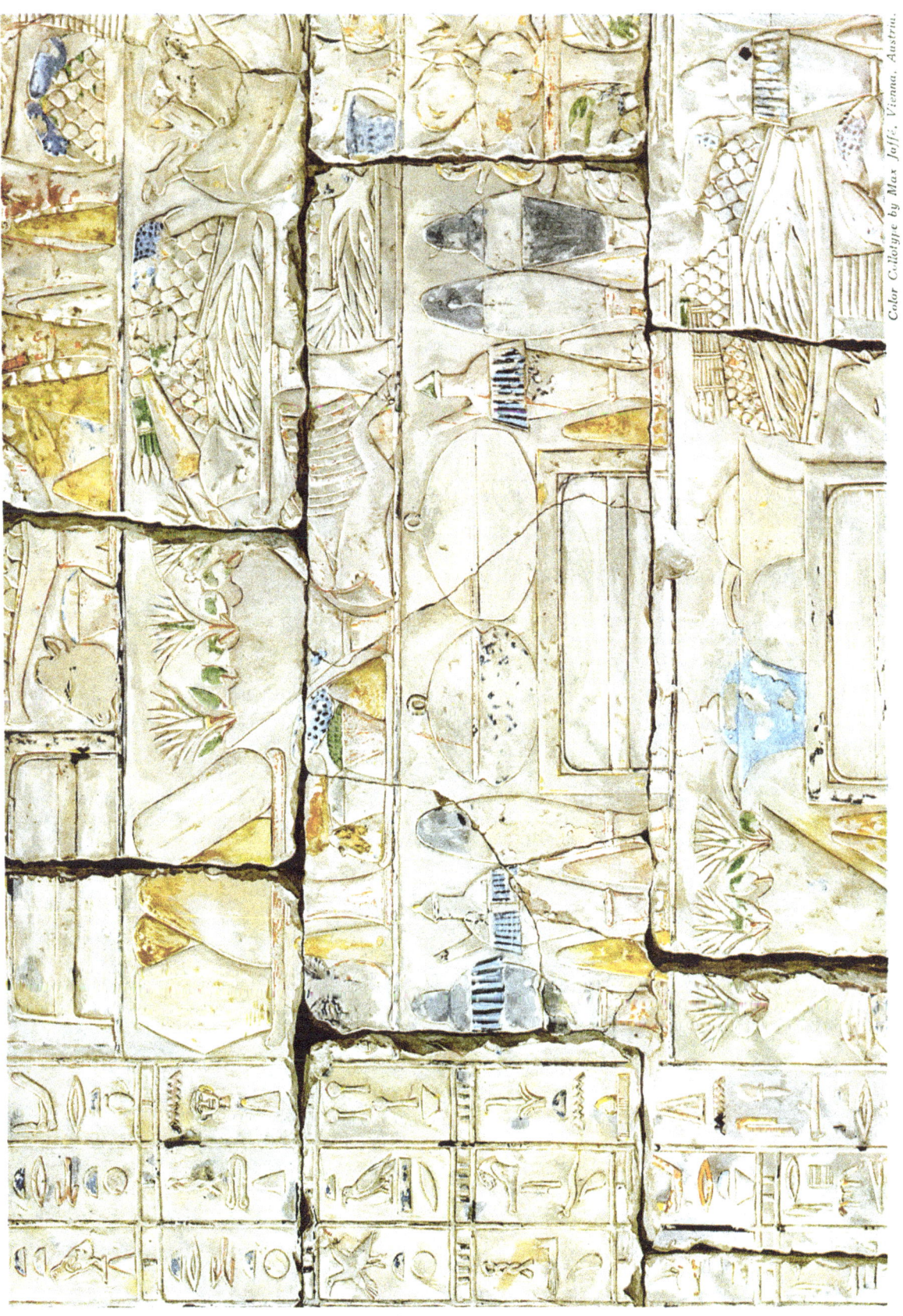

PLATE XII

Color Collotype by Max Jaffé, Vienna, Austria.

PLATE XIII

Section of decoration with colors restored. Tomb of Per-nēb, main chamber, north wall, parts of registers 1, 2, 3, and 4 from top. Compare pls. XI, XII. Painted by Hazel de Berard. Scale 1 : 5. See pp. 10 n. 30, 24, 27 n. 33, 34 n. 75, 34 n. 76, 36, 38 n. 3, 40, 40 n. 15, 41, 42, 43, 44, 45 n. 39, 47, 48-53, 50 n. 84, 52 n. 93, 54 n. 108, 59 n. 130, 60, 60 n. 146, 66, 69 n. 189, 70, 71, 71 n. 207.

PLATE XIII

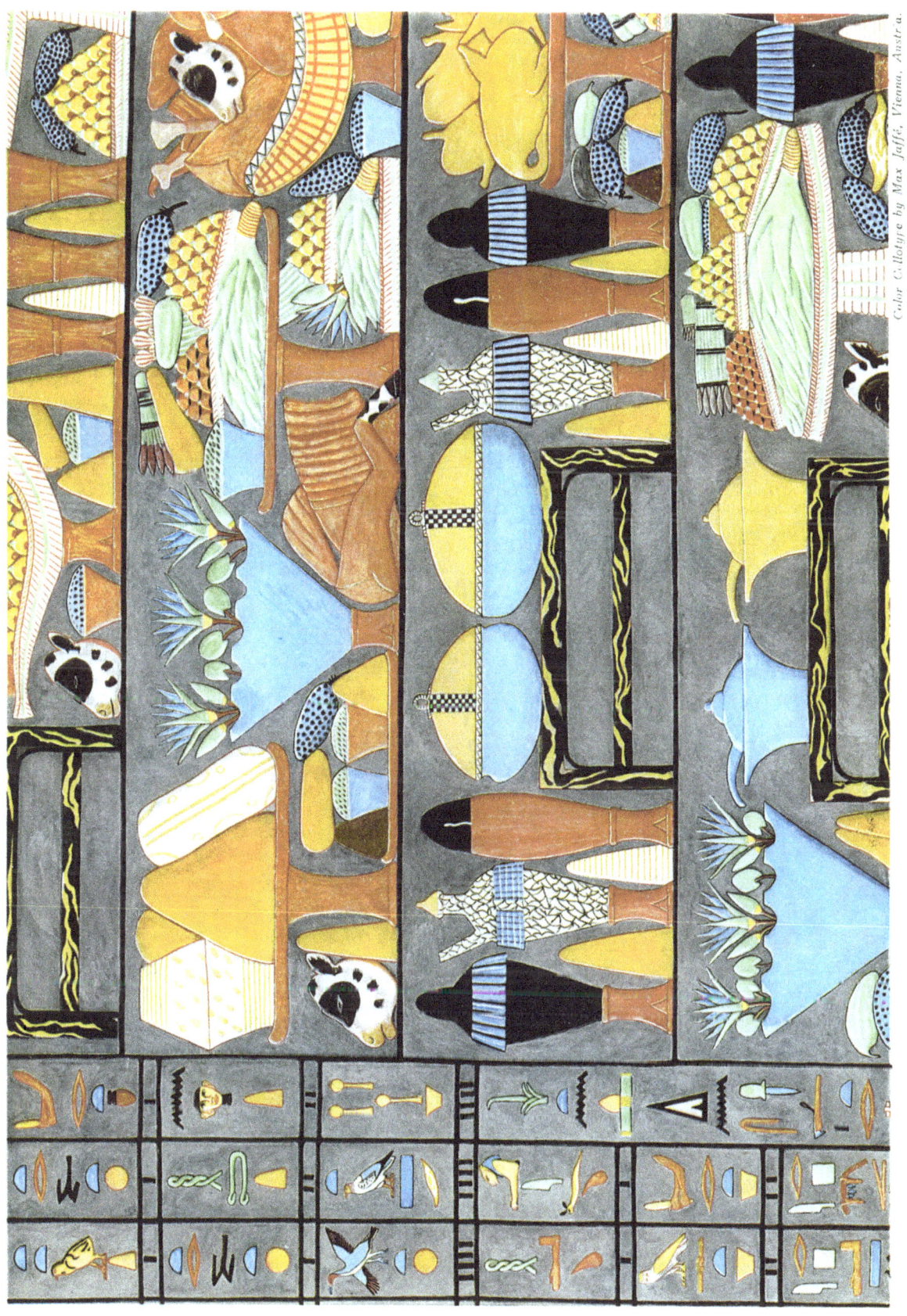

Color Collotype by Max Jaffé, Vienna, Austria.

PLATE XIV

Detail for study of finish of sculptured surface
and lines of second, or painter's, sketch.
Tomb of Per-nēb, main chamber, south wall,
in register 4 from top. Scale 5:6. See pp. 18,
23, 51 n. 91.

PLATE XIV

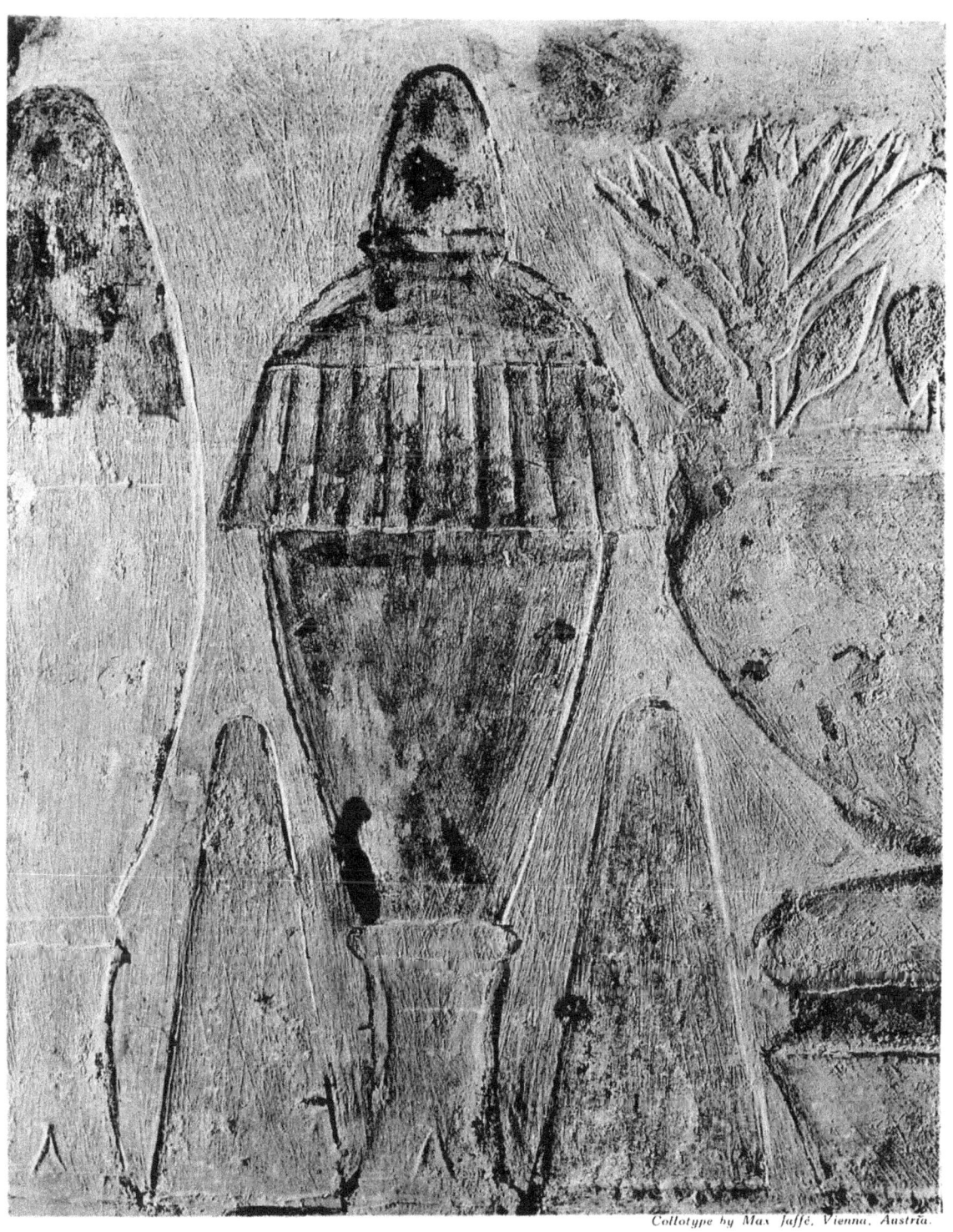

PLATE XV

Detail showing lines of second, or painter's, sketch, and painted final outlines. Tomb of Per-nēb, main chamber, south wall, register 6 from top, offering bearers 3, 4, and 5. Compare pl. xvi. Scale 2 : 5. See p. 23.

PLATE XV

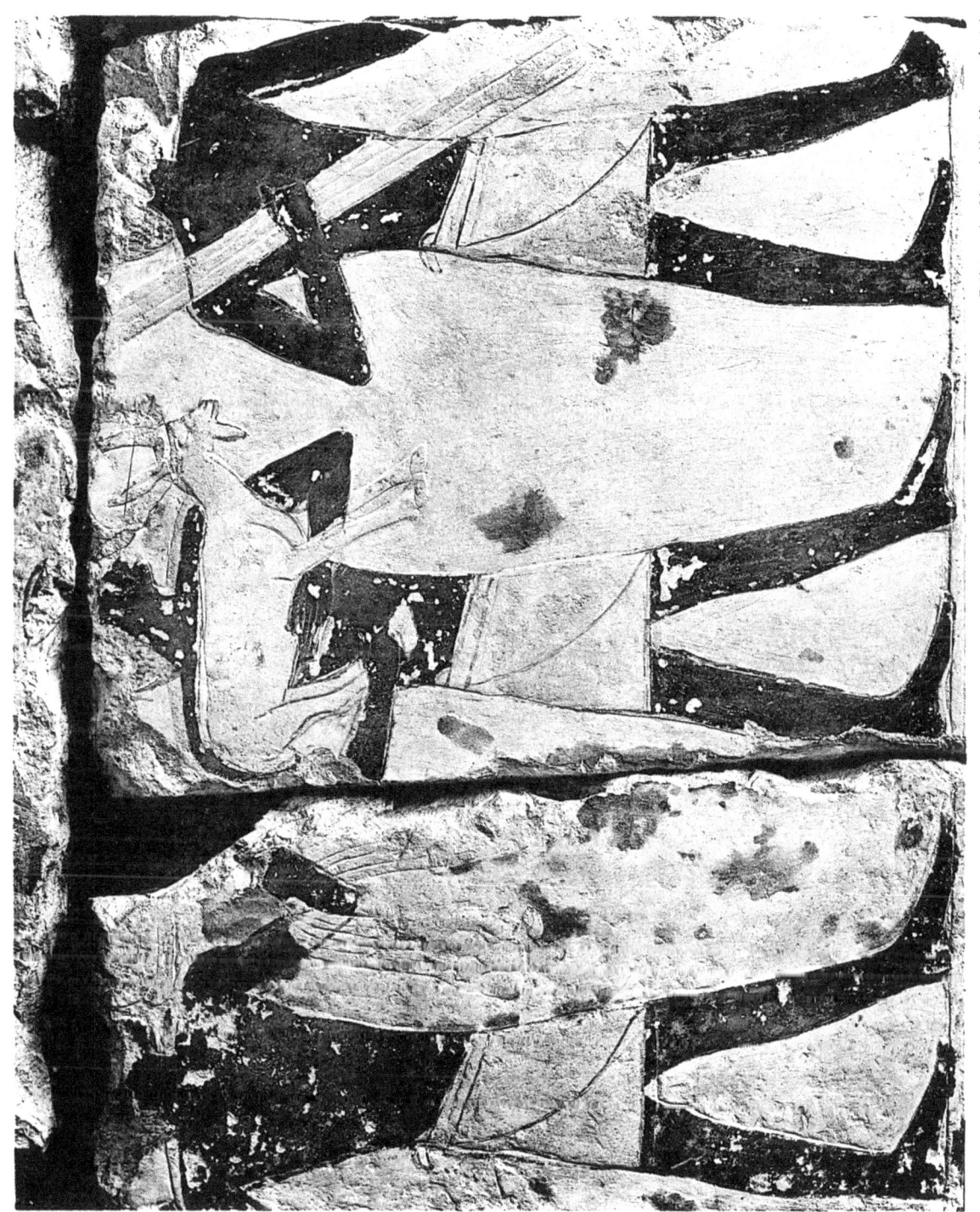

PLATE XVI

Drawing to show relation of second sketch to relief; the former in broken lines, the latter in solid lines. Tomb of Per-nēb, main chamber, south wall, register 6 from top, offering bearers 3, 4, and 5. Compare pl. xv. Drawn by Lindsley F. Hall. Scale 2:5. See p. 23.

PLATE XVI

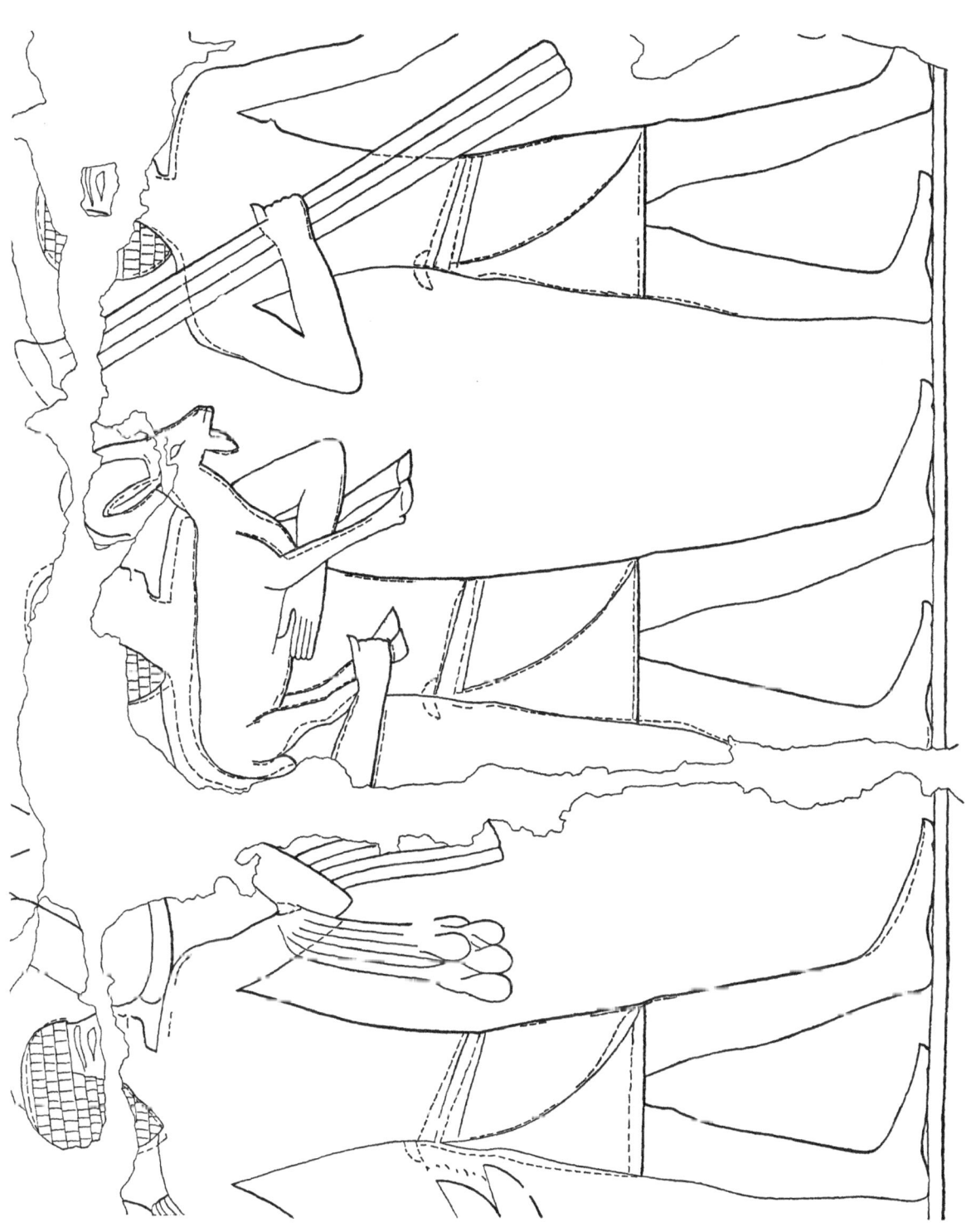

PLATE XVII

Detail for study of ruled lines, painter's sketched and final outlines, and brush strokes. Tomb of Per-nēb, main chamber, south wall, west end. Scale 1 : 5. See pp. 10 n. 30, 23, 34 n. 74, 35-36.

PLATE XVII

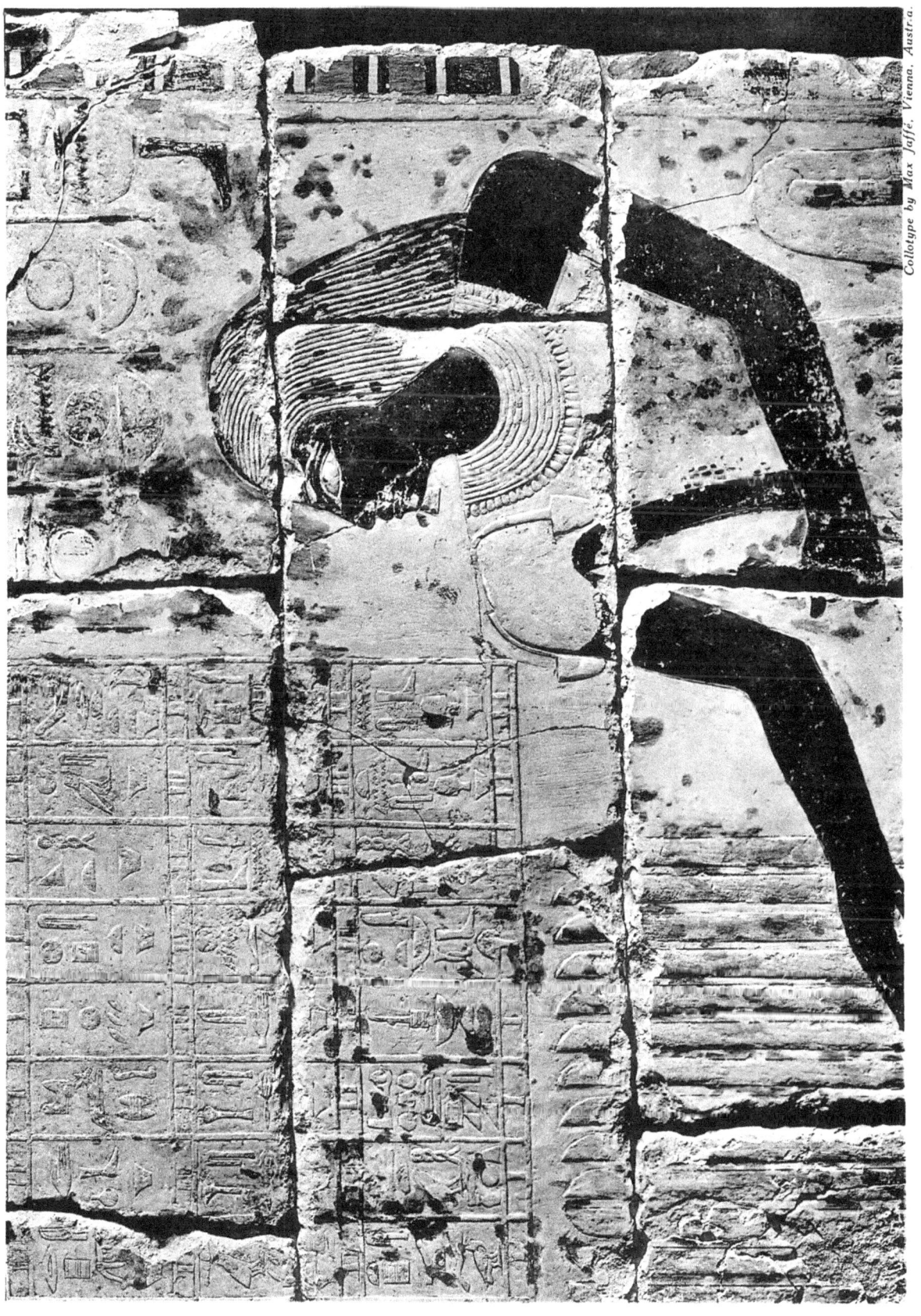

PLATE XVIII

Above, section of final surface well preserved, in upper part unsculptured. Tomb of Per-nēb, main chamber, east wall, parts of registers 1 and 2 from top. Compare pl. xix. Scale 1:5. See page references under pl. xix; also p. 51 n. 91.

Below, detail to show brush lines around design as first process in putting in gray background. Tomb of Per-nēb, main chamber, east wall, bottom register, right end. Scale 1:4. See p. 35.

PLATE XVIII

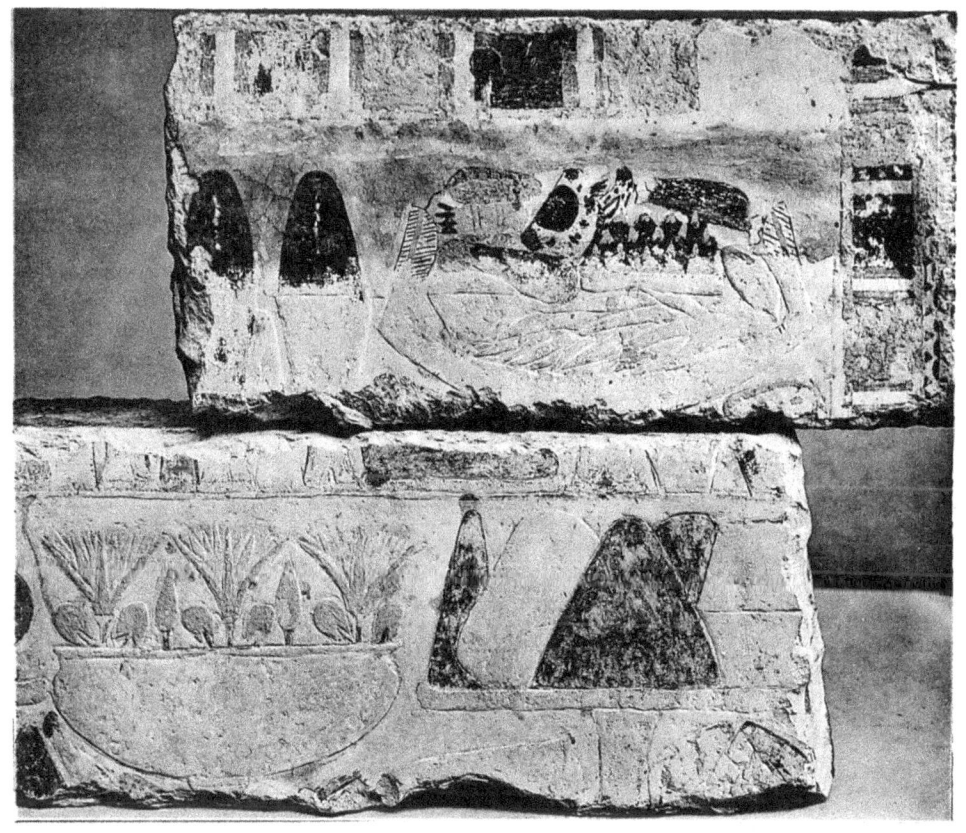

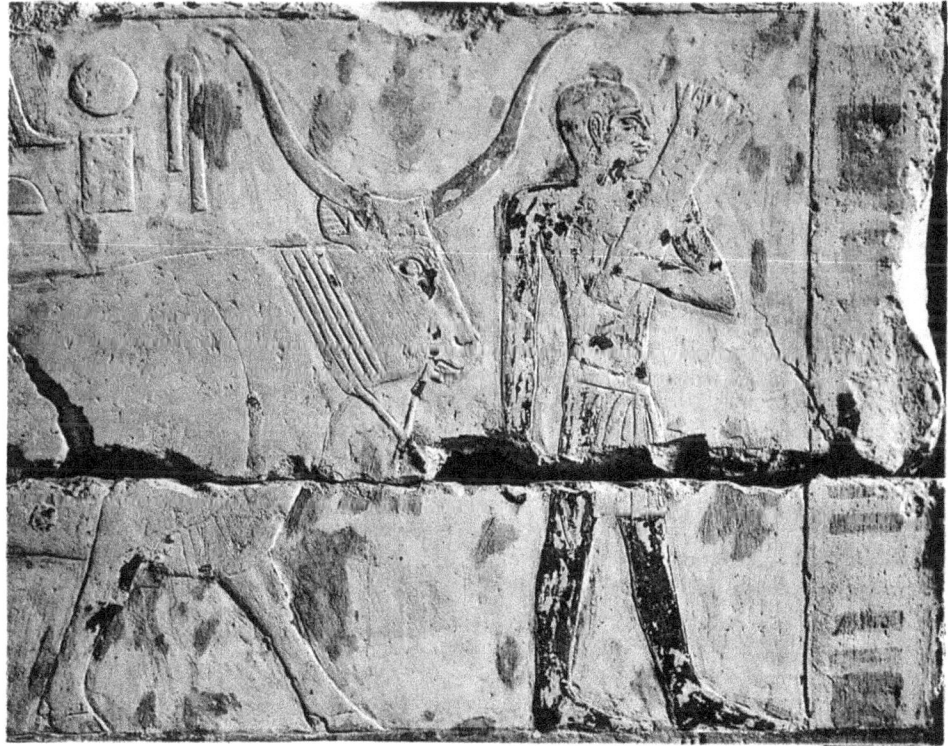

PLATE XIX

Detail of final surface, in upper part unsculptured. Tomb of Per-nēb, main chamber, east wall, in register 1 at top. Compare pl. xviii. Copied by Hazel de Berard. Scale 1:3. See pp. 34 n. 75, 38 n. 3, 40, 41 n. 22, 44-46, 48-50, 52 n. 93.

PLATE XIX

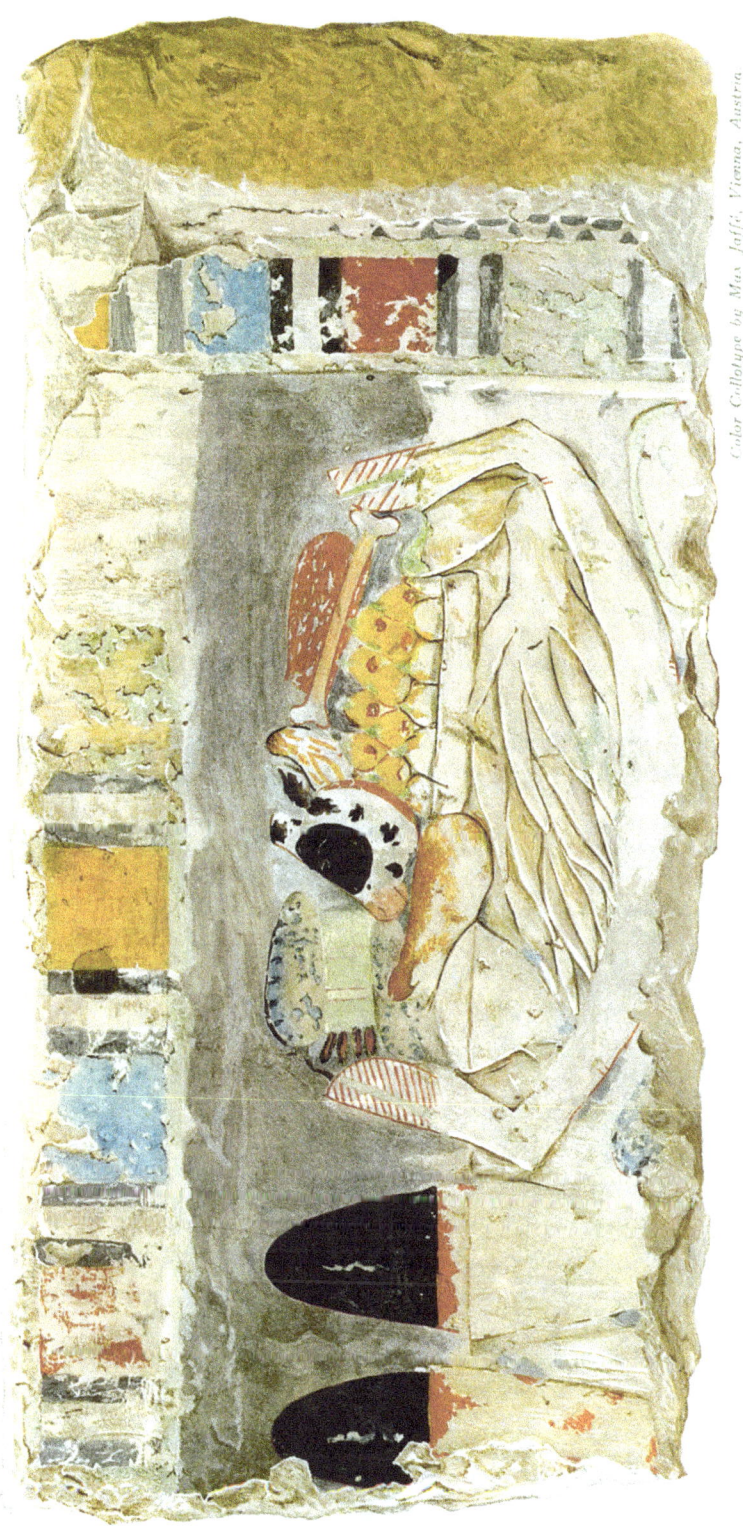

PLATE XX

Shapes and colors of vases among offerings. Tomb of Per-nēb. Drawn by Lindsley F. Hall. To same, but not a determined, scale. See pp. 50-53, 50 n. 86, 51 n. 90, 51 n. 91, 52 n. 93.

PLATE XX

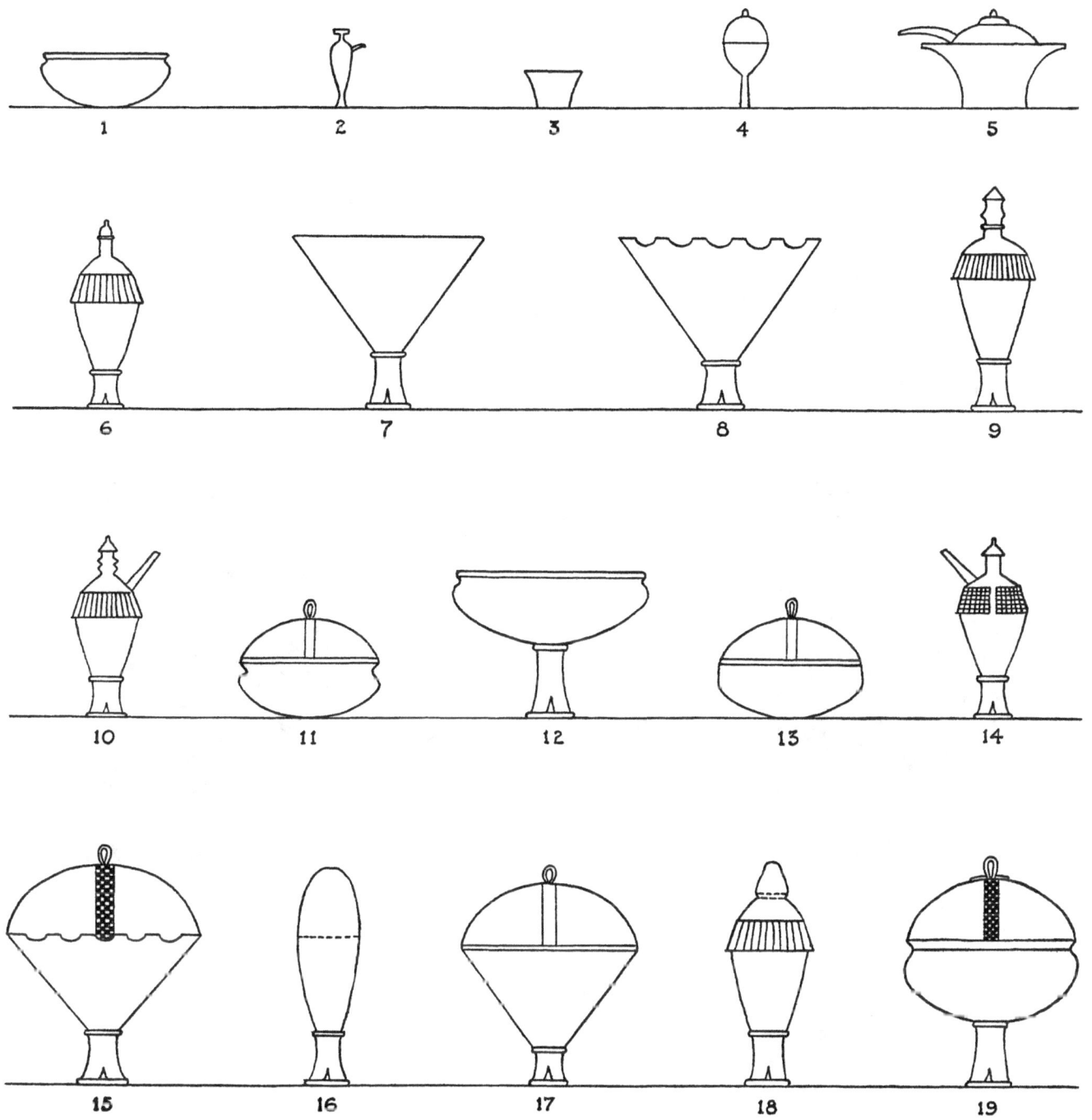

Black: vases, 18; seals, 16, 18; checkers on covers, 15, 19

Blue: vases, 3-9, 11-15, 17, 19; supports, 14; stoppers, 14; wraps, 6, 9, 10, 14, 18

Green: stoppers, 9, 14; checkers on covers, 15, 19

Red: vases, 1, 3, 16; supports, 7-9, 12, 14-16, 18, 19

White: vases, patterned in line, 9, 14; support, patterned in line, 9; loops on top of covers, 15, 19

Yellow: vases, 2, 5, 10, 14; stoppers, 10, 14; supports, 10, 14; main part of covers, 11, 13, 15, 17, 19

Coachwhip Publications
CoachwhipBooks.com

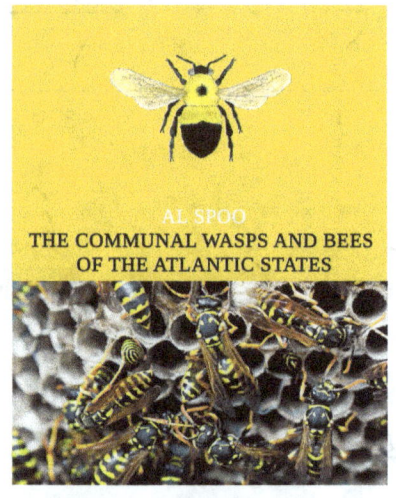

AL SPOO
THE COMMUNAL WASPS AND BEES OF THE ATLANTIC STATES

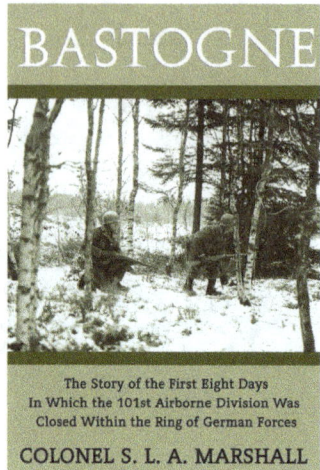

BASTOGNE

The Story of the First Eight Days
In Which the 101st Airborne Division Was
Closed Within the Ring of German Forces

COLONEL S. L. A. MARSHALL

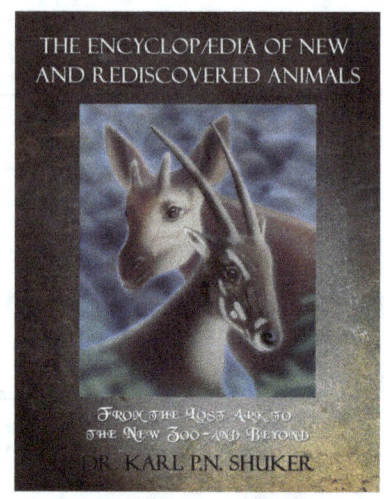

THE ENCYCLOPÆDIA OF NEW AND REDISCOVERED ANIMALS

FROM THE LOST ARK TO THE NEW ZOO—AND BEYOND

DR. KARL P.N. SHUKER

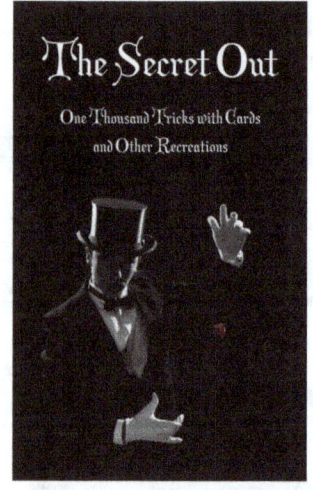

The Secret Out
One Thousand Tricks with Cards
and Other Recreations

TANKS
AND HOW TO DRAW THEM

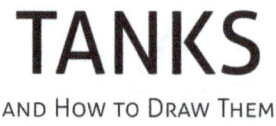

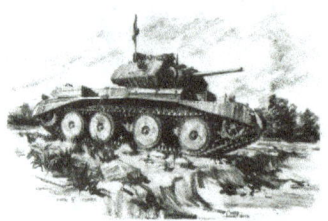

TERENCE T. CUNEO

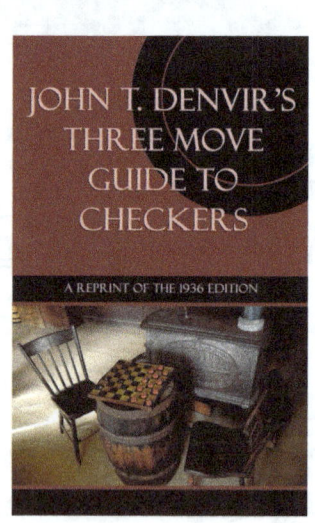

JOHN T. DENVIR'S
THREE MOVE
GUIDE TO
CHECKERS

A REPRINT OF THE 1936 EDITION

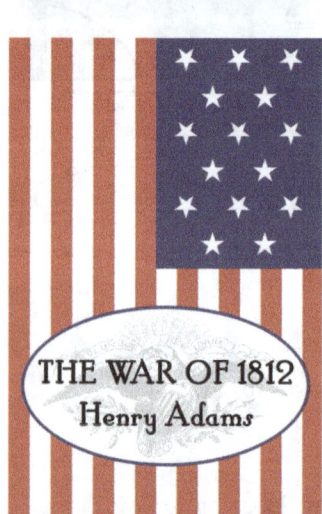

THE WAR OF 1812
Henry Adams

YORKTOWN

THE STRATEGY, PEOPLE, AND EVENTS
SURROUNDING THE FINAL BATTLE IN THE
AMERICAN WAR OF INDEPENDENCE

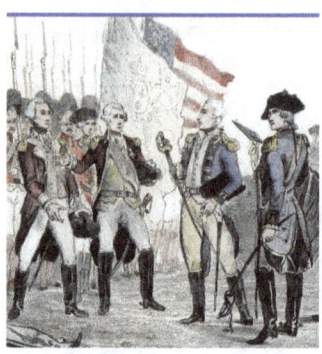

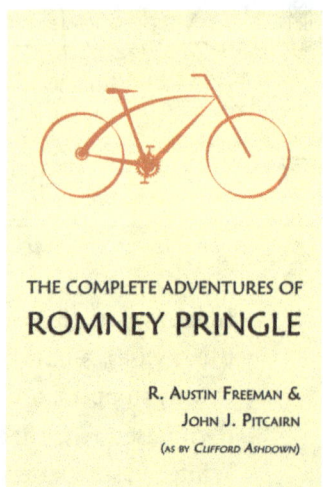

THE COMPLETE ADVENTURES OF
ROMNEY PRINGLE

R. AUSTIN FREEMAN &
JOHN J. PITCAIRN
(AS BY CLIFFORD ASHDOWN)

Coachwhip Publications
CoachwhipBooks.com

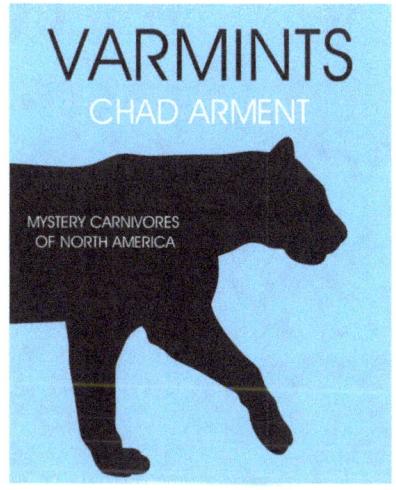

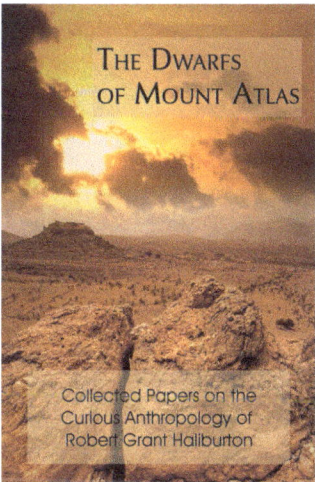

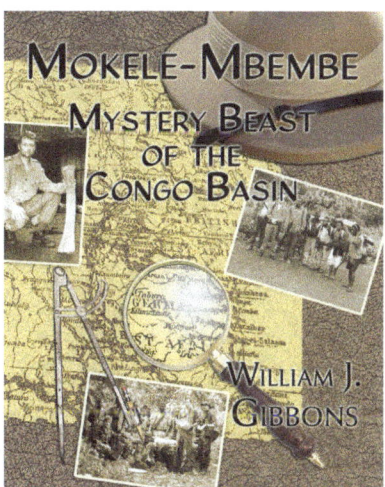

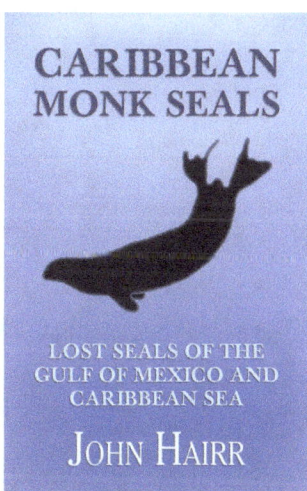

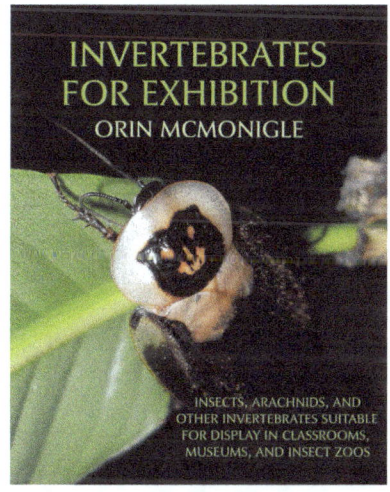

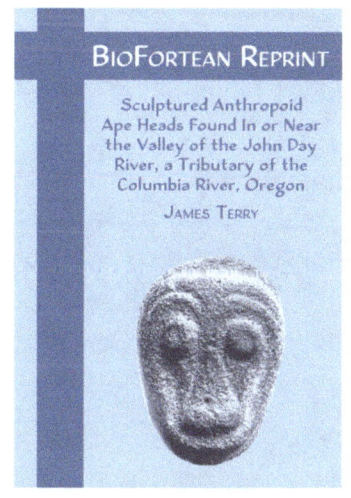

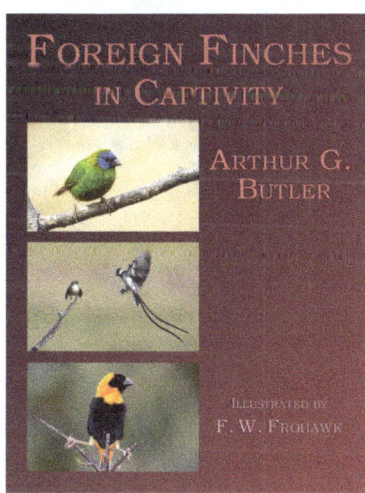

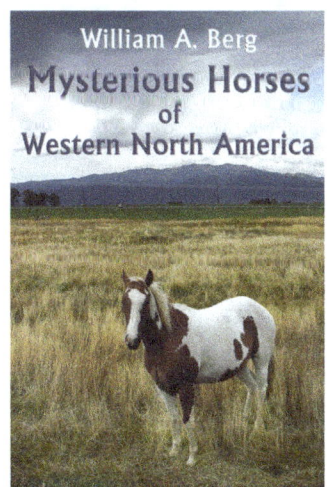

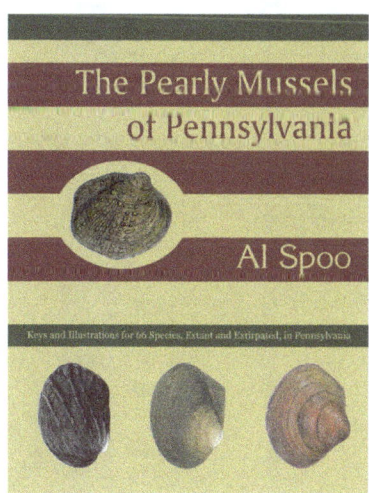